DATE DUE

DEMCO 38-296

HENRI SAUGUET

Henri Sauguet (1901-1989). *From the Fred and Rose Plaut Archives in the Music Library of Yale University.*

HENRI SAUGUET

A Bio-Bibliography

DAVID L. AUSTIN

Bio-Bibliographies in Music, Number 39
Donald L. Hixon, Series Adviser

Greenwood Press
New York • Westport, Connecticut • London

Library of Congress Cataloging-in-Publication Data

Austin, David L.
    Henri Sauguet : a bio-bibliography / David L. Austin.
        p.   cm. — (Bio-bibliographies in music, ISSN 0742-6968 ; no.
    39)
    Discography: p.
    Includes index.
    ISBN 0-313-26564-X (alk. paper)
    1. Sauguet, Henri, 1901-   —Bibliography. I. Title.
    II. Series.
    ML134.S215A95   1991
    016.78'092—dc20   90-29278
    [B]

British Library Cataloguing in Publication Data is available.

Library of Congress Catalog Card Number: 90-29278
ISBN: 0-313-26564-X
ISSN: 0742-6968

First published in 1991

Greenwood Press, 88 Post Road West, Westport, CT 06881
An imprint of Greenwood Publishing Group, Inc.

Printed in the United States of America

The paper used in this book complies with the
Permanent Paper Standard issued by the National
Information Standards Organization (Z39.48-1984).

10 9 8 7 6 5 4 3 2 1

à la mémoire d'Henri Sauguet

Contents

Preface

Henri Sauguet's music remains little known outside his native
France and portions of Belgium. Even there a younger generation of listeners and practitioners only vaguely associates
his name with the ballet Les Forains, the popular song Le
Chemin des forains, and a handful of other minor masterworks.
Yet during his lifetime, impresarios, poets, stage directors,
choreographers, and film directors eagerly sought his collaboration on important projects.

Sauguet's very "Frenchness" contributed to his lack of
recognition outside the Gallic environment. Such refinement,
subtlety, irony, and melancholy as his found few sympathetic
listeners in Germanic or German-oriented societies like England or the United States. The aloof quality of his music
likewise fell on cold ears in the neighboring Romantic countries.

Sauguet also lacked an aggressive publicist such as Jean
Cocteau who, prior to the composer's arrival in Paris, expen-
ded great effort on behalf of "Les Six." Erik Satie, the
crotchety "Maître d'Arcueil," seemed less inclined toward
the end of his life to champion the anti-Wagnerian individu-
alism of young musicians such as Sauguet who gathered around
him. Outside France, Ernst Krenek exhibited a passing interest in Sauguet's stage works. Andrew Porter, in England, and
Virgil Thomson, in the United States, both saw something to
champion in Sauguet's Neo-Romantic music. In the estimation
of his friend and constant supporter, Darius Milhaud, Sauguet's
music fills the gap between the generation of "Les Six" and
that of Olivier Messiaen.

The period between the well-known 1920s and the renewed
interest in French creativity during the late 1950s needs
closer examination if we are to make a full and unbiased evaluation of the twentieth century in the future. A document,
such as this volume in the Bio-Bibliographies in Music Series,
which concerns itself with the life and achievements of a man
whose career spanned the period in question, and who worked
not only in the field of "pure" music, but also in the areas
of stage, broadcast and cinema music, may help in the task.

Finally, while some critics may have deemed Henri Sauguet's music dated in the past, others appreciated the poetic
and sincere qualities of his work. Such qualities can be

perceived and valued by audiences today. Performers may, therefore, find some practical application for the list of Sauguet's works when adding "new" music to their repertoires.

French sources figure prominently in a volume about the life and work of a French composer so little known outside his native country. A problem exists in which of the thirty-three pre-1939 daily Parisian newspapers and various weekly and monthly publications to consult. It lessens somewhat by 1960, with only thirteen daily newspapers on the streets of Paris. The consideration of time and space available re-solved some of the problem; only those extant and generally available in hard copy or on microfilm were consulted. The lack of adequate indexes for French periodical and newspaper literature also presented a problem. Therefore, many cita-tions concerning the life and works of Henri Sauguet probably fall outside the pages of the volume.

The author accepts full responsibility for the transla-tions from the French and German sources. No attempt was made to present them in exact or literal translations unless he deemed the quality of expression worthy of preservation. Space limitations prevented the inclusion of material in the original language with a translation following. Every effort was made, however, to capture the original writer's style and inflection.

The organization of the volume falls into five parts:

1) A brief biography sums up the important events in Henri Sauguet's life.

2) A list of works and performances, more complete than any compiled to date, follows. By the time the author under-took the preparation of the volume Monsieur Sauguet's final illness had advanced to a state which ruled out his advice or assistance in the task. Additional work with the composer's estate, in the possession of Raphaël Cluzel, may reveal more premiere and performance dates. Furthermore, the existence of manuscripts and their availability to researchers and per-formers may also be clarified. Each item within a genre (ope-ra, ballet, concerto, etc.) chronologically follows the name of that kind of work. "W" numbers (e.g., W1, W2, etc.) pre-cede the titles of the work in lieu of any official or formal numbering by the composer. Performances appear chronologi-cally with premieres listed first.

3) The selection of prose writings and speeches by Henri Sauguet makes no attempt at comprehensiveness. Music and dra-ma reviews are presented separately in chronological order un-der the name of the journal in which they appeared. Inclusion of such citations will be helpful to readers who want to gain an understanding of the kind and quality of creative activi-ties presented in Parisian theaters and concert halls during the twenty-year period 1928-1948. A fifth subsection presents the composer's verbal contributions for other publications and events. An "S" number precedes each entry in section three as the "W" number did in section two.

4) Items in the discography section are preceded by "D" numbers. Record manufacturer's labels and numbers dictate, in an alphanumeric sequence, the order of entries in section four.

5) The bibliography of writings about the composer and his music is organized alphabetically by author with anonymous

works inserted alphabetically by title. A "B" number precedes
each entry, and a short annotation, summary, or quote from the
source follows.

Two appendixes follow the work proper. Appendix I organizes the music alphabetically by title and also includes
working titles, subtitles and alternate titles from the compositions. Appendix II organizes the works chronologically
to give a clearer picture of the progression and disposition
of works during the composer's career.

An index to the people, organizations, and events cited
in the body of the document concludes the work. Throughout
the volume "See" references indicate other citations which
bear relationship to that in hand. With both the "See" and
index references the appropriate mnemonic (e.g., W5, S49, D7,
B128) rather than page number refers to the appropriate cita-
tation. Index references to the preface and the biography
are indicated in the traditional lowercase Roman numerals and
Arabic numbers, respectively.

Acknowledgments

The preparation of a volume which relies so much upon source
material that is difficult to find necessarily depends heavily
upon the competent support of a number of people. I would
like to extend my gratitude to those who consciously and un-
consciously lent me aid and encouragement during its production.

Many staff members at my home institution, the University of Illinois at Chicago, participated in one way or another. The Administration of the Library granted support and
academic release time for the project. The Reference Department staff provided answers to my questions sometimes and
helped me think through problems at other times. Phyllis
Warren and her staff at the Periodicals and Microform desk
soon began to anticipate my need for an empty microfilm reel
even before I arrived at the desk. Most of all, however, I
would like to thank Kathleen Killian and her assistants, Jerry Romero and Maria Macias, at the Interlibrary Loan desk.
Their cheerful and willing help cannot be acknowledged enough.

Participation with other libraries stands as the foundation of all interlibrary lending and borrowing services. The
cooperating institutions of which I am most aware are the Ur-
bana-Champaign campus of the University of Illinois and the
Center for Research Libraries. Without access to their holdings and to the holdings of many other libraries around the
country, huge gaps would remain unfilled in the bibliography.

Nearby, the staffs of the Chicago Public Library, the
Newberry Library, the University of Chicago's Regenstein Library, and the Library of Northwestern University, especially
Don Roberts and Shirlene Ward, accommodated my requests with
advice and access to their collections. Outside the immediate
area, Ann Basart of the Music Library at the University of
California, Berkeley, and Jerry Persons of Stanford University
Library helped me with information about and access to their
collections.

Further afield, Joy Stephens, Administrative Assistant
at the University of Louisville Music Library, and Nan Harmon,
Public Relations Director for the Louisville Orchestra, provided information about the commission for Les Trois lys and
the reaction to its premiere. David Gollon, Music Librarian,
Pitkin County (Colorado) Library, provided details about the

Aspen Festival appearance of Sauguet. Monsieur Gérard Boireau, Directeur général, Grand Théâtre de Bordeaux, provided
information about the 1990 posthumous tribute to Sauguet at
the Mai musical de Bordeaux.

Kendall L. Crilly, Public Services Librarian at the Yale
University Music Library provided information about Henri
Sauguet in the Fred and Rose Plaut, and the Virgil Thomson
archives. Florence Roth, Conservateur de la Bibliothèque,
Société des Auteurs et Compositeurs dramatiques, directed me
to the location of the composer's papers.

I am also grateful to Raphaël Cluzel, the adopted son
and heir of Henri Sauguet, for his interest and encouragement
in the project. The late Virgil Thomson, who died only a few
weeks after his friend, fellow critic and composer, Henri
Sauguet, likewise provided his encouragement. Don Hixon and
the editorial staff at Greenwood Press offered welcome advice
during the last stages of my work.

Returning to my home environment, I would especially
like to thank my wife, Joan, for her support, patience, direction, encouragement, and constant good fellowship.

HENRI SAUGUET

Biography

When Henri Sauguet was born to a solid Bordeaux business family in 1901 no one expected him to be unusual. The Dames de
France department store employed his father, Auguste Poupard
as chief clerk in charge of the hosiery section. His mother,
Elisabeth, managed the household and raised the children, as
befit the times. Both parents grew up in families which were
traditionally organized and strongly oriented toward commercial concerns. They carefully planned out their lives and
the lives of their two sons, Henri and Jean.
     The first of the two boys was unusual, however. Even
before the first year of his life he displayed a strong interest in musical sounds. He screamed and cried to be carried to the window to see a goatherd who played a flageolet
to signal his presence to those who wished to buy the fresh-
est milk. By the time he was five his mother conceded to his
entreaties and arranged for her old piano teacher to give les-
sons to the young boy.
     A quick passage through school subjects confirmed an a-
bove average intelligence in Henri. In addition to his academic, piano, and later, organ studies, he also participated
as an altar boy and chorister in one of the churches. As such
he heard and sang the beautiful plaint chant, and harmonies
and polyphonies of the services. His enchantment with the music grew so strong that he decided upon the church as his vocation by the time of his first communion.
     For the first of many times to come a conflict arose be-
tween Henri and his family. Auguste Poupard stepped in and
insisted that his son take a more practical course for his
life. Conforming to his father's wishes, the boy completed
the course work necessary to obtain a diploma in shorthand
typing.
     Music remained the strongest fascination in his life.
Henri's second piano teacher convinced his mother to present
him as an applicant to the Conservatoire at Bordeaux, but his
prudent father decided that his son should seek a more secure
future. When the army called upon Auguste Poupard in August,
1914, the advice seemed wise indeed. Henri needed to rely
upon his commercial training to help support his family. To
do this he applied his secretarial skills at a law firm, a
wine warehouse, a canning factory, and a shipping firm in

succession. He continued such work even after his father returned after the war in 1918.
    Music's attraction grew stronger and stronger during this
period. Bordeaux offered many cultural opportunities, though,
especially since it acted as the administrative center for the
country during the war. Performers and ensembles seldom omit-
ted the city from their tours, and publications of literary
and artistic offerings could be readily and inexpensively pur-
chased. Some even printed new music. Through these Henri
learned of the music and esthetic philosophy of "Les Six" and
Erik Satie. He also learned of Jean Cocteau and the poets of
the day. The dream to be a musician ripened into a passion.
    To fulfill the desire, Henri knew that he needed training.
For a time he lived and worked at Montauban where he studied
with Joseph Canteloube. Once again, however, family responsibility brought him back to Bordeaux.
    The city's artistic life lacked contemporary content. To
remedy what he perceived as a deprivation in his environment,
Henri, Louis Emié, and Jean-Marcel Lizotte founded "Le Groupe
de Trois" in imitation of "Le Groupe de Six." The three young
men studied and talked of new music and poetry, of Satie,
Stravinsky, Falla, and Schoenberg, of Cocteau, Farge, the Dada
movement and surrealism. Not content with mere talk, they
performed music by Satie and "Les Six," as well as their own
creations at a concert. A small and mostly unenthusiastic
audience heard their efforts. Henri's mother and father became impatient with his "hobby" as they saw it. Even Uncle
Arthur Portail, an amateur vocalist who had supported the
young man's interest, found himself less friendly toward the
efforts of "Les Trois." When their next concert featured music of Schoenberg, Webern, and Bartók, among others, they lost
even more allies.
    The situation in Bordeaux continued to grow more restric-
tive; Henri's father refused to allow the association of the
family name of Poupard with such ventures. The young composer
therefore adopted his mother's maiden name, Sauguet. He also
bravely sent off copies of his music to composers in Paris for
their appraisal. He needed to know if his talent could sur-
vive in the highly competitive atmosphere of the capital.
    Darius Milhaud, a member of "Les Six," received some of
the copies of Sauguet's music and responded to the young pro-
vicial with an invitation to visit him. He promised to show
him what creative life was like and introduce him to some of
his colleagues. Henri's parents felt so little sympathy with
his ambition that he could not ask them either their permis-
sion or their support for the trip.
    Guile seemed the only solution, so he notified his em-
ployer that he was ill and, in all probability, would not be
back to work on Monday, perhaps even Tuesday. He informed
his parents that a young couple who heard him play the organ
at church requested him to play for their wedding. Since the
church in which they were to be wed was at a distance, and he
needed to adapt to the church's instrument, he would be away
from home for a few days. Only Uncle Portail, who lent him
some money for the trip, seemed to know what was happening.
On the night of 14 January, 1923, Henri Sauguet left Bordeaux
on a train bound for Paris. The trip changed the course of
his life forever.

The demands on Darius Milhaud's time and talent as a composer and conductor left him little to entertain a young guest. Henri would have to be satisfied with accompanying him through a fairly normal Paris weekend. The young man could have hoped for nothing better. After an afternoon concert by the Orchestre Pasdeloup, where he sat next to Maurice Ravel, they ate dinner and adjourned to the Théâtre des Champs-Elysées. Here Rolf Maré's Ballets suédois presented a double bill with Milhaud's L'Homme et son désir, libretto by Paul Claudel and set and costumes by Fernand Léger, before intermission. In the second half, music by many of the active Parisian composers backed up the action in Jean Cocteau's Les Mariés de la tour Eiffel.

The next evening Henri attended a concert at the Salle Gaveau at which Milhaud conducted the Paris premiere of Arnold Schoenberg's Pierrot lunnaire. Such an even naturally attracted all the social and creative elite of the city, and they, like Milhaud and Sauguet, repaired to the post-concert party at Le Bœuf sur le toit. Here Henri met Erik Satie Francis Poulenc, Raymond Radiguet, Léon-Paul Farge, Pablo Piccaso, André Dérain, Jean Börlin, and, of course, Cocteau. The next morning, as he boarded the train back to Bordeaux, the young man vowed that he would return to Paris, this time for good.

At first his parents, especially his father, adamantly refused to listen to his request for independence, but as time wore on he weakened their resolve. Auguste Poupard now made periodic buying trips to Paris where he made the acquaintance of other business colleagues at Les Grands Magasins de Paris-France and other department stores. Through such connections he secured employment (in a hosiery department) for his son. In return for the assistance he extracted a promise from Henri to give up his interest in music. The young man felt the drive too strongly, however, to keep the promise long, and the ensuing rupture in familial relations endured until the completion of his most complex undertaking, the opera La Chartreuse de Parme.

On his own now in Paris, Sauguet began to find his milieu. The fascinating cubist poet and painter Max Jacob also worked at the same department store. They soon struck up a friendship and Jacob suggested that Henri move to the same building, the Hôtel Nollet, where he lived. In the evenings many creative young people gathered in the rooms of one or the other residents of the apartment building. Such evenings might center around gravely serious discussions of the latest creative or philosophical trends. On the other hand, the participants might devote themselves with equal enthusiasm to silliness of the most absurd variety. Henri and the painter Christian Bérard shared a reputation for an ability to take a lampshade or a bedspread and transform themselves into some of the most bizarre characters of history or fiction.

Sauguet's first Paris friend, Darius Milhaud, continued to look after the young man's progress and act as his unofficial sponsor for social connections. The more important introductions Milhaud made for him included Charles Kœchlin, the Beaumonts, and Erik Satie. Kœchlin provided Sauguet's raw talent with the polish that a more conventional man would have sought, perhaps in vain, at the Conservatoire. Compte and Comptesse Etienne de Beaumont played leading roles in Le

Tout Paris, the cream of the capital's social world, many of
whom vied with each other to sponsor, at at least be seen at,
the latest artistic phenomenon. One year they sponsored evenings of dance performances, entitled Les Soirées de Paris,
at the Théâtre de la Cigale. For the event Sauguet composed
music for Les Roses, the first of many ballets to come. The
association with the Beaumonts unveiled the young composer
to other potential patrons such as the Noailles and the Polig-
nacs.

The introduction to Satie led to even more important artistic and esthetic consequences. Critical judgment, even to
the end of his life, tends to link Sauguet with and compare
him to the older composer, one of the most sardonic and whim-
sical characters in music history. Satie's anti-Wagnerian
philosophy and sparse writing style attracted young avant-
garde French musicians who struggled to break from sover-
eignty which German music enjoyed during the nineteenth century. The group "Les Six" previously achieved their break
from the domination under Satie's guidance, but they grew re-
bellious and separated from him. After their disaffection he
welcomed the attention of Henri Sauguet's younger generation
who conceived of themselves as "L'Ecole d'Arcueil" (The School
of Arcueil) after the suburb in which Satie lived, and chris-
tened him the Master of Arcueil. Other members of the group
included Roger Désormiére, Henry Cliquet-Pleyel, and Maxime
Jacob, though only Sauguet achieved prominence as a composer.
Associations with the crotchety old composer sometimes
grew strained, however. Once, at a performance of Mercure,
Satie, who played piano for his own work, constantly snapped
at his protégé for turning pages at the wrong time. The old
man's directions continued to deteriorate throughout the work.
Although unable to apologize for his behavior, Satie sensed
a need to atone for the treatment of his page turner. To make
amends Satie arranged a luncheon date with Serge Diaghilev
during which he presented Sauguet to the great impresario.
The introduction led to the commission of the music for La
Chatte which the Ballets russes performed in 1927. With the
success of the ballet and the connection to Diaghilev and his
associates established, Henri Sauguet could dedicate his time
exclusively to music. He no longer needed to sell hosiery or
look after the business affairs of the curator of the Musée
Guimet.

Now that his credentials were established Sauguet could
embark upon a supplementary vocation as a critic. His record
of criticism, which spans twenty years, from 1928 to 1948, reveals keen interest in both music and drama and a perceptive
appraisal of all creative trends of his day. As his verbal
skills sharpened he became aware that he possessed the ability to say something in a medium other than music. His natural writing style often exhibits the same biting and wry sense
of humor that people like Christian Dior, Maurice Sachs,
Pierre Gaxotte, and Virgil Thomson heard when they visited
Sauguet or Max Jacob at the Hôtel Nollet.

The composer's flirtation with the stage extended to the
opposite side of the footlights, too. At a 1932 performance
of Satie's Le Piège de Méduse at the Concerts de La Sérénade,
Sauguet played the character of Baron Méduse. When Marcel
Herrand presented his series of historically accurate productions of Molière's plays Sauguet's audition won him the part

of Madame Pernelle in _Tartuffe_. Sauguet even appeared on the boards in New York City, this time as Cardinal Richelieu in the 1953 performance of the ballet _Le Cardinal aux chats_. He enjoyed playing roles, even when he appeared on radio or television programs.

The nineteen-thirties, a period of world-wide economic trouble, witnessed only two major works by the composer. His piano _Concerto_ in A minor achieved immediate acceptance, partly due to Clara Haskil's numerous performances of it in the thirties. The responsibility for the work's long lasting popularity lies with Vasso Devetzi, a student of Marguerite Long. Sauguet awarded Devetzi exclusive performing rights to the work for a number of years as part of her prize for winning the piano division of the Concours du Conservatoire, and she performed it frequently during her tours throughout the world.

Shortly after the premiere of _La Chatte_, the composer's newly found confidence encouraged him to undertake the most ambitious work of his career, _La Chartreuse de Parme_. Between 1927 and 1936 he worked on the opera with his librettist Armand Lunel. Stendhal's novel provided the inspiration, and Sauguet cast it in a more classical form than that currently in vogue. Orchestration tended to reflect the nineteenth century, while harmonies, declamation, and rhythms belonged to the twentieth. The composer's special touch lay in the through-composition of recitatives, arias, duets, etc., which resulted in a "lyrical conversation" that provided too much continuity for the taste of many in the audience at its premiere in 1939. Moreover, a work written between the ages of twenty-six and thirty-five could not help but reflect too much growth and not enough cohesion. The imminence of the war also contributed to its lack of popularity. Audiences felt too uneasy to sit comfortably through a lengthy work of such a serious nature, but many important critics, then and later, recognized touches of genius in some sections. The premiere also marked the first of many successful collaborations between the composer and the designer Jacques Dupont, whose lavish sets and costumes always garnered the highest praise.

The war and consequent occupation caused no more trouble for Sauguet than for the average citizen of France. The army called upon him to help defend his country in the beginning, but when pro-German factions took over the government the military dismissed him from his duty. He lacked sufficient motivation to defend his "new" country from anti-fascist enemies. Moreover, the new army wanted nothing to do with artists and musicians. His lack of interest in politics left him free to write and perform music.

Even during the discouraging and difficult years of the German occupation the people of Paris needed diversions like music. With a few exceptions the composer wisely avoided writing works which required large numbers of performers, but the amount of chamber music and incidental music destined for the consumption by larger audiences increased. Henri Sauguet wrote his first score for a play, _Irma_, by Roger Ferdinand, in 1926. He returned to the genre a few times after that, but in 1939 he entered into what came to be a frequent partnership with Louis Jouvet. Jouvet at the time excelled in the production of new dramatic works by Jean Giraudoux. The success of Giraudoux's _Ondine_ depended on the chemistry Jouvet formulated by mixing together the playwright, the actors,

Jouvet and Madeleine Ozeray, the sets and costumes of Pavel
Tchelitchev, and the music by Sauguet. The success of so many
of the composer's best works turned on similar magical combi-
nations of participants. His music continued to enliven many
of the stage productions that Parisians saw during the war
and for many years after.
    The cinema claimed little of the composer's attention be-
fore the medium improved its technical capabilities. He
thereafter joined other prominent French musicians such as
Milhaud and Georges Auric in providing film with high quality
incidental music. Sauguet's true interest began during the
war, and, although it continued into the sixties, the 1946
production of Farrebique probably stands as his greatest a-
chievement in the area.
    The importance of radio grew during the war, and the
composer's first venture into the field of incidental music
for broadcast also took place then. Several fruitful artistic collaborations began during the period and continued into
the era when television began to dominate broadcasting. Sauguet's visual sensitivity and familiarity with film allowed
him to make an easy and successful transition to that medium.
    Sauguet's most important project during the early 1940s,
the ballet Les Mirages, postponed its premiere from 1944 to
1947 after the German forces, retreating from the Allies' advance on Paris, shut down electricity in all public places,
including theaters. Gradual restoration of economic confidence allowed large scale productions again, and the ballet
Les Forains and the incidental music for the play La Folle de
Chaillot rank as Sauguet's chief contributions to the postwar years.
    La Folle, a play which Louis Jouvet produced in memory
of the author and his late friend, Jean Giraudoux, included
sets and costumes by Christian Bérard. The play marked the
beginning of Bérard's most creative years, and Sauguet gladly
entered into the partnership. He knew the designer from the
Hôtel Nollet days and valued his visual additions to the 1930
ballet, La Nuit, which Sauguet wrote for Charles B. Cochran.
The two men continued their participation in numerous stage
productions until the artist's death in 1949.
    Les Forains remains the best known stage work upon which
the two men bestowed their creative talents. Sauguet's melancholy motive perfectly matched Boris Kochno's scenario and
lighting, while Bérard's sparse set and costumes provided the
exact space necessary for Roland Petit's choreography. Each
element displayed the participants' individual talent. Combined, they exhibited real genius.
    The composer's plaintive score, which depicts the un-
grateful and endless life of itinerant performers as they
travel from town to town to earn a few pennies from their
skills, appealed equally to audiences then as it does now.
The sentiment and melody also caught the attention of Edith
Piaf, who, along with Sauguet and the lyricist Jean Dréjac,
transformed it, as Le Chemin des forains, into one of her
most popular chansons of the 1950s.
    The composer's conception of the ballet developed more
complexly than his approach to any other form. From the fairly conservative music for the more avant-garde production of
La Chatte to his unusual tenor solo and a cappella mixed chorus setting of the more visually conservative La Plus loin

que la nuit et la jour, he challenged classical dance to grow
with the times. Other prominent creative minds willingly
joined with him or sought out his cooperation on important
projects. Throughout his career, in fact, cooperation played
an important part in Sauguet's most successful works.

One area in which his talent shone as a single star,
rather than as a part of a constellation, lies in song writing. Critics consistently praised his contributions to the
solo song and the song cycle, and often compared his works
favorably to those by Francis Poulenc. His special sensitivity to text may be traced back to his earliest ventures in
vocal music. Verbal awareness as a writer and an extensive
exploration of literature and poetry contributed to his com-
petence in the genre. Sauguet also applied this skill to
popular song. His venture into the field of chanson merely
reflects a tradition which he shared with many of his colleagues and which created a standard of quality in popular
music that exceeded levels found in most other countries.

The fifth and sixth decades of our century and of Henri
Sauguet's life witnessed a mature composer who actively involved himself in all creative ventures, including musique
concrète. More symphonic works, incidental music for plays
and broadcasts, and for ballets flowed from his creative mind.
His commissions from music festivals in Aix-en-Provence, Besançon, and even his native Bordeaux grew more frequent. Audiences in cities as distant from Paris as Moscow and Buenos
Aires heard his music. His popularity with listeners outside
France never took root long enough to bear fruit though. Even
New York City, where his stanch supporter Virgil Thomson
lived, fêted him early in 1953 and promptly forgot about his
music a few weeks later. Sauguet's Louisville commission for
Les Trois lys in 1954 and his appearance at the Aspen Festival
in 1962 likewise failed to inspire a faithful following in the
United States.

Numerous awards in his native France recognized his artistic achievements, however. Recordings of Les Forains, the
Quatuor à cordes no. 2, and the Mélodie concertante brought
him honors from the judging panel of the Grand Prix du Disque.
Colleagues elected him president of the Société des Auteurs,
Compositeurs et Editeurs du Musique, the Société des Auteurs
et Compositeurs dramatiques, the Comité national de Musique,
the Société française de Musique contemporaine, and the Société du Droit du Reproduction du Musique. The Académie du
Jazz and the Légion d'Honneur bestowed membership upon him
also. Henri Sauguet received honors from Belgium and the
United States too, but he felt that his election to the Académie des Beaux-Arts in 1976 surpassed them all.

Other composers may have enjoyed such success and recognition in a more relaxed manner than Sauguet did during his
seventies and eighties. The passion which led him to rebel
against his father's authority and forsake a comfortable existence in a stable environment continued to drive him yet.
Two operas, Boule des suif, and Tistou-les-pouces-vert, a few
more song cycles, and several major instrumental chamber
pieces, along with numerous small compositions still needed
his pen to create them.

In 1985 he became ill and found composition an increas-
ingly difficult task to undertake. His mental faculties still
responded to his will, but partial paralysis limited his

body's abilities. Finally, during the night of 12 June, 1989, Henri Sauguet died, only two months after his eighty-eighth birthday. Colleagues and friends honored him on 27 June at the Cathedral of Saint-Roch, and his body joined those of Berlioz, Heine, Offenbach, Delibes, and Stendhal in the Cimetière Montmartre.

Works and Performances

Henri Sauguet's compositions are listed chronologically within the framework of each genre. The "See" references (e.g., See: D17, B12) refer to citations found in the "Discography" section and the "Writings about Henri Sauguet and his Work" section. "See also" references (e.g., See also: W23) refer to other portions in the "Works and Performances" section of the volume.

OPERAS

W1.   **Le Plumet du Colonel** (1929; Rouart, Lerolle)
       See: D4, D31, D58, D62. B29, B90 B167, B220, B279, B294, B306, B350, B351, B352, B362, B414, B415, B422, B501, B502, B507, B510, B551, B638, B639, B640, B702, B714, B744.

Opéra-bouffe militaire in one act
Libretto and text by Henri Sauguet
Commissioned by Mme. Beriza
Dedicated to the composer's mother and father
Composed 1924

Premiere:
1924 (27 April): Paris; Théâtre des Champs-Elysées; Compagnie Beriza; Directed by Medgyès; Set and costumes by Pierre Lardin; Orchestra conducted by Ernest Ansermet.

Selected performances:
1943 (19 May): Paris; Part of "Hommage à Mme. Beriza."

1960 (Spring): Paris; Théâtre Charles-de-Rochefort; Troupe René Loin.

1967 (Summer): Pforzheim; Staatstheater; Conducted by Otto Siebert.

1971 (June): France; Radio broadcast of excerpts.

1981 (November): France; Radio broadcast; Henri
Gallois, conductor.

Excerpt:
"Berceuse créole" (1929; Salabert)
See: B220.

Premiere:
1929 (May): Paris; Ellabelle Davis.

W2.   **Un Amour du Titien** (unpublished)
See: B90, B240, B748.

Operetta in five acts and four scenes
Libretto and text by Max Jacob
Unfinished project; discarded when the collaborators
    decided that a production would be too costly
Composed 1928

W3.   **La Contrebasse** (unpublished; 45 min.)
See: D62. B26, B62, B90, B118, B378, B470, B472,
    B482, B505, B537, B551, B614, B662, B664, B679.

Opera bouffe in two scenes
Libretto by Henri Troyat after the short story by An-
ton Chekov.
Commissioned by Nikita Balieff.
Dedicated to Roger Désormière
Composed 1930

Premiere:
1930: Paris; Théâtre de la Madeleine; Compagnie
    Nikita Balieff; Directed by Serge Komisarjevsky;
    Sets and costumes by Georges Annenkov; Orchestra
    conducted by Raoul Labis.

Selected performances:
1956 (November): Marseille; Opéra de Marseille;
    Directed by Joseph Lazzini; Sets by Raffaelli.

1957 (October): Paris; Théâtre des Champs-Elysées;
    Opéra de Marseille.

1962 (27 July): Aspen, Colorado; Wheeler Opera
    House; Aspen Festival Workshop; Directed by Made-
    leine Milhaud.

1971 (June): France; Radio broadcast of excerpts.

1981 (25 May): Bordeaux; Centre André Malraux; Mai
    musical de Bordeaux; Directed by Guy Coutance;
    Sets by Christine Marest; Conducted by Cyril Died-
    rich.

W4.   **La Chartreuse de Parme** (unpublished)
See: B22, B39, B84, B109, B129, B134, B136, B194,
    B210, B253, B306, B307, B406, B418, B446, B500,
    B508, B509, B583, B610, B639, B657, B666, B676,
    B684, B687, B697, B699, B702, B713, B742, B743.

Opera in four acts and eleven scenes
Libretto by Armand Lunel after the novel by Stendhal
Dedicated to Darius and Madeleine Milhaud
Composed 1927-1936

Premiere:
    1939 (20 March): Paris: Opéra de Paris; Directed
    by Pierre Chereau; Sets and costumes by Jacques
    Dupont; Ballet choreographed by Albert Aveline;
    Orchestra conducted by Philippe Gaubert; Cast
    includes Germaine Lubin, Jacqueline Courtin, and
    Raoul Jobin.

Selected performances:
    1958 (30 January): Paris; Théâtre des Champs-Ely-
    sées; Selections from the performance broadcast
    on radio 6 February.

    1968 (7 February): Grenoble; Winter Olympics;
    Théâtre municipal de Grenoble; Directed by Jean-
    Jacques Etcheverry; Conducted by Henri Sauguet;
    Cast includes Cora Canne-Meyer, Jacques Doucet,
    Christianne Stutzmann.

    1971 (June): France; Radio broadcast of excerpts.

W5.   **La Gageure imprévue** (1948; Max Eschig)
    See: D62. B39, B158, B228, B237, B308, B356, B519,
    B548, B740, B741.

Comic opera in one act
Libretto by Pierre Bertin after a short story by
    Sedaine
Dedicated to Jacques Rouché
Composed 1942

Premiere:
    1944 (14 July): Paris; Opéra-Comique; Directed by
    Pierre Bertin; Sets by Jacques Dupont; Conducted
    by Roger Désormière; Cast includes Odette Turba-
    Rubier; Paul Derenne, Emile Rousseau.

Selected performances:
    1945 (20 April): Paris; Opéra-Comique; details as
    in the Premiere.

    1968 (18 December): New York City; Lincoln Center;
    Directed by Jean-Louis Barrault; Sets by Jacques
    Dupont; Accompanied at the piano by George Schick;
    Cast from the Metropolitan Opera Studio.

    1969 (3 October): Paris; Opéra-Comique; Sets by
    Jacques Dupont; Conducted by Jean-Claude Hartemann;
    Cast includes Caroline Dumas; Michel Termpont,
    André Mallabera.

    1971 (June): France; Radio broadcast of excerpts.

W6.   **Les Caprices de Marianne** (1954; S. A. Ricordi)
See: D62. B65, B78, B97, B132, B160, B170, B192,
B197, B268, B327, B354, B369, B370, B376, B377,
B392, B393, B566, B571, B578, B607, B643.

Opera in two acts
Libretto by Jean-Pierre Grédy after Alfred de Musset
Composed 1953-1954

Premiere:
1954 (20 July): Aix-en-Provence; Festival d'Aix-en-
Provence; Directed by Jean Meyer; Sets and costumes by Jacques Dupont; Orchestre de la Radio
diffusion française conducted by Louis Martin;
Cast includes Graziella Sciutti, Jacques Jansen.

Selected performances:
1955 (December): Naples; Teatro San Carlo; Directed by Livio Luzzato; Sets and costumes by Jacques
Dupont; Conducted by Franco Caracciolo; Cast includes Gena Doria, Francesco Albanese.

1956 (May): Paris; Same particulars as in the Premiere.

1956 (22 June): Buenos Aires, Argentina; Teatro
Colon.

1971 (June): France; Radio broadcast of excerpts.

Excerpt:
"Romance napolitaine" (Amphion)

Premiere:
1962 (September): Aix-en-Provence; Festival d'Aix-
en-Provence; Suzanne Lalique.

W7.   **Soledad** (unpublished)

Musical comedy
Story by Bernard Zimmer and Marc Cab
Alternate title: Peau d'Espagne
Unfinished project
Undertaken August-September, 1963.

W8.   **Le Pain des autres** (unpublished)

Comic opera in two acts
Working title: Le Pain d'autrui
Libretto by Edmond Kinds after Ivan Turgenev
Begun 1967; completed 1973

W9.   **Boule de suif** (unpublished)
See: B230, B231, B232, B557.

Musical comedy in two acts
Libretto by Jean Meyer after a short story by Guy de
Maupassant, with additional couplets by Albert
Husson

Premiere:
>1978 (December): Lyon: Théâtre des Célestins;
Directed by Jean Meyer; Sets and costumes by Jean-
Denis Maclès; Conducted by Claude Lecointe.

W10.   **Tistou-les-pouces-verts** (unpublished)
See: D46. B55.

Lyric tale in one act
Libretto by Jean-Luc Tardieu after the tale by Maurice
Druon
Composed 1980

Premiere:
>1981 (26 March): Paris: Théâtre du Jardin d'Accli-
mation (Carré Sylvia Monfort); Directed by Jean-
Luc Tardieu; Conducted by Jean-Claude Pennetier;
Performance broadcast on television 18 November.

BALLETS

W11.   **Le Marin et la sirène** (unpublished)

Ballet
Composed 1923 but unfinished. Only the Overture (Nocturne) and Danse des matelots remained.

W12.   **La Fortune de Venise** (unpublished)
See: B32, B35.

Ballet
Scenario by Emile Fernandez
Composed 1924 but unfinished

W13.   **Les Roses** (unpublished)
See: B31, B115, B124, B260, B296, B422, B462, B473,
B482, B497, B534, B556, B715.

Divertissement dansé
Based on a waltz by Olivier Metra
Choreography by Léonide Massine
Set and costumes by Marie Laurencin
Commissioned by Compte Etienne de Beaumont
Composed 1924

Premiere:
>1924 (14 June): Paris: Théâtre Cigale; Soirées de
Paris; Conducted by Roger Désormière.

W14.   **La Chatte** (1927; piano score; Rouart, Lerolle; 22 min.)
See: D33. B14, B23, B25, B39, B46, B47, B58, B63,
B66, B70, B94, B95, B114, B124, B128, B131, B153,
B154, B181, B193, B246, B261, B277, B281, B291,
B319, B373, B395, B403, B404, B405, B418, B421,
B438, B440, B452, B476, B480, B481, B497, B499,
B507, B518, B544, B572, B573, B574, B575, B577,
B589, B599, B625, B639, B642, B667, B669, B682,
B693, B694, B695, B702, B716, B737, B743.

Ballet in one act
Scenario by Sobeka (Boris Kochno) after the fable by
    Æsope
Choreography by Georges Balanchine
Set and costumes by Naum Gabo and Antoine Pevsner
Commissioned by Serge Diaghilev
Dedicated to Gaëtan Fouquet
Score and parts (3.3.3.3/4.3.3.1/timp/perc/str) avail-
    able on rental from Salabert
Composed 1927

Premiere:
    1927 (30 April): Monte Carlo; Théâtre de Monte
    Carlo; Ballets russes; Conducted by Marc-César
    Scotto; Cast includes Serge Lifar and Olga Spes-
    sivtzeva.

Selected performances:
    1927 (27 May): Paris; Théâtre Sarah-Bernhardt;
    Conducted by Roger Désormière; Same cast as the
    Premiere, but Alice Nikitina substitues for Olga
    Spessivtzeva.

    1927 (14 June): London; Prince's Theatre; Same
    particulars as the Paris premiere.

    1927 (27 Decmeber): Paris; Théâtre des Champs-Ely-
    sées; Alicia Markova replaces Alice Nikitina.

    1939 (8 June): Paris; Pavillon de Marsan; Program,
    entitled "La Dernière period des Ballets russes
    de Diaghilew," directed by Jean Cocteau; Cast in-
    cludes Nemtchinova, Nicolas Efimov, and Serge
    Lifar.

    1990 (14 May): Bordeaux; Salle Jacques Thibaud;
    Mai musical de Bordeaux; Hommage à Henri Sauguet;
    Choreography by Joseph Lazzini.

W15.   **David** (1928; piano score; Rouart, Lerolle; 40 min.)
    See: B154, B243, B271, B292, B428, B451, B481,
    B492, B497, B526, B589, B716, B743.

Ballet in one act
Scenario by André Doderet
Choreography by Léonide Massine
Sets and costumes by Alexandre Benois
Commissioned by Ida Rubinstein
Score and parts (3.3.3.3/4.4.4.1/timp/perc(2)/cel/hp/
    str) available on rental from Salabert
Composed 1928

Premiere:
    1928 (4 December): Paris; Opéra; Compagnie de Mme
    Ida Rubinstein; Conducted by Walter Straram.

W16.   **Prés du bal** (unpublished)

Divertissement dansé

Choreography by Yvonne Franck
Costumes by Marie Laurencin
Dedicated to Madame Jeanne-René Dubost
Composed 1929

Premiere:
    1929: Paris; Private soirée; Conducted by Henri
    Sauguet.

W17.   **La Nuit** (1930; piano score; Rouart, Lerolle; 12 min.)
        See: B7, B52, B120, B124, B135, B200, B201, B244,
        B277, B310, B327, B328, B366, B400, B403, B404,
        B433, B456, B477, B479, B490, B497, B623, B695,
        B698, B729.

Ballet in one act
Scenario by Boris Kochno
Choreography by Serge Lifar
Set and costumes by Christian Bérard
Commissioned by Charles B. Cochran
Score and parts (1.1.2.1/2.2.1.0/timp/perc/hp/str)
    available on rental from Salabert
Composed 1930

Premiere:
    1930 (31 March): London; Pavilion; C. B. Cochran's
    Revue of 1930; Cast includes Alice Nikitina and
    Serge Lifar; Previously performed in a "try-out"
    at the Palace Theatre in Manchester.

Selected performances:
    1949 (19 April): Paris; Théâtre des Champs-Elysées;
    Ballets des Champs-Elysées; Memorial tribute to
    Christian Bérard; New choreography by Janine Char-
    rat; Cast includes Irène Skorick, Youly Algaroff;
    Later incorporated in world tour of the company.

    1953 (23 April): New York City; Cast includes Maria
    Tallchief, Nicholas Magallanes.

    1980 (25 May): Bordeaux; Centre André Malraux; Mai
    musical de Bordeaux.

W18.   **Caprice** (unpublished)
        See: B143, B627.

Ballet
Choreography by Georges Balanchine
Costumes by Christian Bérard
Composed 1932

Premiere:
    1932 (29 June): Paris; Théâtre des Champs-Elysées;
    Part of a recital by Alice Nikitina.

W19.   **Fastes** (unpublished)
        See: B14, B96, B114, B130, B277, B497, B629, B647,
        B669, B693, B704.

Ballet in one act
Scenario by André Derain
Choreography by Georges Balanchine
Set and costumes by André Derain
Commissioned by Edward James
Dedicated by Edward James
Composed 1933

Premiere:
    1933 (7 June): Paris; Théâtre des Champs-Elysées;
    Les Ballets 1933; Conducted by Maurice Abravanel.

Selected performances:
    1933 (28 June): London; Savoy Theatre; Same partic-
    ulars as in the Premiere.

W20.   **La Dompteur dompté** (unpublished)
        See: B141. See also: W127.

Ballet
Scenario by Jean-Louis Vaudoyer
Choreography by Serge Lifar
Orchestration, 1938, of **Le Jeux de l'amour et du ha-
sard**

Premiere:
    1938 (7 April): Paris; Théâtre des Ambassadeurs;
    Les Ballets de la Jeunesse.

W21.   **Cartes postales** (unpublished)

Scènes chorégraphiques (Suite charactéristique)
Choreography by Pierre Berezzi
Set and costumes by Louis Touchagues
Composed for piano 1941

Premiere:
    1941: Paris; Théâtre Hebertot; Cast includes Ca-
    therine Paul, Pierre Berezzi.

W22.   **La Cigale et la fourmi** (unpublished)
        See: D5.

Ballet in one act for marionettes
Scenario by Jacques Chesnais after a tale by La Fon-
taine
Dedicated to Francis Poulenc
Composed for chamber orchestra (flute, oboe, bassoon,
horn, trumpet, violoncello, piano) 1941

Premiere:
    1948: Rome; Opera del Buratonni di Maria Signorelli.

W23.   **Image à Paul et Virginie** (unpublished)
        See: B437, B512. See also: W137.

Ballet (Pas de deux)
Choreography probably by Roland Petit
Costumes by Marie Laurencin

Dedicated to Roland Petit
Composed for piano 1942; orchestrated 1944

Premiere:
1944: Paris; Cast includes Roland Petit, Janine
Charrat.

W24.   **Les Mirages** (1953; piano score; Salabert; 30 min.)
See: B14, B21, B41, B45, B110, B132, B198, B218,
B224, B227, B235, B273, B277, B280, B300, B309,
B339, B437, B458, B478, B489, B492, B494, B495,
B496, B497, B515, B535, B577, B589, B602, B604,
B649, B655, B656, B737, B743.

Ballet (Choreographic fairy-tale) in two scenes
Scenario by A. M. Cassandre
Choreography by Serge Lifar
Sets and costumes by A. M. Cassandre
Dedicated to Olin Downes
Score and parts (3.3.3.3/4.4.4.1/timp/perc/str) avail-
able on rental from Salabert
Composed 1942-1943

Premiere:
1947 (15 December): Paris; Opéra; Conducted by
Louis Forestier; Cast includes Yvette Chauviré,
Serge Lifar.
Original premiere was postponed when electricity
was shut down in Paris due to the advance of the
allied troups on Paris in 1944.
The ballet remained in the repertoire of the Bal-
lets de l'Opéra. Eventually Nina Vyroubova and
Michel Renault replaced Chauviré and Lifar.

Selected performances:
1948 (21 September): New York City; Tour of the
Ballets de l'Opéra.

1962 (September): Paris; Opéra; Revival of the
ballet; Cast includes Amiel and Flindt.

1977: Paris; Opéra; Part of "Hommage à Serge Lifar"
sponsored by Rolf Liebermann; Cast includes Noëlla
Pontois, Michaël Denard.

W25.   **Les Forains** (1946; piano score; Rouart, Lerolle; 1946;
full score; Salabert; 25 min.)
See: S251. D15, D17, D27, D29, D49. B4, B14, B17,
B24, B36, B38, B41, B54, B69, B71, B74, B78, B81,
B119, B125, B152, B155, B162, B200, B208, B211,
B214, B216, B222, B258, B266, B273, B277, B300,
B304, B311, B326, B327, B328, B332, B357, B371,
B372, B403, B404, B435, B436, B437, B456, B490,
B493, B497, B552, B553, B555, B589, B591, B598,
B599, B601, B632, B655, B656, B667, B695, B726,
B730, B735, B737.

Ballet in one act
Scenario by Boris Kochno

Choreography by Roland Petit
Set and costumes by Christian Bérard
Dedicated to Erik Satie
Score and parts (2.2.2.2/2.2.1.1/timp/perc/cel/pf/
str) available on rental from Salabert
Composed 1945

Premiere:
1945 (2 March): Paris; Théâtre des Champs-Elysées;
Compagnie Roland Petit; Conducted by André Cluytens; Cast includes Roland Petit, Ludmila Tcherina.

Selected performances:
1949 (16-20 December): Florence; Magio· Musical di
Fiorentino.

1950 (October): New York City; National Theatre;
Ballets de Paris.

1960 (May): Marseille; Ballet de l'Opéra municipal
de Marseille; Choreography by Géo Stone.

1963 (15 April): Paris; Théâtre des Champs-Elysées;
Compagnie Serge Golovine; Choreography by Christian Foye.

1964 (Summer): Paris; Concours du Conservatoire
(Danse); Nicole Chouret performs excerpts as part
of her winning performance.

1971 (24-25 April): Tours; Grand Théâtre.

1974: France; Television; Félix Blaska and his
company.

W26.   **La Rencontre** (1949; piano score; Heugel; 1952; minia-
ture score; Heugel; 22 min.)
See: B5, B6, B152, B199, B202, B273, B277, B300,
B311, B329, B403, B404, B412, B435, B456, B459,
B474, B475, B486, B497, B565, B577, B589, B592,
B599, B611, B619, B620, B647, B656, B695, B730,
B736.

Ballet in one act
Scenario by Boris Kochno
Choreography by David Lichine
Set and costumes by Christian Bérard
Dedicated to Boris Kochno and Christian Bérard
Score and parts (2.1.1.1/1.1.1.0/timp/perc/cel/hp/
pf/str) available on rental from Heugel
Composed, Coutras, August, 1948

Premiere:
1948 (8 November): Paris; Théâtre des Champs-Elysées; Conducted by André Girard; Cast includes
Jean Babilée, Leslie Caron.

Selected performances:
1949 (September): London; Prince's Theatre.

1953 (21 April):   New York City; Metropolitan Opera
Theater.

1955 (29 April):   New York City; Metropolitan Opera
Theater; New York Ballet Theatre; Cast includes
Nora Kay, Igor Youskevitch.

1962 (July):   Berlin; Choreography by Tatiana Gsov-
sky; Cast includes Joan Cadzow, Gert Reinholm.

1962 (July):   Paris; Ballet néerlandais; Cast includes Sonja van Beers, Billy Wilson.

1962 (July):   Moscow.

W27.   **Pas de deux classique** (unpublished)

Ballet (Pas de deux)
Commissioned by Jean Guelis
Composed 1951

Premiere:
1951:   Paris; Casino de Paris; Choreography by Jean
Guelis.

W28.   **Les Saisons** (unpublished; 60 min.)
See: B117, B147, B151, B174, B318, B386, B454, B455,
B586, B595, B596, B611, B615, B646, B655, B656.

Ballet in two scenes for chorus, orchestra, and dancers
Scenario by Jacques Dupont and David Lichine
Text by Henri Sauguet
Choreography by Léonide Massine
Sets and costumes by Jacques Dupont
Score and parts (3.3.3.3/4.3.2.1/timp/perc/hp/5 soli/
chor/str) available on rental from Editions fran-
çaises de musique
Composed 1951

Premiere:
1951 (20 May):   Bordeaux; Mai musical de Bordeaux;
Grand ballet du Marquis de Cuevas; Chœurs de la
Maîtresse de la R.T.F.; Orchestre de la R.T.F.;
Conducted by Gustave Cloez; Cast includes Rosella
Hightower, George Zoritch, Harriet Toby, Serge
Golovine, Georges Skibine.

Selected performances:
1952 (20 October):   Paris; Théâtre des Champs-Elysées;   Same particulars as the Premiere, except
Manuel Rosenthal is the conductor.

1990 (14 May):   Bordeaux; Salle Jacques Thibaud;
Mai musical de Bordeaux; "Hommage à Henri Sauguet;"
Choreography of an excerpt entitled "Quatre images
des Saisons" by Joseph Lazzini.

W29.   Cordelia (unpublished)
        See: B2, B29, B132, B147, B430, B490, B579, B647,
        B648, B668, B731.

        Ballet in one act
        Scenario by Henri Sauguet
        Choreography by John Taras
        Set and costumes by Jacques Dupont
        Composed 1952

        Premiere:
        1952 (7 May): Paris; Théâtre des Champs-Elysées;
        Festival du XXe Siècle; Grand Ballet du Marquis
        de Cuevas; Conducted by André Girard; Cast in-
        cludes John Taras, Jacqueline Volmar, Delores
        Starr, Serge Golovine.

W30.   Trésor et magie (unpublished)
        See: B367, B743.

        Ballet (Divertissement chorégraphique)
        Scenario by Serge Lifar after a theme by Lancôme
        Choreography by Serge Lifar
        Set and costumes by Jacques Dupont
        Composed 1952

        Premiere:
        1952 (Spring): Paris; Bal des Petits Lits Blancs;
        Cast includes Claude Bessy, Josette Clavier,
        Jean-Baptiste Lemoine.

        Selected performances:
        1952 (19 July): Aix-en-Provence; Festival d'Aix-
        en-Provence; Conducted by Richard Blareau.

W31.   Le Cardinal aux chats (unpublished)
        See: B190.

        Ballet (Divertissement chorégraphique)
        Scenario by Henri Sauguet
        Choreography by Yvonne Farnck
        Set and costumes by Jacques Dupont
        Commissioned by Baronne de Cabrol
        Composed 1952

        Premiere:
        1952: Paris; Théâtre Marigny; Soirées de l'Essor;
        Conducted by Richard Blareau.

        Selected performances:
        1953 (18 April): New York City; Bal April in Paris;
        Cast includes Henri Sauguet in the role of Cardinal
        Richelieu.

W32.   Le Sacre de l'automne (unpublished)
        See: B150, B157, B183, B209, B484.

        Unrealized ballet
        Scenario by Baron Philippe de Rothschild

Sets and costumes were to be by Salvador Dalí
Choreography was to be by Serge Lifar
Undertaken between 1951 and 1953; work was aborted
  when the participants couldn't agree upon the form
  of presentation

W33.   **Le Caméléopard** (unpublished; 20 min.)
       <u>See</u>: B42, B277, B431, B525, B578, B589, B633.

       Ballet in four scenes
       Scenario by Alain Vigot and Jean Babilée after "The
         Beast with four heads" by Edgar Alan Poe
       Choreography by Jean Babilée
       Sets and costumes by Jacques Noël
       Score and parts (2.1.2.1/2.2.1.0/timp/perc/hp/pf/str)
         available on rental from Ricordi
       Composed June, 1956

       <u>Premiere</u>:
       1956 (19 June): Paris; Théâtre des Champs-Elysées;
         Ballets Jean Babilée; Conducted by Maurice Le
         Roux; Cast includes Jean Babilée, Corinne Reichel,
         Jane Mason.

W34.   **Les Cinq étages** (1957; piano score; Heugel; 42 min.)
       <u>See</u>: B238.

       Ballet in six scenes
       Scenario by Rudolphe Liechtenhan and Wazlaw Orlikow-
         sky after the poem "Les Cinq étages" by Pierre-Jean
         Béranger.
       Choreography by Wazlaw Orlikowsky
       Sets and costumes by Max Bignens
       Score and parts (2.2.2.2/2.2.2.1/timp/perc/cel/str)
         available on rental from Heugel
       Composed January-February, 1957

       <u>Premiere</u>:
       1959: Basel, Switzerland; Opéra de Bâle; Conducted
         by Charles Schwartz; Cast includes Roland April,
         Eva Bajoratis.

W35.   **La Dame aux camélias** (unpublished; 45 min.)
       <u>See</u>: B8, B44, B101, B152, B165, B173, B210, B235,
         B254, B299, B300, B304, B308, B372, B416, B433,
         B434, B491, B541, B589, B593, B606, B610, B661,
         B680, B690, B691, B743, B745.

       Ballet in two acts and five scenes
       Scenario by Tatiana Gsovsky after the novel by Alex-
         andre Dumas, fils
       Choreography by Tatiana Gsovsky
       Sets and costumes by Jean-Pierre Ponnelle
       Score and parts (3.3.3.3/4.3.3.1/timp/perc/hp/pf/str)
         available on rental from Ricordi
       Composed March-September, 1957

       <u>Premiere</u>:
       1957 (September): Berlin; Festival of Berlin;

Inauguration of the new Berlin Concert Hall; Premiere danced by Helga Sommerkamp, but official Gala opening was danced by Yvette Chauviré.

Selected performances:
1960 (3 February): Grenoble; Winter Olympics; Revised version; Sets and costumes by Jacques Dupont; Conducted by Louis Forestier; Cast includes Yvette Chauviré, Georges Skibine.

Selected performances:
1971 (23 April): Havana, Cuba; Teatro Garcia Lorca; New version entitled Nos veremos ayer noche, Margarita; Choreography by Alberto Mendez; Sets and costumes by Salvador Fernandez; Cast includes Alicia Alonso, Jorge Esquivel.

1971 (22 May): Bordeaux; Grand Théâtre de Bordeaux; Mai musical de Bordeaux; Same particulars as in the 23 April performance.

1990 (14 May): Bordeaux; Salle Jacques Thibaud; Mai musical de Bordeaux; "Hommage à Henri Sauguet;" Excerpts entitled "Ballet d'un grand amour;" Choreography by Joseph Lazzini.

Excerpts:
"Lente valse d'amour inquiet" (1960; Ricordi) Excerpt for piano solo

"La Mort de la Dame aux camélias" (unpublished) For orchestra; See also W65.

W36.   **La Solitude** (unpublished; 22 min.)

Ballet for two dancers
Subtitled "Rêverie symphonique" (See also: W66)
Score and parts (1.1.1.1/1.0.0.0/timp/perc/cel/str) available on rental from Heugel
Composed April, 1958

W37.   **L'As de cœur** (unpublished; 25 min.)

Ballet
Scenario based on a tale by Claude Aveline
Choreography by Joseph Lazzini
Set and costumes by Jacques Dupont
Score and parts (2.2.2.2/2.1.1.0/timp/perc/hp/str) available on rental from Editions françaises de musique
Composed September-November 1960; Orchestrated February-march, 1961

Premiere:
1961: Marseille; Opéra de Marseille; Cast includes Alberte Clausier, Michel Bruel, Jean-Paul Comelin, Catherine Verneuil.

W38. **Plus loin que la nuit et le jour** (1961; Salabert)
<u>See</u>: B102, B265, B546, B585, B645.

Cantata-ballet for tenor solo, mixed chorus a cappella
and dancers
Scenario based on "A Mare" by Louis Emié
Choreography by Jean-Jacques Etchéverry
Sets and costumes by Jacques Dupont
Composed November-December, 1960

<u>Premiere</u>:
1961 (May): Bordeaux; Mai musical de Bordeaux; Paul
Derenne; Agrupacíon Choral de camera de Pamplona;
Luis Morondo, conductor; Cast includes Jean-Pierre
Ruffier, Bernadette Ferrasse, Janine Guitton.

W39. **Pâris** (unpublished; 40 min.)
<u>See</u>: B432, B634, B647, B734.

Ballet
Scenario by Boris Kochno
Choreography by Janine Charrat
Set and costumes by Jacques Dupont
Score and parts (1.1.1.1/1.1.1.0/timp/perc(2)/hp/pf/
str) available on rental from Salabert
Composed September, 1964

<u>Premiere</u>:
1964 (25 November): Paris; Théâtre des Champs-Elysées; Festival international de la danse; Ballets
de France; Cast includes Janine Charrat, Tessa
Beaumont; Juan Giuliano; Karl Musil.

W40. **Le Prince et le mendiant** (unpublished; 50 min.)
<u>See</u>: B670.

Ballet-Mimodrama
Scenario by Boris Kochno after <u>The</u> <u>Prince</u> <u>and</u> <u>the</u>
<u>Pauper</u> by Mark Twain
Choreography by Juan Corelli
Score and parts available on rental from Editions
françaises de musique
Composed March, 1965

<u>Premiere</u>:
1965 (September): France; Produced for television
(Première chaîne) by Jean-Pierre Carrère; Conducted by Henri Sauguet.

W41. **La Guirlande de Campra** (unpublished; 20 min.)
<u>See</u>: B48, B337, B338, B460, B736. <u>See</u> <u>also</u>: W60.

Ballet
Based on **Variations sur un thème de Campra** (W60); For
details about the movements see: W60
Choreography by John Taras
Sets by Peter Harvey
Costumes by Esteban Frances
Score and parts (2.2.2.2/2.2.0.0/timp/perc/hp/str)

available on rental from Salabert
Composed 1966

Premiere:
1966 (April): New York City; New York State Theater;
New York City Ballet; Benefit performance to fi-
nance the company's 1966-67 season.

Selected performances:
1966 (December): New York City; New York State Theater; New York City Ballet.

W42.   **Solitude**, new version (unpublished)

Ballet
Scenario by Raphaël Cluzel
Choreography by Skouratof
Composed 1958, revised 1979

Premiere:
1979 (11 March): Bordeaux; Centre Laine.

W43.   **L'Arbre** (unpublished)

Ballet for eleven saxophones and dancers
Scenario by Raphaël Cluzel
Composed 1981

Premiere:
1981 (25 May): Bordeaux; Mai musical de Bordeaux.

INSTRUMENTAL MUSIC, LARGE ENSEMBLES

W44.   **Danse des matelots** (unpublished; 2 min., 30 sec.)
See: B501.

For orchestra (2.1.2.1/2.2.1.1/perc/str)
Possibly from the unfinished ballet, **Le Marin et le
sirène** (W11), or an orchestration of no. 6 from
Trois nouvelles françaises (W143).
Composed 1925?

Premiere:
1941 (10 May): Paris; Concert du Triptyque.

W45.   **La Chatte suite** (unpublished)
See: B153, B246.

Suite for orchestra from the ballet (W14)
Movements: Jeux de garçons; Invocation à Aphrodite;
Hymne final
Composed 1927

Premiere:
1935 (January): Paris.

W46.   **David suite** (unpublished)
See: B243.

Suite for orchestra from the ballet (W15)
Composed 1928

Premiere:
1930 (8 March):   Paris; Théâtre des Champs-Elysées;
Concerts Pasdeloup; D.-E. Inghelbrecht, conductor.

W47.   **La Nuit suite** (unpublished; 12 min.)
See: B112, B244, B506, B508, B520, B587.

Suite for orchestra from the ballet (W17)
Movements: Prélude; La Femme; La Rue; Le Jeune homme;
Valse; Coda
Composed 1930

Premiere:
1930 (30 March):   Paris; L'Orchestre symphonique de
Paris; Pierre Monteux, conductor.

W48.   **Fastes suite** (unpublished)
See: B629.

Suite from the ballet (W19)
Composed 1933

Premiere:
1935 (28 June):   Paris; Concerts de La Sérénade; D.-
E. Inghelbrecht, conductor.

W49.   **Les Mirages suite** (unpublished)

Suite for orchestra from the ballet (W24)
Composed 1943

Premiere:
1945 (December):   Paris; L'Orchestre national de la
R.T.F.; Manuel Rosenthal, conductor.

W50.   **Symphonies de la montagne** (unpublished)
See: B138, B226.

Suite for orchestra extracted from the film score for
Premier de cordée (W366)
Composed 1944

Premiere:
1946:   Lyon; L'Orchestre symphonique de Lyon; René
Corniot, conductor.

W51.   **Image à Paul et Virginie suite** (unpublished)

Orchestral version of the piano nocturne (W137) which
later became the ballet of the same name (W51)
Orchestrated 1944

W52.   **Les Forains suite** (unpublished)
See: B212.

Suite for orchestra from the ballet (W25)

Contents: Prologue; Entrée des forains; Exercises;
Parade; La Répresentation; La Petit fille à la
chaise; Visions d'art; Les Sœurs siamoises; Le Prestidigitateur; Le Prestidigitateur et la poupée; Ga-
lop final; Quête et départ des forains
Composed 1945

Premiere:
1945 (October):   Paris; L'Orchestre national de
France; André Cluytens, conductor.

Selected performances:
1960 (April):   Paris; Société des concerts du Conservatoire; Jean Gittou, conductor.

1964 (March):   Paris; Société des concerts du Conservatoire; Roger Boutry, conductor.

W53.   Symphonie no. 1 (1948; Rouart, Lerolle; 45 min.)
See: B122, B203, B250, B251, B369, B390, B543.

Symphony in four movements (Allegro giusto; Andantino;
Allegro (alla marcia); Lento quasi adagio)
For orchestra (3.3.3.3/4.4.2.1/timp/perc/hp/str)
Alternate title: "Symphonie expiatoire"
Dedicated to the innocent victims of the war
Score and parts available on rental from Salabert
Composed, Paris and Coutras, 1944-1946

Premiere:
1948 (Spring):   Brussels; Radio Belgium concert;
L'Orchestre de la Radio I.N.R.; Franz André, conductor.

Selected performances:
1948 (2 August);   Paris; L'Orchestre Lamoureux; Ernest Bour, conductor.

1948 (Autumn):   Strasbourg; Also broadcast on Radio
France.

W54.   Les Saisons et les jours (unpublished)
See: B226.

Symphonic estracts from the film music for **Farrebique**
(W337)
For orchestra
Composed 1946

Premiere:
1951 (October):   Paris; Concerts Colonne; Richard
Blareau, conductor.

W55.   Stèle symphonique (unpublished)

For orchestra
Commissioned by the Ministre de l'Education Nationale
for a centennial commemoration of the death of Cha-
teaubriand.

Dedicated to the memory of François René de Chateau-
briand.
Composed 1948

Premiere:
1948: Paris; Sorbonne; Conducted by the composer.

W56.   **La Rencontre suite** (unpublished; 22 min.)

Suite for orchestra from the ballet (W26)
Composed 1948

W57.   **Symphonie no. 2** (unpublished; 60 min.)
See: B151, B176, B207, B372, B388, B455, B543.

Symphony in six movements (L'Hiver; Le Printemps; Noc-
turne du Rossignol; L'Eté; L'Automne; Retour de
l'hiver)
For orchestra (3.3.3.3/4.3.2.1/timp/hp/pf/str), mixed
chorus, children's chorus and soprano solo
Alternate title: "Symphonie allégorique"
Score and parts available on rental from Editions
françaises de musique
Later transformed into the ballet **Les Saisons** (W28)
Composed 1949

Premiere:
1949: Paris; Radio concert; L'Orchestre de la Radio
Télévision française; Chœurs de René Alix; Jeanne
Michaud, soprano; Roger Désormière, conductor.

Selected performances:
1959: Paris; Radio concert; L'Orchestre de la
Radio Télévision française; Manuel Rosenthal,
conductor.

Extract:
Les Quatre saisons
See: W191.

W58.   **Tableaux de Paris** (1963; Ahn & Simrock; 28 min., 30
sec.)
See: D29.

Suite for orchestra (2.2.2.sax.1/2.2.1.1./timp/perc/
cel/hp/pf/accordion/str)
Contents: Prélude--Panorama; Matin aux Tuileries;
Quai aux fleurs--Marché aux oiseaux; La Place des
Vosges; Le Canal Saint-Martin; Midi, Place de l'Op-
éra; Lunch au Ritz; Coucher de soleil sur l'Arc de
Triomphe; Soirée à Saint-Germain-des-Prés; Nuit à
Montmartre
Composed for the 2,000th anniversary of Paris
Score and parts available on rental from Ahn & Simrock
Composed 1950

Premiere:
1950: Paris; L'Orchestre de la société des concerts
du Conservatoire; Composer conducting.

W59.   Cordélia suite (unpublished)

Suite for orchestra from the ballet (W29)
Composed 1952

W60.   Variations sur un thème de Campra (1954; limited edition; Salabert; 20 min.)
See: B225, B270, B387, B652.

Collaborative set of variations for orchestra (2.2.2.
2/2.2.0.0/timp/perc/hp/str)
Contents: Thème (orchestrated by Marc Pincerle);
Toccata by Arthur Honegger; Moderato by Daniel-Lesur;
Canarie by Roland-Manuel; Pavane by Germaine Taille-
fere; Matelote provençale by Francis Poulenc; Minuet
by Henri Sauguet; Gigue by Georges Auric
Score and parts available on rental from Salabert
Composed 1952

Premiere:
1952 (August): Aix-en-Provence; Festival d'Aix-en-
Provence; Sudwestfunk Orchester, Baden-Baden; Hans
Rosbaud, conductor.

Selected performances:
1956 (March): Paris; L'Orchestre de la sociéte des
concerts du Conservatoire; Georges Tzipine, conductor.

Transformed by John Taras into the ballet **La Guirlande
de Campra** (W41).

W61.   Les trois lys (1955; Salabert; 8 min.)
See: D27. B133, B384, B514.

Symphonic movement for orchestra (2.2.2.2/2.2.1.1/
timp/perc/hp/str)
Commissioned by the Louisville Orchestra Foundation
Dedicated in tribute to the Louisville Orchestra
Score and parts available on rental from Salabert
Composed in Paris, September, Decmeber, 1953

Premiere:
1954 (September): Louisville, Kentucky; Louisville
Symphony Orchestra; Robert Whitney, conductor.

Selected performances:
1954 (19 December): Paris; L'Orchestre national de
la R.T.F.; Manuel Rosenthal, conductor.

W62.   Symphonie no. 3 (1955; Salabert; 25 min.)
See: B26, B164, B165, B192, B257, B507, B537, B543,
B659, B662, B664, B708.

For orchestra (3.3.3.2/4.3.0.1/timp/perc/hp/str)
Subtitled: "I.N.R."
Dedicated to L'Orcheste de la I.N.R., and its conduc-
tor Franz André
Composed 1955

Premiere:
1955 (September): Venise; Festival de Venise; L'Orchestre de la Radio I.N.R.; Franz André, conductor.

Selected performances:
1961 (November): Paris; L'Orchestre national de la R.T.F.; Manuel Rosenthal, conductor; Broadcast in December.

1962 (July): Aspen, Colorado; Aspen Festival Orestra; Walter Susskind, conductor.

W63.   **Variations sur le nom de Marguerite Long** (1956; Salabert; 24 min.)
See: B119, B142, B212, B229, B379.

Collaborative set of variations for orchestra (3.3.3. 3/4.3.3.1/perc/cel/hp/pf/str)
Theme based on letters from the dedicatee's name
Contributing composers: Darius Milhaud, Daniel-Lesur, Henri Duttileux, Jean Rivier, Francis Poulenc, Georges Auric, Jean Françaix, and Henri Sauguet, whose contribution was "Variations en forme de berceuse"
Dedicated to Marguerite Long
Score and parts available on rental from Salabert
Composed 1956

Premiere:
1956 (6 April): Paris; Sorbonne; L'Orchestre de la société des concerts du Conservatoire; Charles Munch, conductor.

Selected performances:
1960 (April): Paris; L'Orchestre de la société de la concerts du Conservatoire; Jean Gittou, conductor.

W64.   **Les Cinq étages suite** (unpublished)

Suite for orchestra from the ballet (W34)
Composed January-March, 1957

W65.   **La Dame aux camélias suite** (unpublished; 25 min.)
See: B164, B165, B254, B257, B659.

Symphonic suite for orchestra (2.1.2.1/2.1.1.0/timp/ perc/hp/pf/str) from the ballet (W35)
Alternate title: "La Mort de la dame aux camélias"
Score and parts available on rental from Ricordi
Composed March-September, 1957

Premiere:
1961 (November): Paris; L'Orchestre national de l'O.R.T.F.; Manuel Rosenthal, conductor; Concert in honor of Sauguet's 60th birthday. Recorded for broadcast in December.

W66.   **Rêverie symphonique** (1960; Heugel; 22 min.)
       See: D35. B121, B172, B221, B255.

For orchestra (1.1.1.1/1.1.0.0/timp/perc/cel/pf/str)
Concert version of the music for the ballet **La Soli-
tude** (W36)
Dedicated to Jean, La Comtesse de Polignac
Score and parts available on rental from Heugel
Composed 1958

Premiere:
       1958 (8 November); Paris; Semaines musicales inter-
            nationales de Paris; L'Orchestre de la reine Eli-
            sabeth de Belgique; Franz André, conductor.

W67.   **L'As de cœur suite** (unpublished)

Suite for orchestra after the ballet (W37)
Composed November-December, 1960

Premiere:
       1960: Paris; Radio broadcast; Composer conducting.

W68.   **Deux mouvements pour archets** (1964; Editions fran-
       çaises de musique; 15 min., 30 sec.)
       See: D36. B239.

For string orchestra
Contents: Remembrance; Destinée valse
Commissioned by L'Orchestre de la R.T.F.
Dedicated to the memory of the poet Paul Gilson
Score and parts available on rental from Editions
       françaises de musique
Composed January, 1964

Premiere:
       1964: Paris; Radio broadcast by L'Orchestre de la
            R.T.F.; Eugène Bigot, conductor.

W69.   **Promenades espagoles** (unpublished)

Orchestration of music by Roger Désormière
Undertaken April, 1964

W70.   **Symphonie de marches** (unpublished)
       See: D54.
       For orchestra
Commissioned by the Congrès international des Chemins
       de Fer
Composed January, 1966

Premiere:
       1966 (4 July): Paris; XIXe Congrès international
            des Chemins de Fer; L'Orchestre de la S.N.C.F.;
            Robert Blot, conductor.

W71.   **Symphonie no. 4** (1973; Leduc; 35 min.)
       See: B303, B443, B447, B657.

For orchestra (3.3.3.3/4.3.3.1/timp/perc(4)/hp/str)
Three movements: Allegro vivo et marcato; Lento; Al-
legro vivo e scherzando
Subtitled: "Du troisième âge"
Commissioned by Le Ministère des Affaires Culturelles
Score and parts available on rental from Leduc
Composed Coutras and Paris, 29 June-October, 1971

Premiere:
1971 (28 November): Paris; L'Orchestre des concerts
Pasdeloup; Gérard Devos, conductor.

W72.   **Petite valse du Grand échiquier** (1974; Editions françaises de musique; 2 min., 30 sec.)

For orchestra (1.1.1.0/1.1.1.0/timp/perc/cel/hp/str)
Dedicated to Jacques Chancel
Score and parts available on rental from Editions fran-
çaises de musique
Composed 1973

W73.   **Reflets sur feuilles** (unpublished)

For orchestra
Based on Feuilles mortes by Claude Debussy
Commissioned by Union des Conservatoires du Val-de-
Marne.
Composed March, 1979

W74.   **Septembre** (unpublished)

Prelude for orchestra
Orchestration of piano prelude of the same title (W170)
Commissioned by the Collegium Musicum d'Aquitaine
Composed March, 1987

INSTRUMENTAL MUSIC, LARGE ENSEMBLES WITH SOLO

W75.   **Concerto no. 1** (1936; Eschig; 24 min.)
See: D16, D17, D21. B22, B81, B108, B161, B194,
B205, B216, B223, B249, B252, B274, B326, B343,
B359, B383, B468, B553, B613, B632, B656, B660,
B678.

For piano and orchestra (3.3.3.3/4.3.3.1/timp/perc/
str)
Three movements: Andante assai; Lento,quasi adagio;
Allegro moto
Dedicated to Jacques Dupont
Score and aprts available on rental from Eschig
Composed 1933-1934

Private premiere:
1935: Paris; Salon of Princesse de Polignac; Piano,
four-hand version; Clara Haskil and Henri Sauguet
pianos.

Public premiere:
1935: Brussels; L'Orchestre de la Radio I.N.R.;

Paul Collaer, pianist; Franz André, conductor.

Paris premiere:
1935: L'Orchestre des Concerts Lamoureux; Jeanne-
Marie Darre, pianist; Eugène Bigot, conductor.

Selected performances:
1943: Switzerland; Radio Genève.

1946 (December): Paris

1954 (7 February): Paris; Théâtre du Châtelet;
L'Orchestre des concerts Colonne; Vasso Devetzi,
pianist; Richard Blareau, conductor.

1955 (20 June): Paris; Théâtre des Champs-Elysées;
Same performers as 7 February, 1954, performance.

1957 (December): Paris; L'Orchestre des concerts
Pasdeloup; Vasso Devezti, pianist.

1962 (October): Paris; l'Orchestre des concerts Lamoureux; Vasso Devezti, pianist; Jean-Baptiste
Mari, conductor.

1964 (November): Paris; Semaines internationales
de musique de Paris; L'Orchestre national de
France; Vasso Devezti, pianist; Composer conducting.

1971 (February): Prague; Vasso Devezti, pianist;
Jean-Claude Casadesus, conductor.

W76.   **Concerto no. 2** (unpublished)
See: B19.

For piano and orchestra
Subtitled: "Rêverie concertante"
Based on the music of a popular song by Sauguet (W296)
and used in the film, **Les Amoureux sont seuls au
monde** (W342)
Composed 1948

Film version premiere:
1948: Jacqueline Robins-Bonneau, pianist; Henri
Sauguet, conductor.

Concert premiere:
1948: Toulouse; L'Orchestre symphonique de Toulouse;
Dyna August, pianist; Composer conducting.

W77.   **Concerto d'Orphée** (1954; reduction for violin, piano;
Heugel; 25 min.)
See: B24, B107, B164, B165, B192, B257, B267, B347,
B360, B381, B441, B549, B612, B643, B650, B656,
B659.

For violin and orchestra (3.3.2.2/2.1.1.0/timp/perc(2)/
cel/hp/pf/str)
Idea for the concerto suggested by M. Strobel

Score and parts available on rental from Heugel
Composed 1953

Premiere:
    1953 (26 August):   Aix-en-Provence; Festival d'Aix-
    en-Provence; Sudwestfunkorchester; Ludwig Bus,
    violinist; Hans Rosbaud, conductor.

Selected performances:
    1954:   London; BBC Radio broadcast; Louis Kaufmann,
    violinist.

    1961 (21 November):   Paris; L'Orchestre national de
    la R.T.F.; Devy Erlih, violinist; Manuel Rosen-
    thal, conductor; Sauguet's 60th birthday concert.

    1981 (January):   Parsi; L'Orchestre de L'Ile-de-
    France; Hermilo Novelo, violinist; Jacques Hout-
    mann, conductor; Sauguet's 80th birthday concert
    sponsored by La Société française de musique con-
    temporaine.

W78.   **Octave-valse** (unpublished)

For handbells and orchestra
Commissioned by Baronne de Cabrol
Composed 1952

Premiere:
    1953 (23 June):   Soirée du Cirque sponsored by
    Baronne de Cabrol.

W79.   **Concerto no. 3** (1964; reduction for two pianos; Sala-
    bert; 30 min.)
    See: B19, B213, B300, B301, B343, B443, B651.

For piano and orchestra (4.4.3.3/4.3.3.1/timp/cel/hp/
    str)
Subtitled: "Concert des mondes souterrains"
Dedicated to Léon Barzin and L'Orchestre de la Société
    philharmonique de Paris, and Jean Boquet
Score and parts available on rental from Salabert
Composed 1961-1963

Premiere:
    1963 (6 June):   Paris; L'Orchestre de la Société
    philharmonique de Paris; Jean Boquet, pianist;
    Léon Barzin, conductor.

W80.   **Mélodie concertante** (1964; reduction for violoncello
    and piano; Le Chant du monde)
    See: D18, D39. B78, B82, B83, B104, B133, B149,
    B177, B178, B331, B363, B388, B658, B721.

For violoncello and orchestra
One movement
Also published for 'cello and piano by Muzyka, 1967.
Composed December, 1962-November, 1963

Premiere:
   1964 (14 February): Moscow; Moscow Radio Symphony
   Orchestra; Mstislav Rostropovich, cellist; Henri
   Sauguet, conductor.

Selected performances:
   1964 (14 December): Paris; L'Orchestre philharmonique de la Radio; Mstislav Rostropovich, cellist;
   André Girard, conductor; Part of Semaines musicales
   internationales de Paris.

W81.   **Garden's concerto** (1971; Editions françaises de mu-
        sique; 16 min.)
        See: D8, D36. B239, B576, B673.

   For harmonica (or oboe) and chamber orchestra (perc
   (2)/hp/cel/str)
   Three movements: Andantino con grazia; Allegro; Al-
   legro vivace
   Dedicated to Claude Garden
   Composed August-September, 1970

   Premiere:
      1970: Télévision française; Association symphonique
      de chambre de Paris; Claude Garden, harmonica;
      Henri Sauguet, conductor.

W82.   **Sonate d'église** (1986 ; Eschig; 26 min.)
        See: D8. B675.

   For organ and strings
   Three movements: Moderato assai; Lento; Allegro
   Dedicated to Pierre Lacroix and the Festival du Com-
   minges
   Composed 1984-1985

   Premiere:
      1985 (31 July): Comminges; Saint-Bertrand de Com-
      minges; Madame Chaisemartin, organ; Quatuor à
      cordes de Toulouse.

INSTRUMENTAL MUSIC, SMALL ENSEMBLES

W83.   **Quatuor à cordes** (unpublished)

   For string quartet
   Unfinished; Only the first movement (Allegretto) re-
   mained
   Undertaken 1927

W84.   **Près du bal** (1930; Rouart, Lerolle)

   Divertissement for flute, clarinet, bassoon, violin
   and piano
   Contents: Amazone, Flirt, Danseuse en tutu, Soupirs,
   Scherzino
   Dedicated to Madame Jeanne-René Dubost
   Instrumental version of the ballet of the same name
   (W16)

Also arranged for piano; See: W149
Composed April-May, 1929

Selected performances:
1985 (May): Rome; Academia de Santa Cecilia.

W85. Divertissement de chambre (1934; Eschig)
See: D19. B215, B289, B320, B402.

For flute, clarinet, bassoon, viola, and piano
Four movements: Préambule; Sérénade; Aria; Caprice
Dedicated to Roger Faure
Composed 1931

Private performance:
1931: For the inauguration of the Salon de Musique
of Roger Faure.

Premiere:
1931 (December): Paris: Concerts de La Sérénade.

Selected performances:
1985 (May): Rome; Academia de Santa Cecilia.

W86. Cantique en trio (unpublished)

For two violins and violoncello
Composed 1940

W87. Quatuor à cordes no. 1 (unpublished)
See: B91, B275.

For string quartet, in D major
Four movements
Dedicated to the Quatuor Lespine
Composed 1941; complete revision of the composer's
earlier efforts at quartet writing (See: W83)

Premiere:
1942 (5 June): Paris; Conservatoire; Quatuor Lespine.

W88. Six interludes (unpublished)

For organ, guitar, and tambourine
Commissioned by Compte and Comtesse Etienne de Beau-
mont to accompany the reading of poems
Composed 1942

W89. Deux sonnets de Lousie Labé (unpublished)

Arrangement for violin, violoncello and piano of two
of the **Six sonnets de Louise Labé** (W229)
Undertaken 1943

W90. Trio (1948; Editions de l'Oiseau-Lyre)
See: D1, D42.

For oboe, clarinet, and bassoon
Four movements: Allegro scherzando; Andantino

pastorale; Vivo et rustico; Choral varié
Also available in vol. 1 of Les Trios d'Anches de
l'Oiseau-Lyre (1984)
Composed 1946

Premiere:
1947: Paris; trio René-Daraux.

W91.   **Quatuor à cordes no. 2** (1950; Heugel; 21 min., 40 sec.)
See: D18, D24, D56. B73, B103, B180, B182, B185,
B206, B302, B449, B486, B522, B554, B603, B621,
B655, B674.

String quartet
Three movements: Andantino capricioso; Lento molto
espressivo; Tempo di valse (non e leggiero)
Dedicated to the memory of the composer's mother
Composed, Coutras, September, 1947-July, 1948

Premiere:
1949 (July): Aix-en-Provence; Festival d'Aix-en-
Provence; Quatuor Calvet.

Selected performances:
1950 (December): Paris; Société des concerts du
Conservatoire; Quatuor Champeil.

1953 (23 April): New York City.

W92.   **Bocages** (unpublished)
See: B192, B621.

Three caprices, preceeded by three fanfares, for flute,
2 oboes, 2 clarinets, 2 bassoons, 2 horns, and harp
Commissioned by Alexis de Rédé for the opening of the
Galerie Le Brun at the Hôtel Lambert
Dedicated to Baron Alexis Rédé
Score and parts available on rental from Choudens
Composed 1949

Premiere:
1949: Paris; Hôtel Lambert; Chamber ensemble conducted by the composer

W93.   **Golden Suite** (1967; Editions musicales transatlantiques; 12 min., 30 sec.)
See: B651.

For brass quintet
Three movements: Cantilène (Old gold); Chanson varié
(Sweet gold); March (On the gold)
Commissioned by the New York Brass Quintet
Composed March-April, 1963

Premiere:
1963 (June): Paris; New York Brass Quintet

W94.   **Six fanfares** (unpublished)
See: B264, B747.

For two trumpets and four trombones
Composed July, 1969

Premiere:
1969 (7 September): Saint-Emilion; Festival de
Saint-Emilion; Quintet à vent de Paris.

W95.   Danse d'Arles (1969; Editions françaises de musique)

For oboe, percussion, violin, viola, and violoncello
Date of composition unknown, but probably 1969

W96.   Menuet galante (1969; Editions françaises de musique)

For oboe, clarinet, percussion, violin, viola and
violoncello
Date of composition unknown, but probably 1969

W97.   Alentours saxophoniques (unpublished; 10 min.)

For alto saxophone solo, 2 flutes, 2 oboes, 2 clari-
nets, 2 bassoons, and 2 horns
Score and parts available on rental from Choudens
Composed 1976

Premiere:
1976 (30 July): London; Fifth World Saxophone Congress; Christian Thymel, saxophone; Members of
L'Orchestre de Bordeaux; Lucien Mora, conductor.

W98.   Oraisons (1981; Billaudot; 11 min.)

For one saxophonist (playing four saxophones) and organ
Dedicated to Jean-Marie Londiex
Composed June, 1976

Premiere:
1976 (30 July): London; Fifth World Saxophone Congress; Jean-Marie Londiex, saxophonist.

Selected performances:
1980 (26 February): Paris; Union des femmes pro-
fesseurs et compositeurs; Daniel Kientsy, saxophonist; Jacques Maréchal, organist.

W99.   Concert à troi pour Fronsac (unpublished; 12 min.)

For flute, alto saxophone, and harp
Dedicated to Lily Laskine and La Société musicale du
Fronsadais
Three movements: Feuillages; Ramages; Ombrages
Composed March-June, 1979

Premiere:
1979 (24 June): Fronsac.

W100.   Quatuors à cordes no. 3 (unpublished)
See: D24. B73, B185, B446, B674.

For string quartet
Dedicated to the memory of Jacques Dupont
Composed August, 1979

Premiere:
    1980 (25 May):   Bordeaux; Centre André Malraux; Mai
        musical de Bordeaux; Quatuor national d'Aquitaine.

W101.   Méditations à la mémoire de J. Cocteau (unpublished)

For string quartet
Composed 1983

Premiere:
    1983 (18 October):   Saint-Roch; Quatuor; On the oc-
        casion of the 20th anniversary of Jean Cocteau's
        death.

INSTRUMENTAL MUSIC, DUETS

W102.   Sonatine (1927; Rouart, Lerolle)
    See: B31, B501.

For flute and piano
Alternate version for violin and piano (1927; Rouart,
    Lerolle)
Three movements: Allegro; Andante; Presto
Dedicated to Roger Désormière
Composed 1923

Premiere:
    1924:   Paris; Concerts Jean Wiener; Louis Fleury,
        flute; Jean Wiener, piano.

W103.   Sonate (unpublished)
    See: B290.

Unfinished sonata for violin and piano
Undertaken in 1925

W104.   Andantino (unpublished)

For flute and viola
Composed 1934

W105.   Suite (unpublished)
    See: B247, B295.

For clarinet and piano
Alternate version for clarinet solo and eight-part
    clarinet choir
Four movements: Vif; Menuet; Toccata; Rêverie
Composed 1935

Premiere:
    1935 (2 February):   Paris; Concerts de La Sérénade;
        Louis Cahuzac, clarinet; Henri Sauguet, piano.

W106.   **Barcarolle** (1936; Editions sociales internationales; 1986; Hans Sikorski/Le Chant du monde)

For bassoon and harp
Alternate versions for bassoon and piano; violoncello and harp, and violoncello and piano
Composed 1936

Premiere:
   1936 (21 March): Paris; Joël Bernard, bassoon; Raymond Sylvand, harp.

W107.   **Petite chanson** (unpublished)

Sight-reading piece for cornet à pistons and piano for the Concours du Conservatoire, 1942
Composed 1942

W108.   **Plainte** (1950; Lemoine)

For musical saw and piano
Published in: Keller, Jacques, ed. La Lame sonore. Brussels: Lemoine, 1950; Contains original works for musical saw and piano by Charles Kœchlin, Joseph Canteloube, Arthur Honegger, Claude Duboscq, Henri Sauguet and Dom Clément Jacob
Composed 1949

W109.   **Valse** (unpublished)

Sight-reading piece for double bass and piano for the Concours du Conservatoire, 1950
Composed 1950

W110.   **Ballade** (1960; Editions musicales transatlantiques; 7 min., 15 sec.)
   See: D6.

Morceaux de concours for violoncello and piano
Composed February, 1960, for the entrance piece of the Concours du Conservatoire, 1960

W111.   **Sonatine bucolique** (1966; Leduc; 11 min., 30 sec.)
   See: D59.

For alto saxophone and piano
Three movements: Eglogue; Chanson champêtre; Rondeau pastorale
Composed at Coutras, July-August, 1964

Premiere:
   1964 (13 October): Charleroi, Belgium.

W112.   **Sonatine aux bois** (1973; Leduc; 13 min., 30 sec.)
   See: B127.

For oboe and piano
Three movements: D'Oliviers; De Chenes; De Pins

Dedicated to René Daraux and Françoise Bonnet
Composed at Coutras, 1970-1971

Premiere:
1971 (13 December):   René Daraux, oboe; Françoise
Bonnet, piano.

W113.   Romance pour un soir à Saint-Emilion (1973; Leduc; 3
min., 40 sec.)

For bassoon and piano
Single movement: Andante dolce
Dedicated to Gérard Faisandier
Composed at Coutras, August, 1971

Back cover of the Leduc edition contains illustrations
of wine labels from the St. Emilion region.

W114.   Sonatine (unpublished)
See: B234.

For clarinet and piano
Composed April-September, 1972

Premiere:
1973 (November):   New York City; Town Hall; Annie
Kafavian, clarinet; Warren Wilson, piano.

W115.   Six pièces faciles (1977; Leduc)
See: D9, D20.

For flute and guitar
Contents: Petit air doux; Un Bout de valse; La Roue
tourne; Le Sommeil du pâtre; La Barque chinoise;
Pas à pas
Composed July-August, 1975

W116.   Sonatine en deux chants et un intermède (1978; Billaudot; 17 min.)

For clarinet and piano
Two movements (Adagietto and Vivace) with an intermezzo
for solo clarinet
Dedicated to Guy Dagain and Henriette Puig-Roger
Composed 1975

W117.   Cantilène pastorale (1978; Billaudot; 6 min., 20 sec.)
See: B68.

For oboe and piano
Composed 1978, for the Concours du Conservatoire, 1978

W118.   Non moriatur in æternam (1982; Billaudot; 5 min., 30
sec.)
See: B144.

For trumpet and organ
One movement: Allegro moderato
Dedicated to André Jolivet, in memoriam

Part of a work entitled "Hommage à André Jolivet"
composed with Pierre Ancelin and Roger Calmel
Composed June, 1979

Premiere:
1979 (4 August): Sérignan; Eté musical en Langue-
doc; Jean-Jacques Gaudon, trumpet; Jacques Maréchal, organ.

W119.   **Sonate crépusculaire** (unpublished; 15 min.)
See: D43. B70.

For violin and piano
Dedicated to Jean-Michel Damase and Michel Chauveton
Composed 1981

Premiere:
1981 (October): Paris; Salle Gaveau.

W120.   **Une Fleur** (unpublished)

For saxophone and piano
Composed 1984

W121.   **Un Duo** (unpublished)

For flute and piano
Composed 1985 to celebrate the 50th birthday of Pierre
Ancelin

W122.   **Révérence à Jean-Sébastian Bach** (unpublished)

For violoncello and guitar
Published in holograph copy **La Revue musicale** no. 381/
382 (1985), following p.125, as part of a tribute to
Bach on the 300th anniversary of his birth
Composed April, 1985

INSTRUMENTAL MUSIC, KEYBOARD DUETS

W123.   **Première danse nègre** (unpublished)

For piano, four hands
Composed 1919

W124.   **Hommage à Charlot** (unpublished)

For piano, four hands
Composed 1922

W125.   **Bonsoir retraite** (unpublished)

For piano, four hands
Composed 1923

W126.   **Viñes aux mains de fée** (unpublished)

For piano, four hands
Composed in collaboration with Maxime Jacob

Dedicated to Ricardo Viñes
Composed 1925

W127. **Les Jeux de l'amour et du hasard** (1958; Eschig)
See: B141, B245, B342, B513, B562, B569.

For two pianos, four hands
Five movements: Préamble; Poème; Jeu; Nocturne; Sérénade
Commissioned by Princesse Edmond de Polignac
Dedicated to Madame la Princesse de Polignac
Composed 1932

Premiere:
1933 (February): Paris; Concerts de La Sérénade;
Henri Sauguet and Francis Poulenc, pianos.

Selected performances:
1985 (May): Rome; Academia de Santa Cecilia.

The work was later orchestrated as the music for the
ballet, **Le Dompteur dompte** (W20) for the Ballets de
la Jeunesses.

W128. **Valse brève** (1955; Eschig)
See: D22. B315, B342.

For two pianos, four hands
Subtitled "Mouvement de valse modere"
Dedicated to Arthur Gold and Robert Fizdale
Composed September-October, 1949

Premiere:
1949: Arthur Gold and Robert Fizdale.

W129. **La Dame aux camélias** (unpublished)

Transcription of the ballet (W35) for piano, four hands
Transcribed April, 1949, for Yvette Chauviré

W130. **Prière nuptiale** (unpublished)

For organ and harmonium
Composed June, 1962

INSTRUMENTAL MUSIC, KEYBOARD SOLOS

W131. **Deux pièces** (unpublished)

For organ
Composed 1917

W132. **Esquisses** (unpublished)

Three pieces for piano
Composed 1918

W133. Le Passeur (unpublished)

For piano solo
Composed 1918

W134. Trois pièces (unpublished)

For piano solo
Composed 1920

W135. Prélude (unpublished)

For piano solo
Composed 1921

W136. Trois églogues (unpublished)

For piano solo
Composed 1921

W137. Paul et Virginie (unpublished)

Three nocturnes for piano solo
Composed 1922

The second of the nocturnes was later orchestrated by
    Roger Désormière

W138. Cinq inventions (unpublished)

For piano solo
Composed 1922

W139. Préludes (unpublished)

For piano solo
Composed 1922

W140. Les Délices des enfants (unpublished)

Short pieces for piano solo
Composed 1922

W141. Trois françaises (1925; Rouart, Lerolle)
    See: D26. B31, B34, B35, B84, B128, B159, B290,
    B501, B718.

For piano solo
Three pieces: Allegro; Mouvement de marche; Allegro
    moderato
Dedicated to Marcelle Meyer
Composed 1922-1923

Premiere:
    1923 (16 June): Paris: La Baraque de la Chimère;
    Marcelle Meyer, piano.

W142. Quatrième française (unpublished)

For piano solo
Composed 1923

W143.   Trois nouvelles françaises (1925; Rouart, Lerolle)
See: D26. B84, B128.

For piano solo
Three movements: Vif; Andante; Vif et bien rythmé
(Danse de Matelots)
Composed 1924

Premiere:
1925 (21 March):   Paris; Concerts de l'Ecole d'Arcueil; Ricardo Viñes, piano.

The third (Danse de Matelots) was orchestrated (See:
W44) and may have figured as part of the unfinished
ballet, **Le Marin et la sirène** (W11).

W144.   Premier scherzo (unpublished)

For piano solo
Composed 1925

W145.   Sonate en ré majeur (1927; Rouart, Lerolle)
See: D26. B84, B341, B398, B613.

For piano solo
Composed 1926

Premiere:
1926:   Paris; Concerts de l'Ecole d'Arcueil; Henri
Sauguet, piano.

W146.   Nouvel album pour la jeunesse (unpublished)

For piano solo
Composed 1926

W147.   Romance en ut (1930; Rouart, Lerolle)
See: D26.

For piano solo
Alternate title: "Souvenirs des bords du Rhin"
Conposed 1929

W148.   Feuillets d'album (1930; Jobert)
See: D26. B84, B341.

For piano solo
Contents: Un Valse (dedicated to Ricardo Viñes); Un
Nocturne (dedicated to Madame Grunelius); Un Scherzo
(dedicated to Leone Massimo)
Composed 1929

W149.   Près du bal (1930; Rouart, Lerolle)

For piano solo
Contents: Amazone; Flirt; Danseuse en tutu; Soupirs;

Scherzino
Composed 1929

The work was later arranged for chamber ensemble (W84)
and used as the music for the Divertissement dansé
of the same name (W16)

W150.   Chant nuptial (unpublished)

For organ solo
Dedicated to René Laport and Renée Lamon
Composed 1931

W151.   Pièces poétiques pour les enfants (1935; Eschig)
See: D26. B84, B613.

For piano solo
Originally published in two volumes. 1er Cahier (as-
sez facile): Visite à Schumann; Le Chausseur perdu;
Les Cyclistes; Le Juif errant passé; Les Pompiers;
Le Chanteur des rues). 2eme Cahier (plus difficile):
En colère; L'Enfant de troupe; Souvenir des vacances;
Jour de fête)
Composed 1933, 1934

W152.   Nocturne (unpublished)

For piano solo
Composed 1935

W153.   Nuit coloniale sur les bords de la Seine (1937; Deiss)
See: D26, D30, D53. B84, B505, B626.

For piano solo
Dedicated to Marguerite Long
Published as part of a collective work entitled: A
l'exposition (La Seine un martin by Georges Auric;
Diner sur l'eau by Marcel Delannoy; L'Espiègle du
village Lilliput by Jacques Ibert; Le Tour de l'Exposition by Darius Milhaud; Bourée au Pavillon d'Auvergne by Francis Poulenc; **Nuit coloniale sur les
bords de la Seine** by Henri Sauguet; Au Pavillon
d'Alsace by Germaine Tailleferre)
Composed 1937

Premiere:
1937: Paris; Fêtes de la lumière de l'Exposition;
Each piece was performed by a different student
of Marguerite Long.

W154.   Pastorale de septembre (unpublished)

For piano solo
Composed 1940

W155.   Petite marche (unpublished)

For piano solo
Composed 1947

W156.   Espièglerie (1960; Billaudot)

For piano solo
Published in: Les Contemporains. Pièces faciles
    pour le piano collationées et annotées par Lucette
    Descaves. (4 vols.) Paris: G. Billaudot (and
    Pierre Noël), 1960.
Composed 1950

W157.   Pièce, untitled (unpublished)

For piano solo
Composed December, 1958, for the 80th birthday of
    Geneviève Sienkiewicz

W158.   Harmonie du soir (unpublished)
    See: D26.

For piano solo
Composed October, 1961

W159.   Suite royale (1967; Eschig; 19 min., 30 sec.)
    See: D28, D52. B133, B262, B409, B688, B689.

For harpsichord solo
Contents: Réverance; Bavardages; Médisances 2e Ri-
    tournelle; Sarcasmes; 3e Ritournelle; Nostalgies
Dedicated to Sylvia Marlowe and The Harpsichord Music
    Society (of New York)
Composed August, 1962

Premiere:
    1963: Geneva, Switzerland; Sylvia Marlowe, harpsi-
    chord.

Selected performances:
    1964 (15 December): New York City; Carnegie Hall;
    Sylvia Marlowe, harpsichord.

W160.   Oraison nuptiale (unpublished)

For organ solo
Composed for the marriage of Princesse Claude de France
Composed 1964

W161.   L'Esprit de l'escalier (unpublished)

For piano solo
Dedicated to Carlos Muñoz
Composed April-May, 1964

W162.   Chanson du soir (unpublished)
    See: D26. B84.

For piano solo
Composed June, 1964

W163.   A Jean Voilier (unpublished)

Prelude for piano solo
Composed September, 1965

W164.   Le Bestiaire du petit Noé (unpublished)

Ten easy pieces for piano solo
Inspired by the poems of Edwige Pépin
Composed August-December, 1965

W165.   Petite valse du Grand échiquier (1975; Editions françaises de musique)

For piano solo
Dedicated to Jacques Chancel
Composed 1973

Premiere:
1973: France; Radio broadcast by Jacques Chancel;
   Performed by Gyorgy Cziffra, piano

Also extant in a version for orchestra (See: W72)

W166.   Pour regarder Watteau (unpublished)

Suite for harpsichord solo
Composed to accompany an exhibition of paintings by
   Watteau
Composed July-August, 1975

W167.   Portrait-souvenir de Virgil Thomson (unpublished)

For piano solo
Composed March, 1982

W168.   Le Souvenir de Déodat (unpublished)

For piano solo
Dedicated in tribute to Déodat de Severac
Composed, 1983

Premiere:
1983 (16 July): Festival d'Alan-en-Comminges.

W169.   Valse anachronique (unpublished)

For piano solo
Composed for the Lycée de Châteauroux to recall the
   name and spirit of Jean Giraudoux
Composed August, 1985

W170.   Ombres sur Venise (unpublished)

For piano solo
Dedicated to Billy Eidi
Composed March, 1986

W171.   Septembre (unpublished)

For piano solo

Later orchestrated under the same title (See: W73)
Composed August, 1986

INSTRUMENTAL MUSIC, NON-KEYBOARD SOLOS

W172.   Sonate (1957; Ricordi; 11 min.)

For violoncello solo
Three movements: Allegro agitato; Andante lento e
  espressivo; Allegretto scherzando con spirito riso-
  luto
Composed August, 1956

Premiere:
1956 (7 November): Paris; Dmitri Markevitch

W173.   Chant de l'oiseau qui n'existe pas (unpublished)
See: B16.

For flute solo
Composed to illustrate a poem by Claude Aveline
Composed June, 1957

W174.   Soliloque (1961; Ricordi)
See: D25, D40. B174.

For guitar solo
Dedicated to the memory of Manuel de Falla
Composed July-September, 1958

W175.   Trois préludes (1971; Berben)
See: D25.

Three preludes for guitar solo
Contents: Prélude à la mélancolie; Prélude au sou-
  venir; Prélude aux gestes
Dedicated to Angelo Gilardino
Composed July, 1970

Premiere:
1972 (April): Paris; Bobigny; Roman Cueto, guitar.

W176.   Choral varié (1973; Choudens; 5 min., 40 sec.)
See: D3.

Choral and three variations for accordion solo
Dedicated to Alain Abott
Composed October-December, 1972

W177.   Trois pièces (unpublished)

For viola solo
Composed 1972

W178.   Musiques pour Claudel (1975; Editions musicales transatlantiques; 7 min., 30 sec.)
See: D25.

For guitar solo
Published in two volumes. 1re Cahier (En forme d'Ou-
verture; Image; Le Temps qui passé; Caquetage).
2eme Cahier (Cantabile; Les Couleurs: Le Bleu, Le
Rouge, Le Jaune, Le Vert; Contrastes).
Extracted from the incidental music for **Dialogue das
le Loir-et-Cher** (W404)
Dedicated to Sylvia Monfort
Composed 1973

W179. Quelques trilles pour les treilles (unpublished)

For flute solo
Dedicated to Madame Grummer Schlumberger
Composed October, 1982

W180. Cadence (unpublished)
See: D25.

For guitar solo
Dedicated to Alain Prévost
Composed August, 1985

W181. Quatre-vingt-dix notes (unpublished)

For flute solo
For the 90th birthday celebration of Raoul Leven
Composed July, 1986

VOCAL MUSIC, SACRED, UNACCOMPANIED

W182. Requiem æternam (unpublished)

For four-part mixed chorus a cappella
Extracted from the film score for **Tu es Pierre** (W352)
Composed February, 1959

W183. Ecce homo (unpublished)
See: D10.

For mixed chorus a cappella
Extracted from the film score for **Ecce homo** (W358)
Composed January, 1965

W184. Messe jubilatoire (unpublished)

For mixed chorus a cappella
Composed "to evoke the smile of Marie-Blanche, Com-
tesse Blanche de Polignac, on Earth"
Composed January-February, 1983

VOCAL MUSIC, SACRED, ACCOMPANIED

W185. Petit messe pastorale (1946; Rouart, Lerolle)
See; B248.

For two equal voices (women's or children's) and organ
Contents: Kyrie; Gloria; Sanctus; Angus Dei
Composed 1934

Premiere:
1939 (14 March): Paris: Sainte-Trinité; Chorale
Yvonne Gouverné; Olivier Messiaen, organ.

W186. Cantique à Saint Vincent (unpublished)

For three-part chorus and organ
Composed 1940

W187. Je vous salue Marie (1951; Rouart, Lerolle)

For soprano and organ
Alternate title "Salutation angélique"
Dedicated to Madame Félix Ronceret
Composed 1943

W188. Requiem æternam (unpublished)

For voice and organ
Dedicated to the memory of René Laporte
Composed 1954

Premiere:
1954 (3 March): Paris; Funeral of René Laporte.

W189. Pie Jésus (unpublished)

For chorus and organ
Dedicated to the memory of Christian Dior
Composed October, 1957

Premiere:
1957 (29 October): Paris; Funeral of Christian Dior.

VOCAL MUSIC, SECULAR, UNACCOMPANIED

W190. Ma belle forêt (unpublished)

For four-part mixed chorus a cappella
Text by Gérard Pajot
Composed 1943

W191. Les Quatre saisons (unpublished)

For four-part children's chorus a cappella
Extracted from the score of **Symphonie no. 2** (W57)
Score and parts available on rental from Editions
françaises de musique
Composed 1949

W192. Mouton blanc (1954; Salabert)

For four-part men's chorus a cappella
Text by the Princesse Bibesco
Composed 1952

W193. Plus loin que la nuit et le jour (1961; Salabert)

Cantata for tenor and mixed chorus a cappella

Text by Louis Emié
Dedicated to the memory of Claude Debussy
Composed November-December, 1960

Premiere:
    1961 (May): Bordeaux; Mai musical de Bordeaux;
        Musical portion of the ballet of the same name
        (W38).

Selected performances:
    1963 (28-30 June): Spoleto, Italy; Festival of Two
        Worlds.

W194. **Cinq chansons** (unpublished)

For men's or children's chorus a cappella
Text by Louis Emié
Composed September-October, 1964

W195. **L'Espace du dedans** (1966; Eschig)
    See: B413, B445.

Three songs for solo bass voice
Text by Henri Michaux
Contents: Répos dans le malheur; Le Jeune fille de
    Budapest; Dans la nuit
Composed February, 1965

Premiere:
    1965 (8 March): Paris; Concert de l'Eremus; Doda
        Conrad, bass.

W196. **Quatre chœurs** (unpublished; 15 min.)

For mixed chorus a cappella
Texts by Louis Emié
Contents: Le Chevalier du Brouillard; Clair de lune;
    La Pluie; Berceuse
Composed April-June, 1965

Premiere:
    1978 (18 April): Paris; Chœur de l'Opéra de Paris;
        Jean Laforge, conductor.

Selected performances:
    1981 (May): Bordeaux; Mai musical de Bordeaux;
        Collegium Musicum d'Aquitaine; Michel Moureau,
        conductor.

W197. **Toast porte à Henri Barraud** (unpublished)

For men's chorus a cappella
Composed 1965

W198. **Le souvenir, déjà** (unpublished)

Duet for two equal voices
Text by Jean Gacon
Composed, in memory of Henri Cliquet-Pleyel, May, 1966

W199. Trois poèmes (unpublished)

For solo voice
Texts by Pierre-Albert Birot
Composed March, 1968

VOCAL MUSIC, SECULAR, WITH INSTRUMENTS

W200. Complaint (unpublished)
See: B241.

For voice and chamber ensemble
Text and music by Louis Emié
Orchestrated by Henri Sauguet 1921

W201. La Voyante (1939; L'Oiseau-Lyre)
See: D7, D41, D60, D62. B26, B100, B140, B156,
B169, B191, B192, B193, B317, B318, B353, B505,
B537, B559, B568, B570, B610, B621, B733.

For solo woman's voice and small ensemble
Text by Henri Sauguet after Nostradamos
Contents: Cartomancie; Astrologie; Présages tirés des
étoiles; Pour le temps á venir; Chiromancie
Commissioned by Vicomte and Vicomtesse Noailles
Score and parts (flute, booe, clarinet, bassoon, trum-
pet, percussion, violin, viola, violoncello, double
bass) available on rental from L'Oiseau-Lyre
Composed 1932

Premiere:
1932: Hyères; Théâtre municipal de Hyères; Madeleine
Vhita, soprano, ensemble conducted by Roger Désormière; Sets by Christian Bérard; Costumes by Nora
Auric; Directed by Christian Bérard.

Selected performances:
1953 (23 April): New York City; Leontyne Price,
soprano; Jean Morel, conductor.

1954 (August): Cannes; Festival international de
la Radio et de la Télévision; Directed by Bronislaw Horowicz; Elda Ribetti, soprano.

1957: France; Radio broadcast honoring Jane Bathori.

1962 (25 July): Aspen, Colorado; Aspen Festival;
Jennie Tourel, soprano; Walter Susskind, ocnductor.

1964 (11-23 March): Paris; Studio d'Arlequin at the
Théâtre Grévin; Part of Xavier de Courville's Micropéra; Jacqueline Casadesus de Courville, soprano; Vladimir Kojoukharov, conductor.

W202. Enigme (1932; Jobert)

For woman's voice and orchestra
Text by Heinrich Heine
Dedicated to Jean Bertrand

Composed 1932

Premiere:
  1933: Paris; Suzanne Balguerie; L'Orchestre symphonique de Paris.

W203. **Les Ombres du jardin** (unpublished)
  See: B1, B358.

Cantata for soprano, tenor, baritone, bass, male vocal quartet and small orchestra (winds, timpani, percussion, 2 violoncelli)
Text by Joseph Weterings
Dedicated to Paul Collaer
Composed 1938

Premiere:
  1938: Belgium; Private performance for the inauguration of the garden of Paul Collaer's home near Brussels.

Selected performances:
  1942: Brussels; Palais des Beaux-Arts (public premiere.

  1946: Brussels; L'Orchestre de la Radio I.N.R.; Paul Collaer, conductor.

W204. **Madrigal** (unpublished
  See: B92.

For soprano, flute, harp, violin (or viola) and violoncello)
Text by Jean Aubry
Composed 1942

Premiere:
  1942: Paris; Leila ben Sedira.

W205. **Beauté, retirez-vous** (unpublished)

For soprano, flute, viola, violoncello, and harp
Text by Georges Couturier
Extracted from the incidental music for **L'Honorable Mr. Pepys** (W369)
Composed 1943

W206. **Sérénade** (unpublished)

For voice and guitar
Author of text unknown
Composed 1944

W207. **Chant funèbre pour de nouveaux héros** (unpublished)

For tenor and orchestra
Text by Pierre Seghers
Composed 1944

W208. Le Cornette (unpublished)
     See: B168, B204, B213, B256, B300, B301, B330,
     B445, B608, B651.

Cantata for bass voice and orchestra
Text by Rainer-Maria Rilke
French version by Simone Kra
Dedicated to Jacques Dupont
Composed 1950-1951

Song no. 16 is published in a holograph of the composer's MS for voice and piano in **La Revue musicale**
no. 210 (1952) facing p. 125.

Premiere:
     1951: Brussels; L'Orchestre de la radio I.N.R.;
     Doda Conrad, soloist, Franz André, conductor.

Selected performances:
     1952: Paris; L'Orchestre national; Doda Conrad,
     soloist; Roger Désormière, conductor.

     1961 (June): Paris; Centre culturel américaine;
     Doda Conrad, bass; Charles Wadsworth, piano; Pro-
     gram honoring Sauguet's 60th birthday.

     1963 (6 June): Paris; Théâtre des Champs-Elysées;
     L'Orchestre de la société philharmonique de Paris;
     Doda Conrad, bass; Léon Barzin, conductor.

W209. L'Oiseau a vu tout cela (1961; Heugel; 17 min.)
     See: D8, D14. B100, B116, B369, B463, B464, B465,
     B467, B654, B673, B781, B733, B746.

Cantata for baritone and string orchestra
Text by Jean Cayrol
Dedicated to Louis-Jacques Rondeleux, Karl Ristenpart,
and the city of Besançon
Score and parts available on rental from Heugel
Composed at Coutras, April-May, 1960

Premiere:
     1960 (5 September): Besançon; Festival de Besançon;
     Louis-Jacques Rondeleux, baritone; Kammerorchester
     der Saar; Karl Ristenpart, conductor.

Selected performances:
     1963 (1 November): Paris; Jacques Herbillon, bari-
     tone.

     1971 (15 September): Saint-Emilion; Festival de
     Saint-Emilion; Udo Reinemann, baritone.

W210. Chant pour une ville meurtrie (unpublished; 30 min.)

Oratorio for six solo voices, chorus and orchestra
Text by A. M. Monfret
Working title: "Les Pierres vivent"
Score and parts (2.2.2.2/2.2.2.1/timp/perc(2)/hp/str)

available on rental from Editions françaises de musiques
Composed 1966-1967

W211. Trois chants de contemplation de Lao Tseu (1975; Leduc; 9 min., 30 sec.)
<u>See</u>; D61.

For contralto and bass voices with recorder quartet
(or brass quartet, or woodwind quartet, or piano)
Text by Lao-Tseu
French version by Henri Sauguet
Contents: Moderato; Dolce andantino; Andante misurato
Composed 1971

<u>Premiere</u>:
1971 (13 June): Paris; Corinne Petit; Bernard Cot-
tret; Recorder ensemble; Jean Cotte, conductor.

W212. Pour un cyprès (unpublished; 15 min.)

Préambule, three airs, and two interludes for mezzo-
soprano (or baritone), viola and piano
Texts by Lucienne Desnoves
Commissioned by Les Amities artistiques de Bruxelles
Composed October-December, 1972

<u>Premiere</u>:
1974 (26 February): Brussels; Lucienne Tragin,
mezzo-soprano; Bruno Pasquier, viola; Henri Sauguet, piano.

W213. Porte-bonheur (unpublished)

For voice and flute
Text by François Ducaud-Bourget
Composed July, 1974

W214. La Reine aux cheveaux d'or (unpublished; 25 min.)

For soprano and six instruments (flute, oboe, clari-
net, violin, violoncello, and harp)
Text by Maurice Carême
Dedicated to Queen Elizabeth of Belgium
Composed March-May, 1976

<u>Premiere</u>:
1976 (12 November): Brussels; L'Académie des Arts
de Belgique; Private soirée for the birthday of
Queen Elizabeth of Belgium; Lucienne Tragin, mezzo-
soprano; Henri Sauguet, conductor.

<u>Selected performances</u>:
1979 (15 January): Paris; La Société française de
musique contemporaine; Janine Devost, soprano;
Henri Sauguet, conductor.

W215. Par-delà des étoiles (unpublished)

For organ, speaker and chorus a cappella
Accompaniment to the reading of a spoken oratorio by
    Jean-Louis Wallas
Composed January-March, 1982

Premiere:
1982 (24 December): Paris; Saint-Roch

W216. J'Habite le silence (unpublished)

For medium voice and oboe
Text by Michel Manoll
Composed June, 1985

W217. Musique pour Cendrars (unpublished)

For baritone voice and viola
Text drawn from the writings of Blaise Cendrars by
    Raphaël Cluzel
Composed July, 1986

Premiere:
1986 (16 December): Paris; Hommage à Blaise Cen-
    drars; Members of Ensemble Intercontemporain

VOCAL MUSIC, SECULAR, WITH PIANO, CYCLES

W218. Trois poèmes arméniens (unpublished)

For voice and piano
Text by Nahabed Koutebak
Composed 1919

W219. Deux poèmes (unpublished)

For voice and piano
Texts by Jules Romains
Composed 1920

W220. Pronostics de Nostradamus (unpublished)

For voice and piano
Texts by Henri Sauguet
Composed 1920

W221. Oceano roof (unpublished)

For voice and piano
Texts by Jean Cocteau
Composed 1920

W222. Trois cygnes (unpublished)
    See: B241.

For voice and piano
Texts by Louis Emié
Composed 1921

W223. Trois poésies (unpublished)

For voice and piano
Texts by Jean Cocteau
Composed 1921

W224. **Les Animaux et leurs hommes** (1926; Jobert)
  See: D19. B215, B376.

For voice and piano
Texts by Paul Eluard
Contents: Cheval; Vache; Oiseau; Chien; Chat; Poule;
  Porc
Composed 1921

Premiere:
  1923: Paris; Charles Hubbard, tenor.

Selected performances:
  1953 (April): Paris; Part of "Hommage des musiciens
    à Paul Eluard;" Anne Laloë, voice; Henri Sauguet,
    piano.

W225. **Trois poèmes** (unpublished)
  See: B501.

For voice and piano
Texts by Jean Cocteau
Contents: Tour de France; Iles; Miroir des sports
Composed 1922

Revised in 1925 as **Deux poèmes**. "Tour de France" was
  not included in the revision.

W226. **Plumes** (1924; Eschig)
  See: B501.

Three poems for voice and piano
Texts by Georges Gabory
Dedicated to Jane Bathori
Composed 1922

Premiere:
  1923: Paris; Concerts de l'Ecole d'Arcueil; Jane
    Bathori, soprano; Henri Sauguet, piano.

W227. **Trois poésies** (unpublished)
  See: B501.

Three songs for voice and piano
Texts by Raymond Radiguet
Composed 1922

W228. **Cirque** (1926; Rouart, Lerolle)
  See: B298, B501.

Five songs for voice and piano
Texts by Adrien Copperie
Contents: Haut école; Petite écuyère; Ecuyère vol-
  tige; Gymnaste aérien; Cloune étoilé
Dedicated to Gaëtan Fouquet

Composed November, 1925

Premiere:
    1925: Paris; Concerts de l'Ecole d'Arcueil; Ger-
    maine Copperie, soprano; Henri Sauguet, piano.

W229. **Trois mélodies** (unpublished)

For voice and piano
Texts by Friedrich Schiller
Composed 1926

W230. **Six sonnets** (1928; Rouart, Lerolle)
    See: B125.

Six songs for voice and piano
Texts by Louise Labé
Contents: Chasse; A Vénus; Songe; Amour; Printemps;
    Tant que mes yeux
Composed at Toulouse, September, 1927

Another edition, limited to 315 copies, was printed
on special paper with cover illustrations by Christian Bérard. The first fifteen copies were auto-
graphed by Henri Sauguet and Christian Bérard.

Premiere:
    1927: Paris; Jane Bathori.

Selected performances:
    1941 (22 November): Paris; Simon Clouet, soprano;
    Henri Sauguet, piano.

W231. **Quatre poèmes** (1929; Rouart, Lerolle)
    See: B137, B293.

Four songs for voice and piano
Texts by Friedrich Schiller
Contents; Le Souvenir; Le Pèlerin; L'Apparition; Les
    Guides de la vie
Dedicated to the memory of Christian Hardouin
Composed 1928-1929

Premiere:
    1929: Paris; Salle Erard; Jane Bathori, soprano.

Selected performances:
    1942 (December): Paris; Concerts du Triptyque;
        Pierre Bernac, baritone; Francis Poulenc, piano.

W232. **Deux poèmes** (1930; Jobert)

Two songs for medium voice and piano
Texts by William Shakespeare
Contents: Je te vois en rêve; Chanson (à Bruno)
A third, "Mon plus grand trésor" was unpublished
Composed 1929

W233. **Deux mélodies romantiques** (unpublished)

For voice and piano
Contents: "Le Spectre de la rose" (text by Théophile
    Gautier); "A des roses sous la neige" (text by La-
    martine)
The first is dedicated to J. E. Lafollye; the second
    to Christian Dior
Composed 1930

W234. **Polymètres** (unpublished)
    See: B288, B401, B631.

For high voice and piano
Texts by Jean-Paul Richter
Contents: La Muguet; Le Vide de l'instant; La Rose
    palissant au soleil; La Bal d'enfants; Triste jour-
    née
Dedicated to the memory of Robert Schumann
Composed 1931

Premiere:
    1932 (1 February): Paris; Concerts de La Sérénade;
    Jane Bathori, soprano.

W235. **Deux poèmes** (unpublished)

For voice and piano
Texts from Intermezzo by Heinrich Heine
Composed 1932

W236. **Cinq poèmes** (unpublished)

For voice and piano
Texts by Johann Christian Friedrich Hölderlin
French adaptation by Pierre Jean Jouve
Dedicated to Comtesse A. J. de Noailles
Composed 1933

Premiere:
    1934: Paris; Ecole normale de musique; Germaine
    Copperie, soprano.

W237. **Deux poèmes** (unpublished)
    See: B175.

For voice and piano
Texts by Rabindranath Tagore
French version by André Gide
Composed 1937

Premiere:
    1938: Paris; Pierre Bernac and Francis Poulenc.

Selected performances:
    1942 (June): Paris; Pierre Bernac; Francis Poulenc.

W238. **Deux poèmes** (unpublished)

For voice and piano
Texts by Antoinette d'Arcourt
Composed 1938

W239. Six mélodies sur des poèmes symbolistes (1945; Amphion)
See: B453, B709.

For voice and piano
Contents: Renouveau; Tristesse d'Eté (texts by Stéphane Mallarmé); Crépuscule de mi Juillet, huit heures; Clair de lune de novembre (texts by Jules Laforge); two versions of Le Chat (texts by Charles Pierre Baudelaire)
Dedicated to Jacques Dupont
Composed 1938

Premiere:
1942: Paris; Salle Gaveau; Jacqueline Courtin, soprano.

Selected performances:
1938 (March): Italy; Paul Derenne and Henri Sauguet.

W240. Trois duos (unpublished)
See: D19. B179, B215, B710.

For soprano, tenor and piano
Texts by Comtesse Jean Murat
Contents: Lune inconstante; Crépuscule; L'Instant
Commissioned by Comtesse de Polignac
Composed 1939

Premiere:
1941: Paris; Private soirée; Comtesse de Polignac, soprano; Paul Derenne, tenor; Henri Sauguet, piano.

Selected performances:
1942 (19 March): Paris; Salle Chopin; Comtesse Jean de Polignac, soprano; Paul Derenne, tenor; Henri Sauguet, piano.

W241. Les Bonnes occasions (unpublished)
See: B712.

Scène lyrico-réaliste for soprano, tenor and piano
Texts by Georges Courteline
Commissioned by Agnès Capri
Composed 1940

W242. Neiges (unpublished)
See: D19. B215, B263.

Six songs for voice and piano
Texts by Antoinette d'Arcourt
Composed 1942

Premiere:
   1942: Jean-Edmée Lafollye.

Selected performances:
   1942 (16 December): Paris; Ecole normale; Geneviève
   Touraine, soprano; Henri Sauguet, piano.

   1958 (March): Italy; Paul Derenne, tenor; Henri
   Sauguet piano.

   1971 (October): Paris; Paul Derenne and Henri Sauguet.

W243. **Trois mélodies** (unpublished)

For voice and piano
Texts by Abeille Guichard
Composed 1943

Premiere:
   1943: Paris; Ecole normale de musique; Geneviève
   Touraine, soprano.

W244. **Force et faiblesse** (unpublished)
   See: B376.

Seven songs for voice and piano
Texts by Paul Eluard
Composed 1943

Premiere:
   1944: Ginnette Guilamant.

Selected performances:
   1953 (April): Paris; Maison de la Pensée française;
   Hommages des musiciens à Paul Eluard; Ginnette
   Guilamant, soprano, Henri Sauguet, piano.

W245. **La Chèvrefeuille** (unpublished)
   See: B621.

Ten songs for baritone and piano
Texts by Georges Hugnet
Composed 1944

Premiere:
   1948: Besançon; Festival de Besançon; Gérard Souzay, baritone.

Selected performances:
   1952 (10 April): Paris; Pierre Jonneret, baritone;
   Henri Sauguet, piano.

   1953 (May): New York City; Martial Singher, baritone; John de LaMontaine, piano.

W246. **Cinq poèmes** (1949; Heugel)
   See: D13. B80, B89, B276, B368, B486, B538, B654.

For high voice and piano
Texts by Max Jacob
Alternate title: "Les Pénitents en maillots roses"
Contents: A une sainte le jour de sa fête; Jardin
    mysterieux; Marine à Roscoff; La Ville; Ports de
    l'enfer
Dedicated to Pierre Colle ("in memoriam, helas!")
Composed 1944

Also published in an edition limited to 900 copies by
    Editions du Sagittaire. Facsimile of the composer's
    manuscript.

Premiere:
    1945: Paris; Ecole normale de musique; Geneviève
    Touraine, soprano; Henri Sauguet, piano.

Selected performances:
    1956 (April): Paris; Les Amis de la musique de
    chambre; Paul Derenne, tenor; Henri Sauguet, piano.

    1958 (March): Italy; Paul Derenne and Henri Sauguet.

W247. Deux mélodies (unpublished)

For voice and piano
Texts by Paul Valéry
Contents: Le Bois amical; La Ceinture
Composed 1945

W248. Six poèmes (unpublished)

For voice and piano
Texts by André de Richaud
Composed 1946

Premiere:
    1947: Paris; Ecole normale de musique; Suzanne
    Peignot, soprano.

W249. Trois mélodies lyriques sur des textes frivoles (un-
    published)
    See: D34.

For voice and piano
Contents: Elégance sans fortune (text by Jean Fer-
    nandez); Cette attirance dans la brume (anonymous);
    Senteurs (text by Stéphane Mallarmé)
Composed 1937-1947

Premiere:
    1947: Paris; Jean-Edmée Lafollye.

W250. Visions infernales (1950; Heugel; 13 min.)
    See: D12, D50, D51. B49, B189, B287, B329, B374,
    B523, B524, B538, B548, B672.

Six songs for voice and piano
Texts by Max Jacob

Contents: Voyage; Voisinage; Que pense de mon salut;
    Regates mysterieuses; Le Petit paysan; Exhortation
Dedicated to Doda Conrad
Composed 1948

Premiere:
    1948 (28 December): New York City; Town Hall; Doda
    Conrad, bass.

Selected performances:
    1949 (January): Paris: Salle du Conservatoire;
    Doda Conrad.

    1953 (May): New York City; Doda Conrad, bass; Fe-
    lix Wolfes, piano.

    1959 (7 December): Paris; Salle Gaveau; Doda Con-
    rad, bass; Edmond Rosenfeld, piano.

W251. **Mouvements du cœur** (1949; Heugel)
    See: D50, D51. B188, B287, B375, B683.

Suite for voice and piano
Texts by Louise de Vilmorin
Collaborative work undertaken at the suggestion of
Doda Conrad for the centennial commemoration of the
death of Frédéric Chopin
Contents: **Prélude** by Henri Sauguet; Mazurka by Fran-
    cis Poulenc; Valse by Georges Auric; Scherzo im-
    promptu by Jean Françaix; Etude by Leo Préger; Bal-
    lade nocturne by Darius Milhaud; **Postlude (Polo-
    naise)** by Henri Sauguet
Composed 1949

Premiere:
    1949: Paris; Doda Conrad, bass.

Selected performances:
    1949 (November): New York City; Doda Conrad, bass.

    1959 (7 December): Paris; Salle Gaveau; Doda Conrad;
    Edmond Rosenfeld, piano.

W252. **Deux chansons** (unpublished)

For voice and piano
Texts by Pierre Olivier
Composed 1951

W253. **Deux airs à manger** (unpublished)

For voice and piano
Author of texts unknown
Composed for Chez Christofle
Composed 1951

W254. **Deux poèmes** (unpublished)

For voice and piano

Texts by René Laporte
Composed 1954

W255.   Tombeau d'un berger (unpublished)

For voice and piano
Texts by Lucien Jacques
Composed August, 1956

W256.   Deux mélodies (unpublished)

For voice and piano
Texts by Robert Gaillard
Composed 1958

Premiere:
1959:   France: Radio broadcast; Paul Derenne, tenor.

W257.   Mon bien (unpublished)

Three songs for voice and piano
Texts by Georges-Emmanuel Clancier
Composed Spring, 1958

Premiere:
1959:   France; Radio broadcast; Anne Laloë, soprano.

W258.   Trois élégies (unpublished)

For voice and piano
Texts by Marceline Desbordes-Valmore
Composed August, 1959

Premiere:
1959:   France; Radio broadcast; Giselle Guillaumat,
soprano.

W259.   Vie des campagnes (unpublished)
See: B364, B443.

Suite for soprano and piano
Texts by Jean Follain
Commissioned by Alice Esty
Dedicated to Alice Esty
Composed August, 1961

Premiere:
1963 (11 April):   New York City; Carnegie Hall;
Alice Esty, soprano.

W260.   Deux chansons (unpublished)

For voice and piano
Contents: Fantômas (text by Delécluse); La Chanson
des promeneurs (text by Elie Richard)
Composed October, 1961

W261.   Deux sonnets (unpublished)

For voice and piano
Texts by William Shakespeare
Commissioned by Gérard Souzay
Composed April-May, 1964

Premiere:
1964: New York City; Gérard Souzay, baritone.

W262. Deux chansons (unpublished)

For voice and piano
Texts by Alain Saury
Composed May-June, 1969

W263. Trois chants d'ombre (1973; Editions françaises de
musique; 6 min., 30 sec.)

Lyric suite for baritone and piano
Subtitled: "Extraits des hallucinations"
Texts by Henry Jacqueton
Contents: Cette cigarette dans l'ombre; Plein ciel;
Incantaiton, la nuit
Composed July, 1969

Premiere:
1970 (30 January): Paris; L'Union des femmes pro-
fesseurs et compositeurs; Otto Linsi, voice; Dominique Swarowsky-Vichard, piano.

W264. Trois innocentines (unpublished)

For soprano (or tenor) and piano
Texts by René de Obaldia
Contents: Le Secret; Moi, j'erai dans la lune; Les
Jumeaux de la nuit
Composed 1969

Premiere:
1971 (13 December): Paris; Concerts du Triptyque;
Paul Derenne, tenor; Henri Sauguet, piano.

W265. Les Jours se suivent (unpublished)

Suite for voice and piano
Texts by Jacques Baron
Contents: La Tour prend gard; Lied; En attendant
Composed July, 1970

W266. Je sais qu'il existe (unpublished)

Suite for baritone and piano
Twelve poems by Maurice Carême
Composed June-July, 1973

Premiere:
1975: The Netherlands; Radio Hilversum; Ludovic De
San, baritone; Henri Sauguet, piano.

Selected performances:
    1976 (8 July): Narbonne; Festival de la côte
    Languedocienne; Lodovic de San; Henri Sauguet.

W267. Sept chansons de l'alchimiste (unpublished)

For medium voice and piano
Texts by Raphaël Cluzel
Contents: L'Alchimiste au regard d'ambre; L'Alchi-
    miste est dans le grenier; L'Amour sorcier; L'Al-
    chimiste a la voix d'ambre; Dans le jardin de l'al-
    chimiste; Les Yeux d'ambre de l'alchimiste; J'en
    appelle à l'alchimiste
Holography of the composer's manuscript printed in **La
    Revue musicale** (1984)
Composed July, 1978

Premiere:
    1981 (April): Paris; Salle Cortot; Udo Reinemann,
    baritone; Catherine Brilli, piano.

W268. Trois Lieder (unpublished)

For voice and piano
Texts by Jean Tardieu
Composed 1982

Premiere:
    1982: Paris; Centre Pompidou; Anna Ringard.

W269. Quatre sonnets (unpublished)

For voice and piano
Texts by Francis Jammes
Composed July, 1987

VOCAL MUSIC, SECULAR, WITH PIANO, SINGLE SONGS

W270. Le Tabac à priser (unpublished)

For voice and piano
Text by Guillaume Apollinaire
Composed 1920

W271. Carmen (unpublished)

For voice and piano
Text by Jean Pellerin
Composed 1920

W272. Bergerie (unpublished)

Unfinished song for voice and piano
Text by Raymond Radiguet
Undertaken, but abandoned, 1922

W273. Fausse alerte (1922: published in **La Revue horizon**)

For voice and piano

Text by Adrien Copperie
Dedicated to Germaine Copperie
Composed 1922

W274.   Marine (unpublished)

For voice and piano
Text by Henri Sauguet
Composed 1922

W275.   La Vieille image (unpublished)

For voice and piano
Text by Adrien Copperie
Dedicated to Georges Artigues
Composed 1923

W276.   Halte (unpublished)

For voice and piano
Text by Raymond Radiguet
Dedicated to Pierre Lardin
Composed 1923

W277.   La Laboureur (unpublished)

For voice and piano
Text by Friedrich Schiller
Composed 1923

W278.   Inscription pour un portrait (unpublished)

For voice and piano
Text by Henri Rousseau
Dedicated to Erik Satie
Composed 1924

W279.   Equipe de France (unpublished)

For voice and piano
Text by Henri Sauguet
Composed 1924

W280.   Altitudes (unpublished)

For voice and piano
Text by Emile Fernandez
Composed 1924

W281.   Rivière (unpublished)

For voice and piano
Text by Adrien Copperie
Composed 1924

W282.   Amour et sommeil (1930; Rouart, Lerolle)

For high voice and piano
Text by Algernon Swinburne

French version by Gabriel Mourey
Dedicated to Jean Ozenne
Composed 1929

W283.   Présence (1930; Rouart, Lerolle)

For voice and piano
Text by René Laporte
Dedicated to Mme. René Laporte
Composed September, 1929

W284.   Herbst (unpublished)

For voice and piano
Text (in German) by Rainer-Maria Rilke
Composed 1932

W285.   Les Ondines (unpublished)

For voice and piano
Text by Heinrich Heine
French version by Gérard de Nerval
Dedicated to Suzanne Peignot
Composed 1932

W286.   Chanson de marin (unpublished)

For voice and piano
Text by Jean Cocteau
Dedicated to Marianne Oswald
Composed 1933

W287.   Aria d'Eduarda poeta (1936; published in **The Bones of
my hand** by Edward James)
See: D48.

For voice and piano
Text by Edward James
Composed 1934

W288.   Les Enfants du ruisseau (1936; Echiquier)

Chanson valse-musette for voice and piano
Text by Michel Vaucaire
Dedicated to Agnès Capri
Composed 1936

W289.   Un Bouquet à la main (unpublished)

Chanson for voice and piano
Text by Agnès Capri
Composed 1941

W290.   Fumée légère (unpublished)

For high voice and piano
Text by Henry David Thoreau
Dedicated to Jeannine Micheau
Composed 1943

W291.   **Offrande à Hermès** (unpublished)

For voice and piano
Text by Pindar
Composed 1944

W292.   **Bêtes et méchants** (unpublished)

Dissident song for voice and piano
Text by Paul Eluard
Composed 1944

W293.   **Eaux douces** (unpublished)

For voice and piano
Text by Germaine Beaumont
Composed 1945

W294.   **Bergerie** (unpublished)

For voice and piano
text by Léon Chabrillac
Composed 1946

W295.   **Les Amoureux sont seuls au monde** (unpublished)
          See: D44.

Chanson for voice and piano
Author of text unknown
Composed 1947

The chanson achieved some popularity and became the
    basis of both the **Piano Concerto no. 2** (W76) and
    the film of the same name (W34).

W296.   **Le Chalet tyrolien** (unpublished)

Chanson for voice and piano
Text by René Chalupt
Composed 1948

W297.   **Le Chemin des forains** (unpublished)
          See: D45.   B145, B654.

Chanson for voice and piano
Text by Jean Dréjac
Composed 1949

W298.   **Je suis heureuse** (unpublished)

Chanson for voice and piano
Text by Lise Deharme
Composed 1950

W299.   **On pleure aussi dans le Midi** (unpublished)

Chanson for voice and piano
Text by Lou Castel
Composed 1950

W300. L'Eternelle chanson (unpublished)

Chanson for voice and piano
Text by Jean-Pierre Giraudoux
Extracted from the music for the play, **L'Ecole des hommes** (W384)
Composed 1951, for Suzy Solidor

W301. Chanson de la fille de bar (unpublished)

Chanson for voice and piano
Text by William Aguet
Composed 1952 for Radio Lausanne

W302. Isis poignardée (unpublished)

For voice and piano
Text by Armand Lanoux
Composed 1953

W303. Cinq mars (unpublished)

For voice and piano
Text by André Salmon
Dedicated to the memory of Max Jacob
Composed 1953

W304. Sur un page d'album (unpublished)

For voice and piano
Text by Honoré de Balzac
Composed 1954

W305. Valse des si (unpublished)
    See: D23, D47.

Chanson for voice and piano
Author of text unknown
Commissioned by the house of Schiaparelli to promote a new perfume
Composed March, 1956

W306. La Marchande d'anémones (1957; Editions transatlantiques)

Chanson for voice and piano
Alternate title: "Les Anémones"
Text by Sherban Sidery
Composed August, 1956

W307. Image pour Maria Freund (unpublished)

For voice and piano
Text by Maurice Carême
Composed October, 1956, for the 80th birthday of Maria Freund

W308. Un Seul poème (unpublished)
    See: B654.

Chanson ritournelle for voice and piano
Text by Denise Bourdet
Composed November-December, 1959

W309. **Celui qui dort** (unpublished)

For voice and piano
Text by Paul Eluard
Dedicated to Francis Poulenc in memory of forty years
  of friendship
Composed July, 1963, for Alice Esty

W310. **Prière dans le soir** (unpublished)

For voice and piano
Text by Edwige Pépin
Composed August, 1966

W311. **Comme à la lumière de la lune** (unpublished)

For voice and piano
Text by Marcel Proust
Dedicated to G. F. Zaffrani
Composed September-October, 1967

W312. **Dagueréotype** (unpublished)

Chanson for voice and piano
Text by Pierre Laffont
Composed April, 1968

W313. **La Mer est loin de Vienne** (unpublished)

Chanson for voice and piano
Text by Jean Dréjac
Composed September, 1968

W314. **Fado** (unpublished)

For voice and piano
Text by Jacques Deval
Composed October, 1970

W315. **Prélude de la poème sans héros** (1977; In: Akhmatova,
        Anna: Le Poème sans héros. Paris: Librarie des
        Cinq Continents)

For voice and piano
Text by Anna Akhmatova
French version by Elaine Moch-Bickert
Composed 1975-1976

W316. **Love poem** (unpublished)

For voice and piano
Text by William Clift
Composed September, 1976

W317. Chant du feu (unpublished)

For tenor and piano
Text by Léopold Sedar Senghor
Composed December, 1976

Premiere:
1977 (6 February): Dakar, Senegal; Richard Gaillan,
tenor, Henri Sauguet, piano.

W318. Pour Nicolas (unpublished)

For voice and piano
Text by Marie-Alix
Dedicated to Danièle Fontanille in memory of her son
Composed August, 1979

W319. Imploration (unpublished)

For voice and piano
Text by Daniel Boulanger
Composed June, 1981

W320. Arthur Rimbaud (unpublished)

For voice and piano
Text by Louis Amade
Composed December, 1985

W321. Dans la maison de paix (unpublished)

For voice and piano
Text by Raphaël Cluzel
Composed July, 1987

ELECTRONIC MUSIC

W322. Musiques de scènes pour les spectacles de Jean Tardieu
(unpublished)

Musique concrète
Composed 1955 for productions by Tardieu at the Théâtre
de la Huchette

W323. Musique de scène pour les Temps du verbe (unpublished)

Musique concrète
Recorded at the Studio d'essai de la R.T.F.
Composed January, 1956, for a dramatic piece produced
by Jean Tardieu

W324. Aspect sentimental (unpublished)
See: D11. B20, B111, B671.

Musique concrète
Subtitled: "Sous un parapluie"
Composed March-June, 1957, in cooperation with the
Groupe de Recherche de l'O.R.T.F.

W325. **Rêve d'Isa** (unpublished)

Composition métaphonique
Composed February-March, 1962, for the film **Les Amants de Teruel** (W355)

MUSIC FOR THE CINEMA

W326. **L'Epevier** (unpublished)
See: B448.

Music for the film by Marcel L'Herbier
Composed 1933

One song from the film, text by J.G. Auriol, dedicated to Natalie Paley, achieved some popularity.

W327. **La Fortune enchantée** (unpublished)

Music for the animated film by Pierre Charbonnier
Composed 1935

W328. **Péché de jeunesse** (unpublished)
See: B519.

Music for the film by Maurice Tourneur
Composed 1941

The music for the section entitled "Evocation romantique" was modeled on the ballet from **La Chartreuse de Parme** (W4).

W329. **Sur les chemins de Lamartine** (unpublished)

Music for the film by Jean Tedesco
Dedicated to Georges Auric
Composed 1941

W330. **Le Tonnelier** (unpublished)

Music for the film by Georges Roquier
Composed 1942

W331. **Symphonie en blanc** (unpublished)
See: B421, B439, B692, B731.

Music for the film by Serge Lifar
Scenario by Léandre Vaillat and Serge Lifar
Directed by René Chanas and François Adrouin
Orchestra recording the music for the film conducted by Roger Désormière
Cast includes Serge Lifar, Serge Peretti, Solange Schwartz, Lycette Darsonval, and Yvette Chauviré
Composed 1942

The film is presented in two parts: "La Danse éternelle," with music by Sauguet, is an imaginative, evolutionary survey of the dance; "Symphonie en blanc" presents fragments of the ballet in the

repertoire of the Paris Opéra. For this section
the music was arranged and orchestrated by Sauguet
and Francis Poulenc.

Concert performance:
   1979 (12 July): Toulouse; Musique d'été; Grand
   soirée de ballet; Choreography by Lífar; Dancers
   from the Ballet du Capitole, Opéra de Bâle, and
   Opéra de Nice.

W332. L'Honorable Catherine (unpublished)
      See: B498.

Music for the film by Marcel L'Herbier
Screen play based on the play by Solange Terac
Cast includes Edwige Feuillere, Raymond Rouleau
Composed 1942

W333. La Cirque enchanté (unpublished)

Music for the film by Jean Tedesco
Symphonie documentaire no. 3
Composed 1943

W334. Le Charron (unpublished)

Music for the film by Georges Rouquier
Symphonie documentaire no. 5
Composed 1943
Film score orchestrated by Elsa Baraine

A suite of music from the film was arranged and orchestrated by the composer in 1949. Reduced score available from Choudens; full score and parts (1.1.1.1/
1.1.1.0/timp/perc/cel/pf/str) available on rental
from Choudens.

W335. La Part de l'enfant (unpublished)

Music for the film documentary by Georges Rouquier
Symphonie documentaire no. 6
Composed 1943
Orchestrated by Elsa Baraine

W336. Premier de cordée (unpublished)
      See: B138.

Music for the film by Louis Daquin
Screen play based on a novel by Roger Frison-Roche
Dialogue by Alexandre Arnoux
Cast includes André le Gall, Jean Davy, Irène Corday,
   and Mona Doll
Composed 1944

A suite for orchestra, entitled **Symphonie de la montagne** (W50), was later extracted from the film music.

W337. Farrebique (unpublished)
      See: D55. B27, B138, B563, B624.

Music for the film by Georges Rouquier
Alternate title "Les Quatre saisons"
Composed 1946

A suite for orchestra entitled, **Les Saisons et les jours** (W54) was extracted from the film music.

In 1946 the film was awarded the Nice Grand Prix de la Critique International, and the Grand Prix du Cinéma français.

Selected performances:
1971 (May): France; Radio broadcast of excerpts.

W338. **Terre sauvage** (unpublished)

Music for the film by Jacques Marnier
Alternate title: "Sur la Camargue"
Composed 1947

W339. **Clochemerle** (unpublished)
    See: D57.

Music for the film by Pierre Chenal
Screen play based on the novel, Les Médisances de Clochemerle by Gabriel Chevallier
Composed 1947

A suite of 8 minutes for orchestra was extracted from the film music. Condensed score (1948) available for sale from Choudens. Full score and parts (1.1. 2.1/2.2.1.1/timp/perc/pf,str) available on rental from Choudens.

W340. **Les Amoureux sont seuls au monde** (unpublished)
    See: B365, B469.

Music for the film by Henri Decoin
Screen play by Henri Jeanson
Cast includes Louis Jouvet, Renée Devillers, Dany Robin, and Henri Sauguet (as the conductor)
Composed 1947-1948

Music for the film was derived from a popular song by Sauguet (W295) and later formally organized as the **Concerto no. 2** (W76).

W341. **Entre onze heures et minuit** (unpublished)

Music for the film by Henri Decoin
Cast includes Louis Jouvet, Madeleine Robinson, and Robert Arnoux
Composed 1949

Premiere:
1949 (7 June): Paris.

W342. **Ouvrage du fer** (unpublished)

Music for the film documentary concerned with the
smelting of ore and making of steel for various uses
by Simbacha
Composed 1949

W343.   **Au Revoir, Monsieur Grock** (unpublished)

Music for the film by Pierre Billon
Cast includes Grock, Suzy Prim, and Henry Cassidy
Composed 1949

Includes music by Grock, orchestrated by Sauguet

Premiere:
1950 (8 August): Paris.

W344.   **Ce siècle a cinquante ans** (unpublished)
See: B515.

Music for the film documentary by Denise Tual
Montage of events filmed during the first half of the
century
Screen play by Serge Roullet, Lucien Sive, and J. G.
Auriol
Composed, with Georges Auric, 1950

Premiere:
1950 (6 April): Paris.

W345.   **Julie de Carneilhan** (unpublished)
See: B516.

Music for the film by Jacques Manuel
Screen play based on the novel by Colette
Screen play by Jean-Pierre Grédy
Cast includes Edwige Feuillere, Pierre Brasseur, and
Jacques Dumesnil
Composed 1950

Premiere:
1950 (2 May): Paris.

W346.   **Plein-ciel malgache** (unpublished)

Music for a film, maker unknown
Composed 1953

W347.   **Images d'Epinal** (unpublished)

Music for a film by Philippe Agostini
Screen play play by Paul Gilson
Composed 1956
Recorded for the film 24 February, 1956, under the
direction of Henri Sauguet

Selected performances:
1971 (May): France; Radio broadcast of excerpts.

W348.   Don Juan (unpublished)
         See: B622.

         Music for a film by John Berry
         Sets and costumes by Georges Wakhévitch
         Cast includes Fernandel and Carmen Sevilla
         Composed 1956

         Premiere:
         1956 (9 May):   Paris.

W349.   Lorsque l'enfant paraît (unpublished)
         See: B622.

         Music for a film by Michel Boisrond
         Screen play based on the play by André Roussin
         Sets for the film by Raymond Nègre and René Moulaert
         Cast includes Gaby Morlay, André Lugnet, and Brigitte
            Auber
         Composed July, 1956

         Premiere:
         1956 (5 October):   Paris.

W350.   Les Œufs de l'autruche (unpublished)
         See: B622.

         Music for a film by Denys de La Patellière
         Screen play with additional dialogue by André Roussin
         Sets by Paul-Louis Boutie
         Cast includes Pierre Fresnay and Simone Renant
         Composed June, 1957

         Premiere:
         1957 (30 August):   Paris.

W351.   Mosaïques (unpublished)

         Music for a film by Abdul Vahab
         Composed November-December, 1958

W352.   Tu es Pierre (unpublished)
         See: B105, B622.

         Music for a film by Philippe Agostini
         Alternate title: "Tu es Petrus"
         Music performed by Chorale Elisabeth Brasseur
         Composed February, 1959

         Premiere:
         1959 (23 October):   Paris.

W353.   Paul Valéry (unpublished)

         Music for a film by Roger Leenhart
         Composed September, 1960
         Recorded for the film under the composer's direction
            October, 1960

W354. France (unpublished)

Music for a film by Etienne Lallier
Composed January, 1962

W355. Les Amants de teruel (unpublished)
      See: B437.

Music for a section of a film by Raymond Rouleau
Major portion of the film music composed by Mikis
    Theodorakis
The section entitled **Le Rêve d'Isa** (W325) was com-
    posed for the dancer Ludmilla Tcherina
Sets and costumes for the film by Jacques Dupont
Composed February-march, 1962

Premiere:
1962 (15 May): Canne; Canne Film Festival.

Selected performances:
1962 (14 December): New York City.

Film available on video cassette from Kultur Video as
The Lovers of Teruel.

W356. France (unpublished)

New version of the music for the film by Etienne
    Lallier
Composed January, 1963

W357. Au pied de l'arbre (unpublished)

Music for a film by Alain Saury
Composed March, 1964

W358. Ecce homo (unpublished)

Music for a film by Alain Saury
Composed January, 1965

Extract from the film score with the same title for a
    cappella chorus (W183).

W359. L'Heure de vérité (unpublished)

Music for a film by Henri Calef
Composed February, 1965

Selected performances:
1971 (May): France; Radio broadcast of excerpts.

W360. Documents Lumière Angleterre-Amérique (unpublished)

Music for a film by Marc Allegret
Piano improvisation of the music in December, 1966
Music improvised and recorded for producion March,
    1968

MUSIC FOR THE THEATER

W361.   **Irma** (unpublished)
   <u>See:</u>   B77, B505.

   Music for a play by Roger Ferdinand
   Composed 1926

   <u>Premiere:</u>
      1926 (6 February):   Paris; Charles Dullin and his
      company at the Atelier.

W362.   **Le Retour de l'enfant prodigue** (unpublished)
   <u>See:</u>   D32.   B28, B195, B346, B399, B581.

   Music for a play by André Gide
   Dedicated to Jacques Dupont
   Composed 1933

   <u>Premiere:</u>
      1933 (23 February):   Paris; Théâtre de l'Avenue;
      Marcel Herrand, director; Performed in a reading
      without sets or costumes.

W363.   **Le Sicilien ou l'amour peintre** (unpublished)
   <u>See:</u>   B61.

   Music for a play by Molière
   Composed 1934

   <u>Premiere:</u>
      1934:   Aix-en-Provence; Compagnie des Quinze.

W364.   **Ondine** (unpublished)
   <u>See:</u>   B21, B30, B132, B387, B396, B397, B399, B533,
      B536, B542, B577, B727.

   Music for a play by Jean Giraudoux
   Dedicated to Madeleine Ozeray
   Composed 1939

   <u>Premiere:</u>
      1939 (4 May):   Paris; Théâtre Athénée; Direced by
      Louis Jouvet; Sets and costumes by Pavel Tchelit-
      chev; Cast includes Louis Jouvet and Madeleine
      Ozeray; Music recorded for the production by Roger
      Désormière.

   <u>Selected performances:</u>
      1940 (23 March):   Paris; Théâtre Athénée; Production
      reopened after the original 274 performances.

      1941:   Portions of the play performed as part of a
      tour of unoccupied zones of Europe by Jouvet and
      Ozeray.

      1949 (May):   Paris; Théâtre Athénée; Presented with
      original music, sets and costumes;   Cast includes
      Pierre Renoir and Denise Blanchar.

W365. L'Ecole de la médisance (unpublished)

Music for a play by Richard Brinsley Sheridan
Dedicated to Marcel Herrand and Jean Marchat
Composed 1940

Premiere:
   1940: Paris; Théâtre des Mathurins; Music for the
   performances recorded by Roger Désormière.

W366. Les Perses (unpublished)

Music for a play by Æschylus
Dedicated to Louis Jouvet
Composed 1940

Premiere:
   1940: Paris; Théâtre de l'Athénée; Produced by
   Louis Jouvet.

W367. Sigismond (unpublished)
   See: B712.

Music for a play by Georges Courteline
Composed 1940

Premiere:
   1940: Paris; Théâtre Agnès Capri; Produced by
   Agnès Capri.

Selected performances:
   1945 (October): Paris; Théâtre Agnès Capri.

W368. De mal en pis (unpublished)

Music for a play by Pedro Calderon de la Barca
Composed 1942

W369. L'Honorable Mr. Pepys (unpublished)

Music for a play by Georges Couturier
Composed 1943

Premiere:
   1947 (April): Paris; Théâtre de l'Atelier; Produced
   by André Barsacq; Cast includes Jacques Erwin and
   Marie-Hélène Daste.

W370. Ingeborg (unpublished)

Music for a play by Michel Arnaud
Composed 1943

W371. Le Pendu (unpublished)

Music for a play by X. de Christen
Composed 1944

Premiere:
1944: Paris; Produced by Le Groupe d'Art.

W372.   **Passe-temps** (unpublished)

Music for a play by Gilbert Fermont
Composed 1944

Premiere:
1944: Paris; Produced by Le Groupe d'Art.

W373.   **A quoi rêvent les jeunes filles** (unpublished)

Music for a play by Alfred de Musset
Composed 1944

Premiere:
1944: Paris; Théâtre de l'Atelier; Produced by André Barsacq.

W374.   **Monsieur et madame Roméo** (unpublished)
See: B132, B589.

Music for a play by Jean Berthet
Composed 1944

Premiere:
1944: Paris; Théâtre Saint-Georges; Sets by Guillaume Monin.

W375.   **La Folle de Chaillot** (unpublished)
See: B316, B327, B395, B399, B404, B456, B457, B542,
B577, B695, B730.

Music for a play by Jean Giraudoux
Composed 1945

Premiere:
1945 (19 December): Paris; Théâtre de l'Athénée;
Produced by Louis Jouvet; Sets and costumes by
Christian Bérard; Cast includes Louis Jouvet and
Marguerite Moreno.

W376.   **La Voiture versée** (unpublished)
See: B278, B426, B728.

Music for a play by Georges Courteline
Composed 1946

Premiere:
1946 (20 April): Paris; Théâtre des Ambassadeurs;
Collaborative effort for which Sauguet, Jacques
Ibert, Elsa Barraine, Philippe Gérard, Claude Delvincourt, and Darius Milhaud each supplied music
for a short dramatic sketch by Courteline; Directed by Jean Mercure; Sets by Petrus Bride; Costumes by Christian Dior.

W377. Victor (unpublished)
        See: B396.

Music for a play by Roger Vitrac
Alternate title: "Les Enfants au pouvoir"
Composed November, 1946

Premiere:
    1946 (12 November): Paris; Théâtre Agnès Capri;
    Le Thiase directed by Michel de Ré.

W378. Marie-Antoinette (unpublished)

Music for a play by Philippe Erlanger
Composed 1947

Premiere:
    1947: Brussels; Théâtre des Galeries.

W379. Dom Juan (unpublished)
        See: B132, B316, B397, B404, B546, B577, B695.

Music for a play by Molière
Composed 1947

Premiere:
    1947 (24 December): Paris; Théâtre de l'Athénée;
    Produced by Louis Jouvet; Sets and costumes by
    Christian Bérard.

W380. La Tentation de Tati (unpublished)
        See: B632.

Music for a play by Jean Schlumberger
Composed 1949

Premiere:
    1949: Paris; Théâtre Edouard-VII; Directed by Jean
    Mercure; Sets and costumes by Jacques Manuel.

W381. Les Fourberies de Scapin (unpublished)
        See: B132, B316, B397, B577, B695, B730.

Music for a play by Molière
Composed 1949

Premiere:
    1949: Paris; Théâtre Marigny; Produced by Louis
    Jouvet; Sets and costumes by Christian Bérard.

W382. Tartuffe (unpublished)
        See: B397, B577, B582.

Music for a play by Molière
Composed 1950

Premiere:
    1950 (27 January): Paris; Théâtre de l'Athénée;
    Directed by Jouvet; Sets Braques; Costumes Karinski.

W383.   **Théâtre 1950** (unpublished)

Music for a stage work by Xavier de Courville
Work classified as a "Conference-Parade"
Composed 1950

W384.   **Le Roi lepreux** (unpublished)

Music for a play by S. Lilar
Composed 1951

Premiere:
1951:   Brussels; Théâtre du Parc.

W385.   **L'Ecole des hommes** (unpublished)

Music for a play by Jean-Pierre Giraudoux
Composed 1951

Premiere:
1951 (April):   Paris; Théâtre Michel.

The song **L'Eternelle chanson** (W300)   was extracted
from the music for the play.

W386.   **Comme il vous plaira** (unpublished)
See: B132, B578, B580, B594.

Music for a play by William Shakespeare
French adaptation by Jules Supervielle
Composed 1951

Premiere:
1951:   Paris; Comédie-Française; Directed by Jacques
Charon; Sets and costumes by François Ganeau.

W387.   **Robinson Crusoë** (unpublished)
See: B283, B391, B483, B578.

Music for a play by Jules Superville
Composed 1952

Premiere:
1952 (November):   Paris; Théâtre de l'Œuvre; Directed by Jean Le Poulain; Sets and costumes by
Georges Wakhévitch.

W388.   **La Tempête** (unpublished)

Music for a play by William Shakespeare
Composed 1955

Premiere:
1955:   Nante; Festival de Nante.

W389.   **Les Suites d'une course** (unpublished)
See: B578.

Music for a play (pantomime) by Jules Supervielle
Composed 1955

Premiere:
1955 (December):   Paris; Théâtre Marigny; Compagnie
Barrault-Renaud.

W390.   **Un Voix sans personne** (unpublished)

Incidental music, for string quartet, for a play
by Jean Tardieu
Work classified as a "Poème à jouer"
Composed 1956

Premiere:
1956 (4 February):   Paris; Théâtre de la Huchette.

W391.   **Le Lit** (unpublished)

Music for a mime sketch and dance by Béla Reine
Composed october, 1956

W392.   **La Concierge** (unpublished)

Music for a mime sketch and dance by Béla Reine
Composed December, 1956

W393.   **La Nuit des rois** (unpublished)

Music for a play by William Shakespeare
Composed May, 1957

Premiere:
1957:   Paris; Théâtre de Vieux-Colombier; Directed
by Douking.

W394.   **Landscape with figures** (unpublished)
See: B51, B677, B725.

Music for a play by Cecil Beaton
Composed 1959

The play originally appeared in 1951 as The Gains-
borough Girls but was entirely revamped in 1959
under the above title.

Premiere:
1959 (September):   Great Britain (Newcastle, Dublin,
Brighton and Wolverhampton);   Directed by Douglas
Seale; Sets and costumes by Cecil Beaton; Cast
includes Donald Wolfit and Mona Washbourne.

W395.   **Carlota** (unpublished)

Music for a play by Miguel Mihura
French adaptation by Emmanuel Roblès
Composed January, 1960

W396.   Robinson (unpublished)
See also: W387.

New music for a play by Jules Supervielle
Composed October, 1960

Premiere:
1960: Centre dramatique du Nord.

W397.   La Nuit des rois (unpublished)
See: D2. B99. B282, B390. See also: W393.

New music for a play by William Shakespeare
French adaptation by Jean Anouilh
Composed January, 1961

Premiere:
1961 (February): Paris: Théâtre de Vieux-Colombier; Directed by Jean Le Poulain.

W398.   Othello (unpublished)

Music for a play by William Shakespeare
French adaptation by Georges Neveux
Composed April, 1961

Premiere:
1961: Les Tréteaux de France of Jean Danet; Directed by Jean Davy.

W399.   L'Ecole de la médisance (unpublished)
See: B12. See also: W365.

Music for a play by Richard Brinsley Sheridan
French adaptation by Jean-Pierre Grédy and Pierre Ba-
rillet
Composed April, 1962

Premiere:
1962 (May): Paris; Comédie-Française; Directed by
Raymond Gérome; Costumes by Cecil Beaton.

W400.   Un Amour qui ne finit pas (unpublished)

Music for a play by André Roussin
Music for either string quartet or for piano, Hamond
organ and pre-recorded sounds (musique concrète)
Composed January, 1963

Premiere:
1963 (February): Paris: Théâtre de la Madeleine.

W401.   Machinchouette (unpublsihed)

Music for a play by Marcel Achard
Composed July-August, 1964
Recorded by the composer on Hamond organ and mechani-
cal piano for the performance

Premiere:
1964: Paris; Théâtre Antoine.

W402. Le Roi Cymbeline (unpublished)

Music for a play by William Shakespeare
French adaptation by Jean-Louis Sarthou
Composed June, 1967

Premiere:
1967: Paris: Théâtre de l'Ouest; Directed by Jean-
Louis Sarthou.

W403. Scénes d'amour (unpublished)

Music for romantic scenes from the plays of William
Shakespeare
Composed May, 1968

Premiere:
1968: Festival de Sarlat; directed by Julien Ber-
theau; Music performed on the piano by Henri Sauguet.

W404. Dialogue dans le Loir-et-Cher (unpublished)
See: B233.

Music for a play by Paul Claudel
Adapted for the stage by Sylvia Monfort
Composed June-July, 1973

Excerpts from the score published as **Musiques pour
Claudel** (W178).

Premiere:
1973 (September): Directed by Sylvia Monfort; Music performed on the guitar by Raphaël Andia.

W405. Pour Lucrèce (unpublished)

Music for a play by Jean Giraudoux
Composed April-May, 1982

Premiere:
1982 (July): Bellac; Compagnie du Limousin.

MUSIC FOR BROADCAST

W406. Léonce et Lena (unpublished)

Music for a play by Georges Buchner
Adapted for radio by Michel Arnaud
Composed 1941

W407. La Mort de Danton (unpublished)

Music for a play by Georges Buchner
Adapted for radio by Michel Arnaud
Composed 1941

W408. Cinq images pour saint Louis à Damiette (unpublished)

Music for a play by Joinville
Adapted for radio by André Fraigneau
For flute, oboe, trumpet, and harpsichord
Composed 1941

W409. Dix images pour une vie de Jean d'Arc (unpublished)

Music for a radio broadcast
Texts selected by André Fraigneau
For flute, oboe, clarinet, bassoon, horn, trumpet, and
    piano
Composed 1943

W410. Adonis (unpublished)

Music for a poem by Jean de La Fontaine
Adapted for radio presentation by Roger Allard
For small chorus and chamber ensemble
Composed 1943

W411. Le Sport et l'esprit (unpublished)

Music for a radio broadcast
Composed 1944

W412. Les Trente-sept sous de M. Mautaudoin (unpublished)

Music for a play, classified as a "vaudeville," by
    Labiche
Adapted for radio broadcast 6 May, 1945
Composed 1945

W413. Les Enfants terribles (unpublished)

Music for a play by Jean Cocteau
Adapted for radio by Agathe Melta
Composed 1947

W414. Pepe et Carmelita (unpublished)

Music for a radio operetta by William Aguet
Composed 1947

W415. La Pharmacienne (unpublished)

Music for a play by Jean Giraudoux
Adapted for radio by André Beucler
Composed 1949

W416. L'Oiseleur et la fleuriste (unpublished)
       See: B590.

Music for a radio play by Armand Lanoux
Composed 1950

A song from the play, "Chanson de l'Oiseleur" achieved
    some popularity.

W417.   Agathe de Nieul l'espoir (unpublished)

Music for a radio play by Odette Joyeux
Composed 1950

W418.   Tendres canailles (unpublished)

Music for a play by André Salmon
Adapted for radio
Composed 1951

W419.   Robinson Crusoë (unpublished)

Music for a radio operetta by William Aguet
Composed 1951

Broadcast on Radio-Lausanne 1952.

W420.   La Plus long nuit de l'année (unpublished)

Music for a radio mystery by Armand Lanoux
Alternate title: "L'Auberge de la belle étoile"
Composed 1953

Broadcast on Radio française 1953.

W421.   Les Aventures d'Ulysse (unpublished)

Music for a radio broadcast of episodes from the Odys-
sey
Adapted by André Fraigneau
Composed 1954

Broadcast on Radio française 1954.

W422.   L'Ange Dudule (unpublished)

Music for a radio comedy by William Aguet
Composed 1954

Broadcast on Radio française and Radio-Suisse 1954.

W423.   Monsieur Cendrillon (unpublished)

Music for a comic operetta by William Aguet
Composed 1954

Broadcast on Radio-Suisse 1954.

W424.   Lancelot du Lac (unpublished)

Music for a radio play by André Fraigneau
Composed 1954-55

Broadcast on Radio française in ten episodes 1954-55.

W425.   Le Grand écart (unpublished)

Music for a radio adaptation of a novel by Jean Cocteau

Adapted by Alain Tarrancle
Composed February-March, 1956

W426. **Les Mille et une nuits** (unpublished)

Music for a radio adaptation of selected tales from
the Arabian Nights
Adapted by André Fraigneau
Composed August and October, 1956

W427. **Les Folies amoureuses** (unpublished)

Music for a comedy by Regnard
Adapted for television
Composed June, 1957

W428. **Monsieur de Pourceaugnac** (unpublished)

Music for a comedy-ballet by Molière
Adapted for television and directed by Jacques Kerch-
bron
Composed January, 1958

W429. **L'Auberge de la belle étoile** (unpublished)

Music for a mystery by Armand Lanoux
Adapted for television
Composed July-October, 1958

The music for the previous version for radio was also
composed by Sauguet. It was produced under the
title **La Plus longue nuit de l'année** (W416).

W430. **Les Mules du Vice-Roi** (unpublished)

Music for a radio play by Stéphane Audel
Composed January, 1959

W431. **A saint Lazare** (unpublished)

Music for a radio drama by Pierre Devaux
Composed April, 1959

W432. **Le Zébu du zoo** (unpublished)

Music for a radio operetta by William Aguet
Composed November, 1958-June, 1959

Broadcast on Radio-Suisse, 1959.

W433. **Le Chevalier du Brûle-Flamme** (unpublished)

Music for a radio play by Hubert Dumas
Composed March-April, 1961

W434. **Uriel** (unpublished)

Music for a radio mystery by Louis Emié
Composed 1961

Broadcast on Radio Aquitaine 12 June, 1961.

W435.   Monelle de la nuit (unpublished)

Music for a poem by Michel Suffran
Adapted for radio from Le Livre de Monelle by Marcel
   Schwob
Composed November-December, 1961

Broadcast on Radio française 1962.

W436.   Christine, ou la pluie sur la mer (unpublished)

Music for a television comedy by Michel Suffran
Directed by Maurice Château
Composed June, 1963

W437.   Melmoth réconcilié (unpublished)

Music for a television adaptation of the novel by Ho-
   noré de Balzac
Adaptation by Georges Lacômbe
Composed December, 1963

W438.   Destin (unpublished)

Music for a television adaptation of a novel by Fran-
   çois Mauriac
Adapted and produced by Pierre Cardinal
Composed January, 1965

W439.   L'Imposteur (unpublished)

Televised version of the Ballet, **Le Prince et le Mendiant** (W40)
Scenario by Boris Kochno after The Prince and the Pau-
   per by Mark Twain
Composed 1965

Broadcast on Television française 23 March, 1965.

W440.   Max Jacob de Quimper (unpublished)

Music for a television documentary by Camille Arnal
   and André de Beaumont
Composed April, 1966

Broadcast on Television regionale, Rennes.

W441.   Luisa de San Felice (unpublished)

Music for a ten-part radio adaptation of a novel by
   Alexandre Dumas, fils
Adapted by André Fraigneau and Jean Moal
Composed October-December, 1966

W442.   Les Bonifas (unpublished)

Music for an adaptation of Jacques de Lacretelle's novel

Adapted for television by Jean-Louis Bory
Produced and directed by Pierre Cardinal
Score and parts available on rental fron Editions fran-
çaises de musique
Composed April-May, 1967

Selected performances:
1971 (May):   France; Radio broadcast of excerpts.

W443. Les Compagnons de Baal (unpublished)

Music for a television film by Pierre Prévert and
Jacques Champreux
Score and parts available on rental from Editions fran-
çaises de musique
Composed November, 1967-February, 1968

Broadcast on Télévision française in seven episodes
1968.

Selected performances:
1971 (May):   France; Radio broadcast of excerpts.

W444. Le Songe de Dona Clara (unpublished)

Music for a dramatic comedy by Pierre-Alain Tarrancle
Score and parts available on rental from Editions fran-
çaises de musique
Composed November-December, 1968

Broadcast on Télévision française 1969.

W445. Le Desért de l'amour (unpublished)

Music for a television adaptation of a novel by Fran-
çois Mauriac
Adapted and produced by Pierre Cardinal
Score and parts available on rental from Editions fran-
çaise de musique
Composed March, 1969

W446. La Fille qui dit "non" (unpublished)

Music for a television adaptation of a story by Marc-
Gilbert Sauvageon
Adapted by Aimée Mortimer
Score and parts available on rental from Editions fran-
çaise de musique
Composed May-June, 1969

W447. La Ballade de Covendale (unpublished)

Music for a radio comedy by Pierre-Alain Tarrancle
Composed December, 1969

W448. Les Thibault (unpublished)
    See: D38.

Music for a television adaptation of the novel by Roger Martin du Gard
Adapted for broadcast in three episodes by Louis Guilloux
Produced and directed by André Michel
Score and parts available on rental from Editions françaises de musique
Composed 1972

W449. L'Oiselet vert (unpublished)

Music for a musical comedy by Denise Lemaresquier based on the play by Carlo Gozzi
Produced for television by Claude Deflandre
Score and parts available on rental from Editions françaises de musique
Composed April-November, 1972; Originally undertaken in 1963

W450. Salavin (unpublished)

Music for a television adaptation of a novel by André Michel
Adapted by Georges Duhamel
Produced and directed by Michel Suffran
Composed 1974

W451. La Mémoire en marche (unpublished)

Music for a television film
Composed September, 1983

Broadcast on Télévision d'Aquitaine, 1983.

SUPPLEMENT

W452. March au Lieutenant Pourchasse (unpublished)

Instrumentation and function unknown
Composed 1940

W453. Petit air tendre (unpublished)

Instrumentation unknown
Alternate title: "Soixante-dix-notes"
Composed for the 78th birthday of Geneviève Sienkiewicz
Composed October, 1956

W454. C'est ça l'amour (unpublished)

Instrumentation unknown; probably a chanson for voice and piano
Text by Pierre Devaux
Composed January, 1958

Broadcast on Radio française 1958

W455.   **Petit vœu musical** (unpublished)

Instrumentation unknown
Composed for Madame X X X
Composed May, 1958

W456.   **Pâques fête de la joie** (1982; Printed in holograph of
the composer's manuscript in: Robin, Armand: <u>Pâques</u>
<u>fêtes</u> <u>de</u> <u>la</u> <u>joie</u>.   Quimper: Calligrammes, 1982.)

Instrumentation unknown
Composed to accompany an exhibition of photographs by
Armand Robin
Probably composed 1982

W457.   **Quatre-vingt notes** (unpublished)

Instrumentation unknown
Composed for the 80th birthday of Isabelle Gouin
Composed July, 1983

Writings by Henri Sauguet

Henri Sauguet was a prolific writer of words as well as music. Between 1928 and 1948 he wrote criticism for four journals, **L'Europe nouvelle**, **La Revue hebdomadaire**, **La Bataille**, and **La Jour et Echo de Paris**. Criticism for each journal is listed chronologically under the names of each title. A concluding section of "Writings" includes articles and speeches for other publications and events and follows the standard alphabetical presentation.

REVIEWS FROM **L'EUROPE NOUVELLE**

S1.   Les Programmes de la saison--Les Concerts. No. 558
         (15 October, 1928): 1412-1413.
             Sauguet's first review. The editor introduces him
         to the readers and cites his credentials. Among other
         items, Sauguet cites upcoming premiers by Honegger
         (Rugby), Poulenc (Concert champêtre), Stravinsky (Sym-
         phonie, Etude, Apollon musagète), Nicolas Nabokov
         (Ode), and Vittorio Rieti (Orphée).

S2.   Le Premier concert de l'Orchestre symphonique de Paris
         --Mme Elisabeth Schumann. No. 560 (29 October,
         1928): 1504.
             Arthur Honegger's Rugby is premiered at the first
         concert of the Orchestre symphonique de Paris. Ernest
         Ansermet and Louis Forestier conduct the concert. Eli-
         sabeth Schumann presents a song recital.

S3.   Une Audition du "Martyr de Saint Sébastien" aux Con-
         certs Pasdeloup--Un Concert de l'Orchestre sympho-
         nique de Paris. No. 562 (12 November, 1928): 1567-
         1568.
             D.-E. Inghelbrecht conducts Debussy's Martyr de
         Saint Sébastien at Concerts Pasdeloup. Ernest Anser-
         met and l'Orchestre symphonique de Paris premier the
         "Overture" and "Sarabande" from Marcel Delannoy's Le
         Fou de la dame.

S4.   M. Otto Klemperer à l'Orchestre symphonique de Paris--
         Une Audition du "Sacre du Printemps," dirigée par M.

E. Ansermet. no. 569 (5 January, 1929): 11.
        Otto Klemperer leads the Orchestre symphonique de
Paris in performances of Paul Hindemith's Konzertmusik
for wind instruments and Ernst Krenek's Petite symphonie. Ernest Ansermet's interpretation of Igor Stravinsky's Sacre du printemps is well received.

S5.   La "Messe du couronnement' de Mozart aux Concerts Pas-
        deloup--Mme Marcelle Meyer à l'O.S.P. No. 570 (12
        January, 1929): 43-44.
            D.-E. Inghelbrecht leads Concerts Pasdeloup in a
        varied program which includes Mozart's Coronation Mass
        and fragments from Emmanuel Chabrier's Roi malgré lui.
        Marcelle Meyer performs the Burlesque by Richard
        Strauss with the Orchestre symphonique de Paris.

S6.   A l'O.S.P. audition de l'"Ode" de Nicolas Nabokoff et
        du "Baiser de la Fée" d'Igor Stravinsky   No. 576
        (23 February, 1929): 237.
            Ansermet conducts a varied program with new works
        well represented.

S7.   "L'Eventail de Jeanne" à l'Opéra--Une Récital de Jane
        Bathori. No. 578 (3 March, 1929): 310-311.
            L'Eventail de Jeanne was composed for Jeanne Dubost
        by Maurice Ravel, Florent Schmitt, Darius Milhaud,
        Georges Auric, Francis Poulenc, Albert Roussel, Roland
        Manuel, Marcel Delannoy, Jacques Ibert, and P.-O. Fer-
        roud. It is performed at the Opéra. Jane Bathori pre-
        sents a recital at the Comédie des Champs-Elysées which
        includes Debussy's Chansons de Bilitis and Darius Mil-
        haud's Poèmes de Léo Latil.

S8.   "Le Mas" de J. Canteloube à l'Opéra. No. 583 (13 Ap-
        ril, 1929): 477.
            Joseph Canteloube's three act opera, Le Mas is
        warmly received by the public.

S9.   Albert Roussel--A l'Orchestre symphonique de Paris:
        Concerts de printemps: M. P. Monteux. No. 584 (20
        April, 1929): 508.
            Concerts Straram presents a concert of Roussel's
        music in honor of his 60th birthday, La Revue musical
        publishes a special number about his life and works,
        the Opéra-Comique presents Le Festin de l'araignée,
        and the Opéra presents Pâdmavâti. Alfred Cortot con-
        ducts the Orchestre symphonique de Paris in an unex-
        citing program.

S10.   Au Théâtre Danou, une opérette de Georges Auric: "Sans
        façon"--Concerts. No. 585 (4 May, 1929): 575-576.
            Georges Auric's operetta, Sans façon (libretto by
        Jean Alley, with additional couplets by H.-R. Lemar-
        chand, and sets by Paul Collin), opens at the Théâtre
        Danou. Pierre Monteux presents a good performance of
        Claude Debussy's Nocturnes with the Orchestre sympho-
        nique de Paris.

S11.   A l'O.S.P. le "Concert champêtre" de Francis Poulenc-
        -La Saison de printemps. No. 587 (11 May, 1929):
        602.
            Wanda Landowska performs the premier of Francis
        Poulenc's Concert champêtre with the Orchestre sympho-
        nique de Paris. An outline of the spring season of
        concerts and ballets follows.

S12.   Premiers concerts de la saison. No. 610 (19 October,
        1929): 1394-1395.
            Philippe Gaubert's Chants de la mer is premiered.
        Concerts Pasdeloup performs Fragment symphonique de
        Goldoni by Francesco Malipiero. Pierre Monteux leads
        the Orchestre symphonique de Paris in performances of
        a concerto by Paul Hindemith and a work by Pierre Cop-
        pola.

S13.   Mme Elisabeth Schumann chez Lamoureux. No. 611 (26
        October, 1929): 1428-1429.
            Pierre Monteux and l'Orchestre symphonique de
        Paris present a premier of a work by Gustav Holst.
        Why does Monteux choose Holst to represent England when
        Constant Lambert exists. Why Coppola to represent
        Italy when Vittorio Rieti exists?

S14.   Un beau programme à l'O.S.P.--Reprise de Guillaume
        Tell à l'Opéra. No. 612 (2 November, 1929): 1455.
            Monteux and l'Orchestre symphonique de Paris pre-
        mier Milhaud's Mélodies hébraïques. Gioacchino Ros-
        sini's Guillaume Tell is performed at the Opéra.

S15.   Madame Wanda Landowska--A l'O.S.P.: M. Mengelberg.
        No. 613 (9 November, 1929): 1492.
            Wanda Landowska presents her first concert of the
        season. Mengelberg conducts l'Orchestre symphonique
        de Paris. Emmanuel Chabrier's Le Roi malgré lui is
        performed at l'Opéra-comique.

S16.   Un Festival Honegger-Milhaud aux Concerts Pasdeloup.
        No. 614 (16 November, 1929): 1520-1521.
            Concerts Pasdeloup performs Arthur Honegger's Pa-
        cific 231, Rugby, Le Chant de Nigamon, fragments from
        L'Impératrice aux rochers, and the piano Concertino;
        and Darius Milhaud's La Création du monde, Saudades
        do Brazil (selections), Second symphonique suite
        (Protée), and Six chants populaires hébraïques.

S17.   Concerts de la semaine. No. 615 (23 November, 1929):
        1563.
            Lotte Lehman sings at Concerts Lamoureux. Georg
        Schnevoigt conducts l'Orchestre symphonique de Paris.
        Coming attractions are revealed.

S18.   Sur un festival Debussy-Florent Schmitt aux concerts
        Pasdeloup--Concerts divers. No. 617 (7 December,
        1929): 1629.
            Debussy's Martyre de Saint Sébastien and Schmitt's
        Psaume xlvii are performed at Concerts Pasdeloup.
        Frans von Hoesslin conducts l'Orchestre symphonique

de Paris in a performance which features Marcelle Meyer
in Grieg's Piano concerto.

S19.   Quatre concerts à l'Orchestre symphonique--Le Groupe
        des Six. No. 620 (18 December, 1929): 1759.
            Ernest Ansermet leads l'Orchestre symphonique de
        Paris in a performance of Poulenc's Aubade and Stra-
        vinsky's Capriccio. The first of a series of formal
        concerts of the works of Les Six featured Georges Au-
        ric's Les facheux and Germaine Tailleferre's Concerto.
        Darius Milhaud's Deux Psaumes and works by Arthur Hon-
        egger were recently performed at Concerts Siohan.

S20.   A l'O.S.P.: Une Audition de "L'art de la Fugue," de
        J.-S. Bach--A l'Opéra: "Les Créatures de Prométhée,"
        ballet de Beethoven, chorégraphie de Serge Lifar.
        no. 621 (4 January, 1930): 11-12.
            Hermann Scherchen conducts l'Orchestre symphonique
        de Paris in Glaeser's orchestration of Bach's Kunst
        der Fuge. Serge Lifar choreographs Beethoven's Crea-
        tures of Prometheus for a performance at l'Académie
        national de musique.

S21.   Deux concerts à l'Orchestre symphonique de Paris--Chez
        Lamoureux, "Bolero" de Maurice Ravel. no. 623 (18
        January, 1930): 119.
            L'Orchestre symphonique de Paris, under Georgesco,
        performs a concerto by Brahms, Strauss' Sinfonia do-
        mestica, and two premiers: Ring by Filip Lazar, and
        Ronde burlesque by Florent Schmitt. Concerts Lamou-
        reux premiers the concert version of Ravel's Bolero
        under the composer's baton.

S22.   Concerts à l'Orchestre symphonique de Paris--Deux vir-
        tuoses. No. 627 (15 February, 1930): 285.
            Pierre Monteux leads l'Orchestre symphonique de
        Paris in Neues vom Tag by Paul Hindemith and a sym-
        phony by Vittorio Rieti. Marcel Dupré participates
        in the dedication of the new organ in Salle Pleyel.
        Robert Casadesus and Zino Francescati perform recitals.

S23.   La "Symphonie lyrique" de N. Nabokoff, à l'Orchestre
        symphonique de Paris. no. 629 (1 March, 1930): 370.
            L'Orchestre symphonique de Paris performs Nicolas
        Nabokov's Symphonie lyrique among other compositions.

S24.   Concert de la Société J.-S. Bach--"Le Sacre du prin-
        temps" dirigé par M. Monteux--Mme Concita Supervia
        à l'Opéra. No. 635 (12 April, 1930): 570.
            The Société J.-S. Bach celebrates its 25th anni-
        versary with a concert. Pierre Monteux' direction of
        Le Sacre du printemps wins admiration. Conchita Su-
        pervia and an Italian company perform Rossini's Bar-
        biere di Sevilla and L'Italiana in Algeria.

S25.   "Au temps des valses," à l'Apollo--Un "Concerto" pour
        orgue et orchestre de P. Hindemith. No. 636 (19
        April, 1930): 625-626.
            Au temps des valses an adaptation by Saint-Granier

of Noel Coward's <u>Bitter Sweet</u> which was produced in
London by Charles B. Cochran, now plays at the Apollo.
Concerts Straram premiers Paul Hindemith's <u>Organ</u> <u>con-
certo</u>.

S26. Fondation à Paris d'une "Société d'Etudes Mozartiennes."
      No. 638 (3 May, 1930): 698.
         Modeled on that founded in Salzburg by Lilli Leh-
      mann, Mme Octave Homberg outlines the foundation and
      goals of the new Société d'Etudes Mozartiennes.

S27. Création à Berlin de "Christophe Colomb," opéra en 2
      actes, de Paul Claudel et Darius Milhaud. No. 641
      (24 May, 1930): 790-791.
         German premier of darius Milhaud's <u>Christophe</u> <u>Co-
      lomb</u> at the Staatsoper Unter den Linden.

S28. Concerts du mois. no. 642 (31 May, 1930): 828-829.
         Highlights are Nabokov's <u>Symphonie</u> <u>lyrique</u>, Hin-
      demith's <u>Neues vom Tag</u>, the overture to the second
      act of Milhaud's <u>Euménides</u>, Rieti's <u>Concerto napolitan</u>,
      Germaine Tailleferre's <u>Mélodies</u>, and Manuel de Falla's
      <u>El retablo de maese Pedro</u>.

S29. Un concert d'orchestre au Théâtre Pigalle--La "Cantate"
      d'Igor Markevitch. No. 644 (14 June, 1930): 894-895.
         Igor Markevitch's <u>Cantate</u> (on a text by Jean Coc-
      teau) is placed between the <u>Acante</u> <u>et</u> <u>Céphise</u> (suite)
      by Rameau and Satie's <u>Aventures</u> <u>de</u> <u>Mercure</u>.

S30. Un "Salut Solennel" à la Société de Musique d'Autre-
      fois--Récital de chant par M. Reinhold de Warlich--
      Les Fêtes Pastorales" chez Wanda Landowska. No. 646
      (28 June, 1930): 970-971.
         Roger Désormière conducts performances at the
      Société de Musique d'Autrefois. Reinhold de Warlich
      continues to present a series of recitals entitled
      <u>Aspects</u> <u>du</u> <u>romantisme</u>, and Wanda Landowska performs
      the first of her concert series entitled <u>Fêtes</u> <u>Pasto-
      rales</u>.

S31. A l'Apollo: "La Revue milliardaire"--A l'Opéra-com-
      ique: Nouveau spectacle. No. 647 (5 July, 1930):
      1003-1004.
         De Rougemont's <u>La Revue milliardaire</u> features Damia
      and Jack Forester. L'Opéra-Comique presents Jacques
      Ibert's <u>Angélique</u>, Marcel Delannoy's <u>La Fou de la dame</u>,
      and Manuel Rosenthal's <u>Rayon de soieres</u>.

S32. Trois concerts de Wanda Landowska--Erik Satie. No.
      650 (26 July, 1930): 1125.
         Landowska presents the last two of her <u>Fêtes</u> <u>pas-
      torales</u>. In memorial commentary of the fifth anniver-
      sary of Erik Satie's death Maxime Jacob's article on
      the composer in the July issue of <u>Vigile</u> is recommended.

S33. Un Nouveau livre sur Claude Debussy--Le 10e anniver-
      saire de la mort de Déodat de Severac. No. 655 (30
      August, 1930): 1247.

Maurice Boucher's new book on Debussy is reviewed. The 10th anniversary of Severac's death is acknowledged along with the formation of Amis de Déodat de Severac, but the composer's music is still neglected in performance.

S34.   Les Grands concerts--Au Théâtre Antoine, "La Petite Catherine," par Alfred Savoir, musique de scène de Nicolas Nabokoff. No. 661 (11 October, 1930): 1465-1466.
Concerts Lamoureux, under D.-E. Inghelbrecht, performs Jeu du Furet by Roger-Ducasse. Alfred Savoir's La Petite Catherine has incidental music by Nicolas Nabokov.

S35.   Au Théâtre de l'Atelier: "Les Fils de Don Quichotte," par Pierre Frondaie. No. 662 (18 October, 1930): 1495-1496.
A lengthy review of Frondaie's play.

S36.   Au Théâtre Montparnasse: "Opéra de Quat' sous"--Au Théâtre Pigalle: "Donogoo." No. 664 (1 November, 1930): 1576-1578.
A comparison between the Dreigroschenoper by Bertold Brecht and Kurt Weill and John Gay's Beggar's Opera. Jules Romains' Donogoo is reviewed.

S37.   Au Théâtre de l'Athénée: "Un Ami d'Argentine," de M. Tristan Bernard et Max Maurey. No. 667 (22 November, 1930): 1696-1697.
Lengthy review of Un Ami d'Argentine.

S38.   A l'Atelier: "Musse ou l'Ecole de l'Hypocrisie"--Au Théâtre des Mathurins: "Browning." No. 668 (29 November, 1930: 1729-1731.
Jules Romains' Musse, directed by Charles Dullin and sets and costumes by Barsacq, replaces Fils de Don Quichotte at l'Atelier. Browning by Mario Duliani and Jean Refroigney, after the story of O. de Klemm, opens at the Mathurins.

S39.   Au Théâtre Edouard-VII: "L'Assemblée des femmes"--A l'Apollo: "Matricule 33." No. 669 (6 December, 1930): 1761-1762.
L'Assemblée des femmes by Maurice Donnay is an adaptation of an Aristophanes' play. Bertin supplies scenery and Félix Fourdrain adds incidental music. Matricule 33 by Alex Madis and Robert Boucard opens at the Apollo.

S40.   "La Femme de minuit," "Les Aventures du Roi Pausole," "La Brouille," "Boën." No. 671 (20 December, 1930): 1824-1825.
Two new operettas have opened. Raoul Moretti's La Femme de minuit has a libretto by André Barde; Arthur Honegger's Roi Pausole has a libretto by Albert Willemetz after the novel by Pierre Louÿs and includes scenery by Picasso and Foujita. Charles Vildrac's play La Brouille opened at the Comédie-française, and

Jules Romains' Boën opened at the Odéon.

S41.   Sur trois festivals de musique contemporaine--Au Thé-
       âtre Montparnasse, reprise du "Dibbouk"--382e repre-
       sentation du "Sexe faible." No. 672 (27 December,
       1930): 1852-1853.
          At the Prokofiev festival the Orchestre symphonique
       de Paris performs the Second Symphony, Second piano
       concerto, the Scythian Suite and an overture. Concerts
       Pasdeloup performs Milhaud's Deux hymnes de Sion, Car-
       naval d'Aix, and Saudades do Brazil and Honegger's Le
       Roi David and Judith. Concerts Siohan performs suites
       from Stravinsky's Petrouchka, Pulcinella, and Oiseau
       de Feu and the Piano Concerto. Dibbouk by An-Ski is
       performed by the Compagnie Gaston Baty. While on his
       way to attend the Institut de Beauté at the Théâtre
       de la Potiniere the reviewer stopped off to see the
       382nd performance of Le Sexe faible.

S42.   "Le Jour," de M. Henri Bernstein. No. 674 (10 January,
       1931): 43-44.
          Lengthy review of Bernstein's play.

S43.   Au Théâtre Tristan-Bernard: "Que le monde est petit!"
       --A l'Opéra: "Virginie"--Mort de Jean Börlin. No.
       675 (17 January, 1931): 80-81.
          Tristan Bernard's Que le monde est petit! opens at
       his usual theater. Alfred Bruneau's Virginie opens at
       the Opéra to a libretto by Henri Duvernois. Aveline
       choreographs the dance in the opera. Jean Börlin dies
       in New York but will be buried in Père-Lachaise. Bör-
       lin's contributions to dance and his place in Rolf
       de Maré's Ballets suédois are noted.

S44.   A l'Atelier: "La Quadrature du cercle"--"Fraternité."
       No. 677 (31 January, 1931): 140-141.
          La Quadrature du cercle by Valentin Kataev opens
       in a French translation by E.-M. Hunzbucler. Fernand
       Fleuret and Georges Girard's Fraternité opens.

S45.   A la Comédie-française: "Le Maître de son cœur." No.
       679 (14 February, 1931): 206-207.
          Le Maître de son cœur by Paul Raynal opens at the
       Comédie-française.

S46.   "La Folle du logis," au Théâtre de l'Œuvre--Terraine
       vague," au Théâtre Montparnasse. No. 680 (21 Feb-
       ruary, 1931): 240-241.
          La Folle du logis by Frank Vosper, in a French
       translation by Nozière and Galland is directed by
       Lugné-Poe. Terraine vague by Jean-Victor Pellerin
       and Le Sourd ou l'auberge pleine by Pierre Choudard-
       Desforges are also discussed.

S47.   A l'Opéra et à l'Opéra-Comique: nouveaux spectacles--
       "Idoménée" à la Société d'Etudes Mozartiennes. No.
       681 (28 February, 1931): 266-267.
          Guy Ropartz's ballet, Prélude dominical et Six
       pièces a danser pour chaque jour de la semaine opens

at the Opéra with choreography by Serge Lifar along
with his steps for L'Orchestre en liberté by Sauve-
plane and L'Illustre Fregona by Laparra. Roger-Ducasse's setting of Raymond Escholier's Cantegril opens
at the Opéra-Comique. The performance of Mozart's
Idomeneo at La Société d'Etudes Mozartiennes is conducted by Paul Dacher.

S48.   Au Théâtre Edouard-VII: "Les Trois chambres"--Au Thé-
       âtre Daunou: "La Belle amour!--Au Théâtre de la
       Potinière: "La Tuile d'argent." No. 682 (7 March,
       1931): 298-299.
          Les Trois chambres by Henry-René Lenormand, La
       Bell amour! by Léopold Marchand, and La Tuile d'argent
       by Lucien Descaves and Henri Duvernois are discussed.

S49.   A l'Apollo: "Balthazar"--Au Théâtre Fontaine: "La
       Condottiere"--Au Théâtre Mogador: "La Vie pari-
       sienne." No. 684 (21 March, 1931): 388-389.
          Balthazar by Léopold Marchand and La Condottiere
       by Turpin and Paul Fouriere are dramatic offerings of
       the week. A production of Jacques Offenbach's La Vie
       parisienne opens at the Théâtre Mogador.

S50.   "Pierre ou Jack!" de M. Francis de Croisset, à l'A-
       thénée. No. 685 (28 March, 1931): 418-419.
          Lengthy review of Croisset's play.

S51.   "Palais-Bourbon"--Les Nouveautés en revue--"Narcisse"
       --"Don Pasquale"--Concerts. No. 686 (4 April, 1931):
       470-471.
          Palais-Bourbon by Léon Treich and Paul de Mont
       opens at the Théâtre des Mathurins. Henri Jeanson's
       Revue opens at the Théâtre des Nouveautés. Comment
       l'esprit vient aux garçons by Jacques Dapoigny opens.
       Nini Belucci leads an Italian company and the Orchestre
       symphonique de Paris in a performance of Gaetano Doni-
       zetti's Don Pasquale. Concerts Lamoureux performs
       Milhaud's Cinq chants hébraïques and La Création du
       monde. Orchestre symphonique de Paris presents Conrad
       Beck's Symphony no. 5 and fragments from Alban Berg's
       Wozzeck.

S52.   Au Théâtre des Arts: reprise de "L'Otage," de Paul
       Claudel. No. 687 (11 April, 1931): 504.
          Lengthy review of Claudel's play.

S53.   "La chaîne" au Théâtre Antoine; "Tout va bien" au
       Théâtre Saint-Georges; "Kiki" au Théâtre Daunou.
       No. 689 (25 April, 1931): 580-581.
          La Chaîne by Stève Passeur, Tout va bien by Henri
       Jeanson, and Kiki by André Picard are reviewed.

S54.   Au Théâtre des Arts: "La Charrette de pommes"--Au
       Théâtre de l'Atelier: "Atlas-Hôtel"--Au Théâtre
       Montparnasse: "Le Beau Danube rouge"--Au Théâtre
       Pigalle: "Le Plus beaux yeux du monde." No. 690
       (2 May, 1931): 617-618.
          Reviews of La Charrette de pommes (The Apple Cart)

by George Bernard Shaw, Armand Salacrou's <u>Atlas-Hôtel</u>
(with sets by Vakalo), Bernard Zimmer's <u>Beau Danube</u>
<u>rouge</u> (with sets by Emile Bertin) and <u>Les Plus beaux</u>
<u>yeux</u> <u>du</u> <u>mond</u> by Jean Sarment.

S55. Spectacle du Théâtre Tristan Bernard. No. 691 (9 May,
1931): 644-645.
   <u>La</u> <u>Partie</u> <u>de</u> <u>bridge</u>, <u>La</u> <u>Crise</u> <u>ministèrielle</u>, and
<u>Les</u> <u>Jumeaux</u> <u>de</u> <u>Brighton</u>, by Tristan Bernard, open.

S56. "Comtesse Maritza" at Théâtre des Ambassadeurs--"L'A-
mour à la blague" at Théâtre Fontaine--Concerts.
No. 692 (16 May, 1931): 683.
   <u>Comtesse</u> <u>Maritza</u> by Emmerich Kalman (Libretto by
Max <u>Eddy</u> and <u>Jean</u> Marietti) and <u>L'Amour</u> <u>à</u> <u>la</u> <u>blague</u>
by Pierre Sabatier are reviewed. Concerts conducted
by Felix Weingartner and Furtwängler are mentioned in
passing.

S57. A l'Opéra: "Guercœur" et "Othello"--Théâtres de quar-
tier--Elisabeth Schumann. No. 693 (23 May, 1931):
709-710.
   <u>Guercœur</u> by Albéric Magnard (with major portions
orchestrated by Guy Ropartz) is conducted by Ruhlmann.
Verdi's <u>Othello</u> is conducted by Philippe Gaubert. <u>Le</u>
<u>Coup</u> <u>de</u> <u>Trafalgar</u> by Guy D'Abzac opens at the Théâtre
Moncey, and Elisabeth Schumann sings a recital of Mo-
zart vocal music.

S58. "Bourrachon," au Théâtre Antoine--"Les Tribulations
d'un Chinois en Chine," au Théâtre Sarah-Bernhardt
--Concert privé à l'Ecole normal de musique. No.
694 (30 May, 1931): 738-739.
   <u>Bourrachon</u>, whose author, Laurent Doillet dies
during the run, plays at the Antoine. Sauguet always
associates Diaghilev with the Sarah-Bernhardt. Con-
sequently, he's always sad when a performance doesn't
come up to expectations there. So it is with <u>Les</u> <u>Tri-</u>
<u>bulations</u> <u>d'un</u> <u>Chinois</u> <u>en</u> <u>Chine</u> by Claude Farrère and
Charles Mére, based on the novel by Jules Verne. The
Association amicale de l'Ecole normale de musique presents Schumann's Dichterliebe, the premier of Nicolas
Nabokov's <u>Overture</u>, Julien Krein's <u>Concerto</u> for violoncello and orchestra, and Schubert's <u>Symphony</u> <u>no.</u> <u>5</u>.

S59. L'Opéra-Ballet de Michel Benois at Théâtre Pigalle.
No. 695 (6 June, 1931): 772.
   Michel Benois presents <u>Opéra-Ballet</u> at the Théâtre
Pigalle. It is composed of arranged and choreographed
versions of <u>On</u> <u>ne</u> <u>s'avise</u> <u>jamais</u> <u>de</u> <u>tout</u> by Monsigny
(based on a libretto by Sedaine, and arranged by Léon
Tarle, with sets by Natalie Gontscharova), <u>Giannina</u> <u>et</u>
<u>Bernardone</u> by Cimarosa (directed by Komisarjevsky),
Prokofiev's <u>Classical</u> <u>Symphony</u> (sets and costumes by
Larionov and choreography by Thadée Slavinsky). All
works are conducted by Roger Désormière.

S60. "L'Eau fraîche" à la Comédie des Champs-Elysées--"Le
sang de Danton" à la Comédie-française. No. 696

(13 June, 1931): 804.
Brief comments about L'Eau fraîche by Drieu La
Rochelle, and Le Sang de Danton by Saint-Georges de
Bruhélier. About the latter, in a word, "Helas!"

S61.   A l'Opéra-Comique: "Les Brigands"--In memorian Jean
Huré--Œuvres de Virgil Thomson. No. 698 (27 June,
1931): 886-887.
Offenbach's Les Brigands (Libretto by Meilhac and
Halevy) is reviewed. A short appreciation of the
little known composer, Jean Huré, is accompanied by a
brief list of works. A concert of the works of Virgil
Thomson at the Salle Chopin includes the Sonata for
violin and piano, the String quartet, Air de Phedre,
Stabat Mater, Oraison funèbre, and Cinq inventions.

S62.   A l'Opéra: "Bacchus et Ariane" avec Serge Lifar--Cinq
causeries de M. D.-E. Inghelbrecht. No. 699 (4
July, 1931); 918.
Ballet master Serge Lifar choreographs Albert
Roussel's Bacchus et Ariane, with costumes and sets
by Georgio di Chirico, at L'Académie nationale de musique. D.-E. Inghelbrecht gives five tips on how not
to interpret Carmen, Faust, and Pelléas.

S63.   Un Entretien avec Mme Régina Camier; Le Théâtre Eclair;
ses projets. No. 700 (11 July, 1931): 949-950.
Régina Camier, star of Cocu magnifique by Fernand
Crommelynck, and founder of "Le Théâtre Eclair," out-
lines her plans for the future.

S64.   Quand Mme Cécile Sorel joue "Poliche" au mois de juillet à la Comédie-française. No. 701 (18 July, 1931):
986-987.
Sauguet expresses great admiration for Cécile Sorel's
performance in Henry Bataille's Poliche. A triptych
entitled Légends et réalities takes the boards at
Théâtre Eclair. Parts are Légend de sainte Rosaline
de Villeneuve by A. de Badet, L'Icone by Maurice Rostand, and Les Sonnettes by Paul Ginistry.

S65.   Le Théâtre et la musique. Petit bilan de l'année.
No. 702 (25 July, 1931): 1013-1014.
The recently completed theater season is reviewed
along with that for music. Highlights included were
Igor Markevitch's Concerto grosso, the Symphonie de
psaumes by Igor Stravinsky, and Paul Hindemith's Harp
concerto conducted by Roger Désormière.

S66.   "Le Sot du tremplin," par M. Lugné-Poe. No. 703 (1
August, 1931): 1048.
Review of the memoires of Lugné-Poe.

S67.   L'Opéra-Comique. No. 706 (22 August, 1931): 1145-1146.
An appraisal of the impact of the appointment of
a new director of l'Opéra-Comique, Louis Masson.

S68.   Trois livres sur Igor Strawinsky: celui de M. P. Collaer; celui de M. A. Schaeffner; celui de M. C.-F.

Ramuz. No. 707 (29 August, 1931): 1177-1178.
Reviews of Stravinsky by Paul Collaer; Stravinsky
by André Schaeffner; and Souvenirs sur Igor Strawinsky
by C.-F. Ramuz.

S69. Dialogues. No. 708 (5 September, 1931): 1208-1209.
Sauguet asks questions of himself concerning the
dramatic and the musical theater. For example: How
often do you go to the theater these days, and is it
worth it? What's good and bad about music these days?

S70. Théâtres de province. No. 710 (19 September, 1931):
1273-1274.
While on vacation, Sauguet notices that the cinema
has all but killed live theater in the provinces. In
the past provincial theaters were interested in producing new drama and music, but now they are only interested in the large, popular productions of the past
that are sure to draw large paying crowds.

S71. La Musique et "l'art muet." No. 712 (3 October, 1931):
1304-1341.
Sauguet sees the advent and growth of sound films
as detrimental to live music. Silent films employed
more instrumentalists and musicians to accompany them
and write music for them.

S72. "Fabienne"--"Les Autres"--"La Revue du Canard." No.
713 (10 October, 1931): 1366.
Reviews of Fabienne by Jacques Natanson (which is
very similar to Gian Carlo Menotti's Telephone) which
uses the telephone as a prop in a monologue; Les Autres
by Georges Berr; and La Canard enchaîne by André Dahl
and Maurice Maréchal.

S73. Pile ou face--Papavert--Machiavel--Le Général Boulanger. No. 714 (17 October, 1931): 1403-1404.
Reviews of Pile ou face by Louis Verneuil; Papa-
vert by Chas K. Gordon and Loïe Le Gouriadée; Machia-
vel by Alfred Mortier; and Le Général Boulanger by
Maurice Rostand and Pierre Mortier.

S74. Nuit d'enfer--La Belle hôtesse--La Duchesse de Padoue
--La Vision de Mona--Concerts--Musique nègres à
L'Esposition coloniale. No. 715 (24 October, 1931):
1431-1433.
Reviews of Nuit d'enfer by Guido Stacchini, translated into the French by Max Daireaux; La Belle hôt-
esse by Goldoni in a French version by Benjamin Cré-
mieux; La Vision de Mona (at the Académie national de
musique) with music by Louis Dumas and libretto by
Desveaux-Vérité and Fragerolle; and La Duchesse de
Padoue with music by Maurice Le Boucher and libretto
by Grosfils after the play by Oscar Wilde. The new
season of concerts features Stravinsky's Violin Concerto and Ravel's Concerto for the left hand. On 17
October, L'Institut international des Langues et Civ-
ilizations africaines sponsored a concert of music

and songs from black Africa. The event was moderated
by Dr. Stèphen-Chauvet.

S75.   "La Tragédie d'Alexandre"--Reprise de "La Pomme"--Ren-
trée de Mlle. Mistinguett au Casino de Paris. No.
716 (31 October, 1931): 1469-1470.
        Reviews of Tragédie d'Alexandre by Paul Demasy;
La Pomme by Louis Verneuil; and a revue entitled Paris
qui brille by Varna and Earl Leslie and featured Mistinguett.

S76.   "Un Taciturne"--"Tsar Lenine"--Concerts. No. 718 (14
November, 1931): 1531-1532.
        The plays reviewed are Un Taciturne by Roger Mar-
tin and Tsar Lenine by François Porche. Concerts Poulet performs a Symphony by Nicolas Nabokov. D.-E. Inghelbrecht conducts Concerts Pasdeloup in a performance
of Debussy's La Mer; Roger Désormière conducts a concert of music by Lully and Monteverdi at the Galerie
Mazarine in the Bibliothèque du Conservatoire sponsored
by Elizabeth Sprague Coolidge.

S77.   "Judith"--"La Mauvaise conduit"--"Sous son bonnet"--
"Le Mariage secrète" à l'Opéra-Comique. No. 719 (21
November, 1931): 1562-1563.
        Jean Giraudoux's Judith is performed at Le Théâtre
Pigalle. Louis Jouvet directs, and Moulaert designs
the sets and costumes. The Compagnie des Quinze performs La Mauvaise conduit by Jean Varlot which is based
on Ménechme by Plautus. Sous son bonnet, a revue by
Rip, plays at the Théâtre des Bouffes-Parisienne; and
the Opéra-Comique performs Cimarosa's Il Matrimonio
segreto.

S78.   "L'Homme, la Bête et la Vertu"--Conversation avec M.
Pirandello--"La Banque Nemo"--"Les Cent jours." No.
720 (28 November, 1931): 1596-1597.
        Sauguet interviews Luigi Pirandello whose L'Homme,
la Bête et la Vertu plays at the Théâtre Saint-Georges
in a translation by Max Maurey. Louis Verneuil's La
Banque Nemo and André Mauprey's adaptation of Forzano's
Les Cent jours are also discussed.

S79.   "Bataille de la Marne"--"La Vie en rose"--"Mes femmes."
No. 722 (12 December, 1931): 1657-1658.
        Compagnie des Quinze performs Armand Salacrou's
La Vie en rose (with sets by Lucien Contaud) and André
Obey's Bataille de la Marne. Mes femmes by Pierre
Veber and Alfred Duthil plays at the Palais-Royal.

S80.   "Fanny"--"Village." No. 723 (19 December, 1931):
1688-1689.
        Fanny by Marcel Pagnol plays at the Théâtre de
Paris, and Charles Dullin presents André de Richaud's
Village at the Théâtre de l'Atelier.

S81.   "Asie"--"Le Roi masqué"--Le Concerto pour violon de
Igor Strawinsky. No. 724 (26 December, 1931): 1723
-1724.

H.-R. Lenormand's <u>Asie</u> starts its run. Louis
Jouvet directs Jules Romains' <u>Le Roi masqué</u> with sets
by Moulaert. Samuel Dushkin performs Igor Stravinsky's
<u>Concerto</u> for violin and orchestra with l'Orchestre
symphonique de Paris for the first time in France.

S82.   "Grand Hôtel"--Nouveau spectacle at Théâtre Tristan
        Bernard. No. 725 (2 January, 1932): 13.
        Lucien Besnard's adaptation of Vicki Baum's Grand
Hôtel plays at the Théâtre des Folies-Wagram. Tristan
Bernard mounts two new works at his theater: <u>Deux
histoires anciennes</u> (<u>L'Aimable Dalila</u> and <u>Salomon le
Sage</u>) and <u>On Nuit esclave</u>, written in collaboration
with Jean Schlumberger.

S83.   A l'Opéra: "Maximilien," de Darius Milhaud--Au Théâtre
        de l'Œuvre: "Le Mal de la jeunesse." No. 726 (9
        January, 1932): 42-43.
        Darius Milhaud's <u>Maximilien</u> premiers at the Opéra.
The libretto is by R.-S. Hoffmann (after Franz Werfel)
in a French adaptation by Armand Lunel. Pedro Pruna,
who designed the sets and costumes, worked for Diaghilev. Bruckner's <u>Le Mal de la jeunesse</u> plays at the
Théâtre de l'Œuvre.

S84.   Vingt-quatre heurs de la vie d'une femme--Mon double
        et ma moité--Mademoiselle--Festival Ravel. No. 728
        (23 January, 1932): 112-113.
        <u>Vingt-quatre heures de la vie</u> d'une femme by Ste-
fan Szweig and Sacha Guitry's <u>Mon double et ma moité</u>
(subtitled "Vingt-quatre heures de la vie d'une homme")
for a double bill at Théâtre de la Madeleine. Théâtre
Saint-Georges hosts Jacques Deval's <u>Mademoiselle</u>. The
long-planned Ravel festival takes place in the Salle
Pleyel.

S85.   Le "Concerto pour piano" de Maurice Ravel--Festivals
        Bach and Strawinsky--Un Jeune fille espagnole--Les
        Evénements de Béotie--La Cadets--Jean III. No. 729
        (30 January, 1932): 146-148.
        Maugurite Long performs Ravel's <u>Piano concerto</u> with
Concerts Pasdeloup. Igor Stravinsky conducts l'Or-
chestre symphonique de Paris in his own works. Gustave
Bret conducts an unfortunate performance of Bach's
<u>Magnificat</u>, along with better performances. Maurice
Rostand's <u>Une Jeune fille espagnole</u> plays at Théâtre
Sarah-Bernhardt. <u>Les Evénements de Béotie</u> by Georges
Berr and Louis Verneuil plays at Théâtre de l'Athénée.

S86.   Le Voyageur et l'amour--Amitié--Domino--Giselle--Le
        Spectre de la rose. No. 730 (6 February, 1932):
        175-176.
        Comédie-française premiers Paul Morand's first
work for the stage, <u>Le Voyageur</u>. Raymond Rouleau directs a production of Michel Mourguet's <u>Amité</u>, with
sets by Bertin. Marcel Achard's <u>Domino</u> plays at the
Comédie des Champs-Elysées. At the Opéra Serge Lifar
and Olga Spessitzeva perform in <u>Giselle</u> and <u>La Spectre
de la rose</u>.

S87.   A propos de la reprise d'"Orphée aux Enfers"--Musique
       ancienne et instruments anciens--Quelques concerts.
       No. 732 (20 February, 1932): 245-246.
           Offenbach's Orphée aux Enfers stars the actor Max
       Dearly and contains choreography by Georges Balanchine.
       Roger Désormière directs La Société de Musique d'Autre-
       fois in a program which incorporates early instruments.
       Wanda Landowska and an orchestra conducted by G. Cloez
       present a Bach Festival. L'Orchestre symphonique de
       Paris performs Milhaud's Création du monde and a pre-
       mier of Conrad Beck's Innominata at Concerts Straram.
       Germaine Copperie premiers songs by Nicolas Nabokov,
       Leone Massimo, and Henri Sauguet.

S88.   Concerts de la Société Mozart--Musique américaine à
       l'O.S.P.--Deuxième concert de La Sérénade. No. 734
       (5 March, 1932): 298-299.
           Louis Cahuzac and Elisabeth Schumann, among others,
       perform at the concerts of the Société d'Etudes Mo-
       zartiennes under Félix Raugel. Nicolas Slonimsky con-
       ducts l'Orchestre symphonique de Paris in works by
       Charles Ives, Dane Rudhyar, and Alejandro Caturla.
       La Sérénade performs Erik Satie's Piège de Méduse with
       Madeleine Milhaud, Pierre Colle, and Raoul Leven and
       choreography by Serge Lifar. Francis Poulenc's Trois
       poèmes de Louise Lalaune (Apollinaire), Quatre poèmes
       d'Apollinaire and Chansons gaillards. Fleury plays
       Darius Milhaud's organ Sonata, and Cahuzac and Doyen
       play his clarinet Sonata. Roger Désormière conducts
       Stravinsky's Octuor.

S89.   "Elektra," à l'Opéra--Mme Helba Huara, danseuse péru-
       vienne--Concerts divers. No. 735 (12 March, 1932):
       335-336.
           Jacques Rouché shows his intelligence by producing
       Strauss' Elektra in its French premier at the Opéra.
       Philippe Gaubert conducts the orchestra. The Peruvian
       dancer, Helba Huara, performs in Paris, and Belgian
       Lucienne Fragin performs a lieder recital. Concerts
       Siohan performs Stravinsky's Symphonie de psaumes and
       Germaine Copperie sings Debussy's L'Enfant prodigue
       and other works.

S90.   "La femme nue" à l'Opéra-Comique--Les Concerts--Les
       Ballets russes de Monte-Carlo. No. 743 (7 May, 1932):
       595.
           The Opéra-Comique hosts Henri Fevrier's La Femme
       nue with a libretto by Louis Payen after the play by
       Henry Bataille. Alfred Cortot and Wanda Landowska per-
       form an evening of music by Joseph Haydn. Furtwängler's
       Berlin Philharmonic and Mengelberg's Concertgebouw
       perform in Paris. The old Ballets russe is now at Monte-
       Carlo under the management of Réne Blum and W. de
       Basil with the counsel of Boris Kochno and the choreo-
       graphy of Georges Balanchine and Léonide Massine.
       Items on their programs include Auric's La Concurrence
       and Chabrier's Cotillon with sets and costumes by Chris-
       tian Bérard.

REVIEWS FROM **LA REVUE HEBDOMADAIRE**

S91.   Sur Saint-Saëns. 44, no. 45 (9 November, 1935): 242-
        245.
             If music is only an art of assembling sound in an
        intelligent and learned manner Saint-Saëns is undoub-
        tedly a very great composer. But if, as Stendhal tells
        us, music is our emotion, there are many greater than
        he.

S92.   La Création artistique, don de la nature.   45, no.
        16 (18 April, 1936): 332-339.
             Editor's note: recently, at the Galerie Rive
        Gauche, Sauguet presented several thoughts on artistic
        creation and sensitivity to creative efforts in con-
        junction with the opening of an exhibit at the gallery.
             Sauguet describes his aesthetic philosophy. The
        Conservatoires, the Académies, and the Ecoles des
        Beaux-Arts do not create art producers. The ability
        to do these things and to write poetry, literature,
        and music come as a gift from nature. The process of
        creativity does not differ from medium to medium.

S93.   La Musique--Décadence de l'Opérette française. 46,
        no. 8 (20 February, 1937): 372-374.
             The concert given by the Associations des concerts
        Pasdeloup of French operetta music is not worthy of
        comment. It was so much like the music heard at least
        ten times daily on the radio. There are, unfortunate-
        ly no more Messagers, Offenbachs, Chabriers or Lecoqs
        today.

S94.   Chronique musicale--A l'Opéra-Comique: Le Roi malgré
        lui--Le Testament de la tante Caroline--La Nativité
        du Seigneur, d'Olivier Messiaen. 46, no. 13 (27
        March, 1937): 494-498.
             Bigot conducts Chabrier's Le Roi malgré lui. Rous-
        sel's Testament is directed by Pitoëff, and Roger Dé-
        sormière conducts the orchestra. Messaien performs his
        Nativité du Seigneur on the great organ of Sainte-Trin-
        ité.

S95.   Le Théâtre--Numance--Le Mari singulier--Liberté! 46,
        no. 20 (15 May, 1937): 362-366.
             Jean-Louis Barrault directs Cervantès Numance at
        the Théâtre Antoine. Luc Durtain's Le Mari singulier,
        which was inspired by Cervantès, opens at the Théâtre
        de l'Odéon. Liberté! is a mediocre spectacle or tab-
        leau mounted for the benefit of people attending the
        Exposition.

S96.   Le Théâtre--electre--La Vérité dans le vin--£ 12--
        Boubourouche. 46, no. 23 (5 June, 1937): 116-120.
             Jean Giraudoux's Electre stars Madelaine Ozeray.
        Louis Jouvet directs, and Vittorio Rieti supplies the
        incidental music. Georges Courteline's Boubourouche
        opens at the Comédie-française. It is accompanied on
        the same bill by £ 12 by James Barrie. La Verité dans
        le vin is an 18th century farce by Collé.

112   Henri Sauguet

REVIEWS FROM **LE JOUR ET ECHO DE PARIS**

S97.   De Hændel á Maurice Yvain.   29 March, 1938, 6.
        Under Charles Munch, l'Orchestre de la Société
        Philharmonique performs Handel's Dettingen Te Deum
        and the premiers of Albert Roussel's Bardit des Francs,
        Lourié's First Symphony and Jaubert's Cantate pour le
        temps pascal. Among other items Concerts Colonne per-
        forms Maurice Yvain's Trois chansons ("Brouillard,"
        "Les trois filles," "Porquerolles").

S98.   Le Chanteurs de Lyon et Francis Poulenc.   5 April,
        1938, 6.
        The varied repertoire of the program includes Re-
        naissance part-songs and works by Poulenc: Sept chan-
        sons, the premier of Sécheresses (on a text by Edward
        James) and the Mass in G major.

S99.   Æneas.   6 April, 1938, 6.
        Albert Roussel's Æneas, to a libretto by M. J.
        Weterings, is premiered. Serge Lifar choreographs the
        production.

S100.   Les Ballets de la Jeunesse.   10 April, 1938, 6.
        A review of the dance troup which performed Le
        Dompteur de dompte (W20), although that is not dis-
        cussed. The Basque dance company Eresoïnka also re-
        ceives notice.

S101.   Fin de saison.   13 April, 1938, 6.
        Highlights of the past season included a homage
        to Albert Roussel.

S102.   Le Marchand de Venise.   4 May, 1938, 6.
        Reynaldo Hahn's opera, with a libretto by Zamacoïs
        after Shakespeare, is discussed.

S103.   Le Bon roi Dagobert.   5 May, 1938, 6.
        Marcel Samuel-Rousseau's musical comedy on a lib-
        retto by André Rivoire is conducted by Bigot at the
        Opéra-Comique. Guy Arnoux supplies sets.

S104.   Les Deux concerts de Furtwaengler.   13 May, 1938, 6.
        Traditional fare is offered by Furtwängler.

S105.   Le Concert Fausto Maganini.   15 May, 1938, 6.
        Maganini conducts Concerts Pasdeloup in a perfor-
        mance of Pizzetti's Concerto dell'Estate among other
        more usual items.

S106.   Jeune France.   17 May, 1938, 6.
        Roger Désormière conducts a concert at l'Ecole
        normale which includes Olivier Messiaen's Poèmes pour
        mi, Daniel-Lesur's Pastorale, André Jolivet's Poèmes
        pour l'enfant and Jeux d'enfant, and Yves Baudrier's
        Elenora.

S107.   M. Bruno Walter dirige "Fidelio." 19 May, 1938, 6.
        Performance appraisal of a famous work conducted
        by a well-established conductor.

S108.   Les Marrons du feu. 21 May, 1938, 6.
        Robert Darène presents part of Alfred de Musset's
        Les Marrons du feu in its original version and part
        of it in a musical setting by Gaston Doin.

S109.   Dans la Chapelle de Versailles. 22 May, 1938, 6.
        A review of the first concert of the Festival de
        Versailles.

S110.   En écoutant Bruno Walter. 24 May, 1938, 6.
        The critic registers his reactions to Bruno Wal-
        ter's interpretations.

S111.   Deux concerts á Versailles. 3 June, 1938, 6.
        Société des concerts de Versailles is conducted
        by Gustave Cloez; organist Alexander Ceilier is the
        soloist. Philippe Gaubert conducts a performance
        featuring the singer Germaine Martinelli and the
        harpsichordist Roesgen-Champion.

S112.   La Messe en si de Bach. 4 June, 1938, 6.
        Ernst Lévy conducts Le Chœur philharmonique de
        Paris, l'Orchestre de nouvelle Association symphonique
        and soloists in a performance of Bach's B-minor Mass.
        Vhita, who premiered La Voyante (W201) is one of the
        soloists.

S113.   Salambô. 5 June, 1938, 6.
        François Ruhlmann conducts a performance of Rous-
        sel's work at the Opéra.

S114.   Festival Strawinsky. 11 June, 1938, 6.
        As part of La Sérénade Stravinsky oversees perfor-
        mances of Dumbarton Oaks Concerto, Octet, Suite from
        l'Histoire du soldat, and the Concertino for string
        quartet.

S115.   Concours du Conservatoire, 16 June, 1938, 6.
        Contest for woodwind instruments.

S116.   Concours du Conservatoire. 17 June, 1938, 6.
        Dance, double bass and viola competitions reviewed.

S117.   Concours du Conservatoire, 18 June, 1938, 6.
        Competition for violoncello reviewed.

S118.   Berlioz aux Invalides. 19 June, 1938, 6.
        Charles Munch conducts Hector Berlioz' Requiem at
        Les Invalides.

S119.   Festival Gabriel Fauré. 22 June, 1938, 6.
        Fauré's music performed by La Société des Amis de
        Fauré at the Salle Pleyel.

S120.   Concours du Conservatoire. 24 June, 1938, 6.
         The Violin competition for women is reviewed.

S121.   Concours du Conservatoire. 25 June, 1938, 6.
         Men's competition for violin follows that for women.

S122.   Sur l'école française du piano. 26 June, 1938, 6.
         Five young piano finalists for the Prix du Conser-
         vatoire present a recital at the Salle Erard.

S123.   Concours du Conservatoire. 28 June, 1938, 6.
         Men's competition for the vocal prize is discussed.
         A notice for the premier of **La Chartreuse de Parme** (4)
         appears in the column next to the review.

S124.   Concours du Conservatoire. 29 June, 1938, 6.
         Winners and jury for the women's vocal competition
         are noted.

S125.   Concours du Conservatoire. 30 June, 1938, 6.
         Fifty-three entrants start off the women's com-
         petition in piano.

S126.   Concours du Conservatoire. 1 July, 1938, 6.
         Survivors of the women's piano competition are
         listed along with those in harp. Winners of the men's
         competition, into which only thirteen entered, are
         also listed.

S127.   Heurs et malheurs de la "Saison de Versailles." 2
         July, 1938, 6.
         La Scala Opera's performance of A<u>ï</u>da in Neptune's
         Basin, directed by Bruno Walter, was not very success-
         ful. Performances of early music by La Société des
         concerts de Versailles were better.

S128.   <u>Banquet</u> (nouveau ballet). 5 July, 1938, 6.
         <u>Banquet</u> by J. Larmangeat is performed at the Opéra-
         Comique. Constantin Tcherkas choreographs the work.

S129.   Resurrection d'un musicien français. 6 July, 1938, 6.
         Abbé Delporte conducts La Chapelle française in a
         performance of Antoine de Fevin's <u>Messe</u> <u>Ave</u> <u>Maris</u>.

S130.   Concours du Conservatoire. 7 July, 1938, 6.
         Men compete for a place in the Opéra-Comique.

S131.   Concours du Conservatoire. 8 July, 1938, 6.
         Men's competition for Opéra-Comique ends. Female
         winners are also announced.

S132.   Concours du Conservatoire. 9 July, 1938, 6.
         Particulars for the men's and the women's competi-
         tion for positions at the Opéra are outlined.

S133.   L'Activité de nos orchestres. Ce qu'elle a été et ce
         qu'elle pourrait être. 25 July, 1938, 6.
         Concerts for the coming season mostly continue
         with ordinary repertoire. A few conductors like Munch

with the Société philharmonique will perform works by
composers such as Berg and Schoenberg.

S134.   Des réformes au Conservatoire. Elles s'imposent. On
les attend impatienment. 28 July, 1938, 6.
The impact and anticipated benefits of reforms pro-
posed for the Conservatoire are discussed. The critic
hopes that Maurice Yvain's proposal for a course in
operetta will be adopted. Gaston Poulet started one
in Bordeaux, and it was successful.

S135.   A l'Opéra. Alceste. 8 October, 1938, 6.
Review of Gluck's opera.

S136.   Concerts "Classiques." 15 October, 1938, 6.
Guy Ropartz has two compositions performed on the
same day. One is his Nocturne.

S137.   A l'Opéra. "Dans Tristan et Isolde . . . " 16 October, 1938, 6.
Kirsten Flagstadt stars as Isolde.

S138.   Les Grands concerts. Sous le signe de Bizet. 19 October, 1938, 6.
Concerts for the celebration of Bizet's centennial
expose the listener to something other than Carmen.
The Symphony in C is a little heard, quality work that
deserves more exposure.

S139.   Actualité de Georges Bizet. 25 October, 1938, 6.
Sauguet compares Bizet to Berlioz and Gounod and
finds his music to be more "French" than theirs.

S140.   Deuxième gala Georges Bizet. 27 October, 1938, 6.
Two concerts celebrate Bizet's centennial. Audiences hear performances of Patrie, Variations chroma-
tiques, Carmen, Symphony in C, an unpublished overture,
L'Arlesienne, and Jeux d'enfants.

S141.   Troisième Gala Bizet. 28 October, 1938, 6.
Les Pêcheurs de perles and Djamileh are performed.

S142.   Plaisir à "Carmen." 30 October, 1938, 6.
Carmen is performed during the Bizet centennial.

S143.   De l'inédit chez Pasdeloup. 1 November, 1938, 6.
L'Orchestre de Pasdeloup performs unpublished
French music: Rouen by Georges Sporck, Les Voix du
vieux monde by Albert Doyen, Trois mélodies ("J'ai mis
mon cœur à la fenêtre," "L'Oiseau s'est tu," "Robin
des bois") by Henri Büsser, Quatre kakemonos ("Pandor-
ma," "Geistas," "Temple au crépuscule," "Fête") by
Mariotte.

S144.   Chœurs et orchestres. 3 November, 1938, 6.
Reviews of Colonne, Lamoureux and Pasdeloup concerts. Pasdeloup performs Prélude et Fables de Flo-
rian by P. Vellones.

S145. Le "cas" Wagner. 8 November, 1938, 6.
       Concerts feature too much music by Richard Wagner.
       Even when a concert is not wholly of his music it is
       linked with another (Germanic) composer. Concerts
       Pasdeloup performs Les Douze by Wornoff.

S146. M. Bruno Walter dirige le "Requiem" de Verdi. 15 No-
       vember, 1938, 6.
       Walter conducts the Requiem by Verdi, and the Amer-
       ican conductor, Benjamin Grosbayne, makes his first
       Paris appearance.

S147. Les Santons. Ballet de M. Tomasi. 20 November, 1938,
       6.
       Henri Tomasi's Les Santons (libretto by René Dumes-
       nil) premiers. Sets and costumes are by Hellé, and
       choreography is by Aveline.

S148. La Mémoire de Schubert. 23 November, 1938, 6.
       Société des Concerts, conducted by Charles Munch,
       honors 110th anniversary of Schubert's death. Amer-
       ican conductor Isaïe Dobrowen conducts l'Orchestre
       Pasdeloup. Sauguet finds his gestures too florid.
       Concerts Colonne premiers Jean Clergue's Ballade for
       violin and orchestra.

S149. La Prise de Troie de H. Belioz. 27 November, 1938, 6.
       Philippe Gaubert at the Opéra.

S150. Apparences. 29 November, 1938, 6.
       In Hermann Scherchen's series of six concerts Igor
       Markevitch's Le Nouvel âge is the highlight. Concerts
       Lamoureux premiers Marcel Dupré's Organ Concerto.

S151. Un Grande semaine musicale. 6 December, 1938, 6.
       Charles Munch conducts Société des Concerts du Con-
       servatoire in the premier of Karol Szymanowsky's Sta-
       bat Mater. Gertrude Herliczka leads l'Orchestre de
       Société de Paris in a premier of Ballade et Passacaille
       by Kurt Atterberg. La Sérénade presents songs by Nico-
       las Nabokov, Poulenc's Trois lieder de Louise de Vil-
       morin (sung by Princesse de Polignac), the piano sou-
       venirs of the 1937 Exposition by foreign composers,
       Georges Auric's Trio for wind instruments, and Darius
       Milhaud's Suite après Corette.

S152. Les Grands concerts. Furtwaengler et Mengelberg. 7
       December, 1938, 6.
       Among other items, Furtwängler conducts Hans Pfitz-
       ner's Katchen von Heilbronn. Mengelberg conducts Ber-
       nard Wagenaar's concert overture Cyrano de Bergerac in
       a varied program.

S153. Les grand concerts. Mozart, Bach et quelques autres.
       26 December, 1938, 6.
       The Weihnachts Oratorium by Bach is performed by
       the Berlin Philharmonic Chorus. Performances of La
       Société d'Etudes Mozartiennes are cited. Brief men-
       tion also made of Schmitt's Stèle pour le tombeau de
       Dukas.

REVIEWS FROM **LA BATAILLE**

S154.   Le Souvenir de Maurice Ravel. 4, no. 6 (4 January,
        1945): 6.
            In the closing days of December, 1944, Manuel Ro-
        senthal and Charles Munch lead their orchestras in
        concerts of Ravel's music as a commemoration of the
        seventh anniversary of his death. Munch also conducts
        a concert of J. S. Bach's music which includes Maurice
        Duruflé's orchestration of three chorales and Ottorino
        Respighi's Passacaille. Under the title "Arlequin,"
        Xavier de Courville and Jacqueline Pianavia perform
        early French songs.

S155.   De Beethoven à Romain Rolland. 4, no. 7 (11 January,
        1945): 6.
            Beethoven remains the favored name on concert pro-
        grams, and conductors continue to crank out cycles of
        his symphonies. Romain Rolland continues as a proli-
        fic author. Histoire de l'opéra en Europe avant Lul-
        li, Voyage musical au pays du passé contribute to the
        series "Musiciens d'Aujourd'hui," and biographies of
        Scarlatti and Handel in the series "Musiciens d'Autre-
        fois," are among his credits.

S156.   A l'Opéra-Comique. 4, no. 8 (18 January, 1945): 4.
            Roger Désormière conducts performances of Darius
        Milhaud's Le Pauvre Matelot (libretto by Jean Cocteau),
        Jacques Ibert's Angélique (orginally premiered by Com-
        pagnie Beriza) and Emmanuel Chabrier's L'Education man-
        quée at the Opéra-Comique. Mélodies by Henri Dutilleux
        is performed by Gérard Souzay at the Société des con-
        certs.

S157.   Deux concerts. 4, no. 9 (25 January,1945): 4.
            André Girard conducts a chamber orchestra concert
        in a varied program. Fernand Oubradous conducts a
        chamber and symphonic ensemble in performances that
        include Albert Roussel's Concerto, op. 34, and songs
        by Capdevielle, Suz, Demarquez, and Sauguet.

S158.   Musique soviétique. 4, no. 10 (1 February, 1945): 4.
            The rage for Soviet music gives rise to a badly
        organized concert which features Prokofiev's Concerto
        for piano, trumpet and strings, a string quartet by
        Kartzew, and Vassilenko's Chansons des peuples de l'U.
        R.S.S.

S159.   Musique de chambre . . . froide. 4, no. 11 (8 Febru-
        ary, 1945): 4.
            Concerts warm up the cold days of February. The
        Société privée de musique de chambre performs Lully's
        Alceste and Purcell's Diocletian. Roger Désormière
        conducts. The Société national celebrates its 600th
        concert with music by d'Indy, Messiaen, Delvincourt,
        and Ibert.

S160.   Falla et Strawinsky. 4, no. 12 (15 February, 1945): 4.
            The two greatest composers of the day have concerts

dedicated to their music. Manuel Rosenthal conducts
Les Noces (Geneviève Joy, Monique Haas, Poulenc and
Pierre Sancan on the four pianos), the Capriccio and
fragments from Pulcinella. Henri Tomasi conducts de
Falla's El Retablo de maese Pedro, Chansons espagnoles, Noches en los jardines de España, and El amor
brujo.

S161. De la flûte au tambour. 4, no. 13 (22 February, 1945):
4.
The Théâtre de la Gaité Lyrique presents Jacques
Offenbach's La Fille du Tambour-Major.

S162. Quelques interprètes. 4, no. 14 (1 March, 1945): 4.
M. Peyron performs Joseph Canteloube's Chants de
France. Jacques Dupont's Cenci-symphonie is premiered
at Concerts Lamoureux on the same day that he accom-
panies Yvonne Astruc in a recital of violin sonatas.
Other recitals are also cited.

S163. Musiques de la semaine. 4, no. 15 (8 March, 1945): 4.
Adrian Boult conducts La Société des Concerts in
a performance of Alan Rawsthorne's Piano Concerto. Roger Désormière conducts La Société privée de musique
de chambre in Stravinsky's Danses Concertantes, Darius
Milhaud's Quatre esquisses, Luigi Dallapiccola's Tre
Lauda, and Serge Nigg's Concertino for piano. Roland
Petit's dance recital at the Théâtre des Champs-Elysées
includes Rumba by Claude Pascal, Trois fables de La
Fontaine by Jean Huteau, Liszt's Mephisto valse (with
Jean Cocteau's costumes), and Henri Sauguet's Les Forains, for which Christian Bérard designed costumes
and set.

S164. Semaine anglaise. 4, no. 16 (15 March, 1945): 4.
Paris hosts the Sadler's Wells Ballet which performs, among other more usual items, Arthur Bliss'
Miracle in the gorbals, choreographed by Robert Help-
mann. Benjamin Britten also visits to oversee performances of his Les Illuminations, Serenade, and Sin-
phonia da requiem. Other concerts during the week
include the first of a new group, La Musique de chambre
de Paris, and a homage to Max Jacob with performances
of songs by Cliquet-Pleyel, Joliver, Poulenc, Auric,
and Sauguet, for which Jacob wrote text.

S165. Troisième festival Strawinsky. 4, no. 17 (22 March,
1945): 4.
Since the Liberation three programs dedicated exclusively to the music of Igor Stravinsky have been
heard in Paris. The current one features Jeu de
cartes, Le Faune et la Bergère, Quatre impressions
norvegiennes, and the Symphonie de psaumes.

S166. Visites et retours. 4, no. 18 (29 March, 1945): 4.
Reflections and admiration for the Sadler's Wells
Ballet's visit are registered. Concert life in Paris
is healthy and features, among other things, Roussel's
Third Piano Concerto. Some performers who were in

exile during the war are now returning to France.   The
climate is more favorable these days.

S167.   De l'avenir au présent.   4, no. 19 (5 April, 1945): 4.
        The Director of the Conservatoire, Delvincourt,
and his assistant, Obey, have been charged with refor-
ming concert life in France.   One of the tasks necessary to their goal is to teach the children of France
to sing.   Paul Armer and M.-R. Clouzot's published
harmonizations of French songs should help in culti-
vating more sophisticated taste.   Francis Poulenc's
Cantate was premiered by the B.B.C. during the war,
and it is reviewed here.

S168.   Sur Olivier Messiaen.   4, no. 20 (12 April, 1945): 4.
        The recent performance at Sainte-Trinité of Mes-
siaen's La Nativité du Seigneur prompts a discussion
of his music, including Poèmes pour dire, Quatuor pour
la fin des temps, Visions de l'Amen, and Vingt regards
sur l'Enfant Jésus.

S169.   "L'Affaire" Stravinsky.   4, no. 21 (19 April, 1945): 4.
        While it would be nice to hear more new French mu-
sic, one would be foolish to pass up an opportunity to
hear some recent music by Stravinsky at least.

S170.   Musique française contemporaine.   4, no. 22 (26 April,
        1945): 4.
        The Orchestre national included performances of
Georges Auric's Cinq chansons françaises and Quatre
chansons de la France malheureuse in its concert.
Jean de Rohozinski, a young conductor, directs music
by young French composers: Jacques Besse's Piano
Concerto, Michel Ciry's Symphonie pour cordes, and
Carmen by Pierre Barbaud.   Concerts de La Pléiade in-
cludes Poulenc's Un Soir de neige, and Messiaen's
Trois petites liturgies.

S171.   Martinu, Barraud, Poulenc.   4, no. 23 (3 May, 1945):
        4.
        Manuel Rosenthal's crusade for contemporary music
results in performances of Bohuslav Martinu's Concerto
for string quartet and orchestra and Le Diable à la
Kermesse by Henri Barraud.   Suzanne Balguerie and
Pierre Bernac perform songs by Francis Poulenc.

S172.   La 7e symphonie de Chostakovitch.   4, no. 24 (10 May,
        1945): 6.
        Dmitri Shostakovich's Seventh Symphony (The "Le-
ningrad") receives its Paris premier under the baton
of Charles Munch.   Léon Zighera conducts a concert
which features Le Grand Barrage by Arthur Honegger and
Martinu's Concerto for piano.

S173.   Le Centennaire de Gabriel Fauré.   4, no. 25 (17 May,
        1945): 4.
        A centennial concert series features a large num-
ber of works by Gabriel Fauré.

S174.   Avec un peu d'Espagne autour . . . . 4, no. 26 (24
        May, 1945): 4.
            Ernest Ansermet conducts Willy Burkhard's Hymne,
        Aubade by A.-F. Marescotti, Musique de Mai by Jean
        Binet, Pierre Wissmer's Mouvements pour cordes, and
        Arthur Honegger's Symphony no. 2. The Fauré centen-
        nial celebration concerts continue. Anne Laloé sings
        works by Robert Caby, and Nino de Cadez performs fla-
        menco dances.

S175.   Autour d'une querelle. 4, no. 27 (31 May, 1945): 4.
            A controversy has arisen concerning Manuel Rosen-
        thal's Stravinsky concerts. Joseph Canteloube will
        lead a conference concerning the folk songs of France
        on 8 June.

S176.   Semaines musicales françaises. 4, no. 28 (7 June,
            1945): 4.
            The Comité national de propagande promotes a
        series of concerts of French music. Among those works
        heard is Messiaen's La Nativité du Seigneur. A festi-
        val of Paul Hindemith's works includes Nobilissima
        visione, the violoncello Concerto and the Symphony in
        mi bémol. Other concerts of contemporary music in the
        near future will feature Martinu, Beck, Harsányi,
        Tcherepnine, and Mihalovici.

S177.   De Versailles au Kremlin. 4, no. 29 (14 June, 1945):
            7.
            The concert at Versailles features music appropri-
        ate to the court of Louis XIV. Serge Prokofiev's Hom-
        mage à Staline is premiered along with Manuel Rosen-
        thal's Musique de table. Ernest Ansermet conducts
        performances of Le Sacre du printemps and La Mer.

S178.   Compositeurs et virtuoses. 4, no. 30 (21 June, 1945):
            4.
            The Opéra-Comique performs Jacques Ibert's Roi
        d'Yvetot. Daniel-Lesur and Olivier Messiaen present
        works representative of "Jeune France."

S179.   Soirées de ballets. 4, no. 31 (28 June, 1945): 4.
            Roland Petit and Boris Kochno present a dance re-
        cital at the Théâtre Sarah-Bernhardt which features
        Le Poète by Benjamin Godard (orchestrated by Charles
        Kœchlin and has sets by Lucien Coutaud), Le Rendez-
        vous by Tibor Kosma on a scenario by Jacques Prevert,
        Quadrille by Georges Auric (orchestrated by Tibor Har-
        sányi, sets by Valentine Hugo), and **Les Forains** (W25)
        André Girard fills in at the last moment for André
        Cluytens.

S180.   Vive Satie! 4, no. 32 (5 July, 1945): 4.
            The critic contributes some memoirs and a memorial
        tribute to Erik Satie who died twenty years earlier.

S181.   Adieu, Œdipe . . . . 4, no. 33 (12 July, 1945): 4.
            The seventh and last concert of the Stravinsky
        Festival features Œdipus Rex.

S182. A l'Opéra-Comique. Malvina. 4, no. 23 (19 July,
1945): 4.
The Opéra-Comique presents Reynaldo Hahn's Malvina
(libretto by Duvernois and Donnay). Guy Armoux designs
sets and costumes.

S183. Ballets à l'Opéra. 4, no. 35 (26 July, 1945): 4.
Serge Lifar supplants Aveline as ballet master of
the Opéra. Arthur Honegger's Appel de la montagne (on
a scenario by Favre Le Bret) is choreographed by Serge
Peretti. Sets and costumes are created by Roger Wild,
and the orchestra is conducted by Roger Désormière.
Yvette Chauviré's dancing adds the necessary ingrediet
to make it work.

S184. Un Moine musicien: Dom Clement Jacob. 4, no. 36 (2
August, 1945): 4.
The critic pays tribute to Maxime Jacob, a fellow
member of L'Ecole d'Arceuil.

S185. Bilan d'une saison. 4, no. 37 (9 August, 1945): 4.
A review of the past season which included Sau-
guet's La Gageure imprévue (W5), Paul Le Flem's Le
Rossignol de Saint-Malo, and Reynaldo Hahn's Malvina
at the Opéra. Other high points included Stravinsky's
Danses concertantes and Messiaen's Liturgies.

S186. Sur deux musiciens français. 4, no. 39 (23 August,
1945): 4.
Sauguet reviews Gabriel Fauré by Gabriel Fauré,
and Jehan Alain by Bernard Gavoty.

S187. Pitie pour elle! . . . 4, no. 40 (30 August, 1945):
4.
Radio broadcasts display a cavalier attitude toward serious music.

S188. La Jeunesse et la musique. 4, no. 41 (6 September,
1945); 4.
The conservative, German oriented, music heard
during the Occupation may have seriously dulled the
ears of the young generation and made it less recep-
tive to new (French) music.

S189. Festival de musique international de Lucerne. 4,
no. 42 (13 September, 1945); 4.
The Lucerne International Festival of Music starts
up again in 1945. It was founded in 1938, but shut
down again in 1939 because of the war.

S190. Prochaine saison lyrique. 4, no. 43 (20 September,
1945): 4.
Maurice Lehman announces the next season at the
Opéra. It will include Ariane et Barbe-bleu by Paul
Dukas, Antar by Gabriel Dupont, Padmâvati by Albert
Roussel, and Verdi's Masked ball. At the Opéra-Comique
the new season will feature Verdi's Falstaff, Lucifer
by Claude Delvincourt, Diane de Poitiers by Jacques
Ibert, Médée by Darius Milhaud, Marchand de Venise by

André Bloch, L'Heure Espagnole by Maurice Ravel, and Fragonard by Gabriel Pierné.

S191. Jeune musique américaine. 4, no. 33 (27 September, 1945): 4.
Europeans have become familiar with music by young American composers through the Voice of America broadcasts. Representative composers cited include Virgil Thomson (Three Saints in Four Acts), Roy Harris (Ode to Friendship), and William Schuman (American Festival Overture). Curiosity is expressed about John Cage and Aaron Copland.

S192. Prix de Rome. 4, no. 45 (4 October, 1945): 6.
L'Académie des Beaux-Arts awards two Prix de Romes this year. Marcel Bitsch and Claude Pascal are winners.

S193. Premiers concerts. 4, no. 46 (11 October, 1945): 6.
Marcel Mihalovici's Symphonies pour le temps présent, and Virgil Thomson's suite from the ballet, Filling Station are premiered on the Orchestre national concert.

S194. Quelques cris. . . . 4, no. 47 (18 October, 1945): 6.
Indignation: Lack of French music on programs presented in Paris.
Admiration: Franz André conducts l'Orchestre national in Oscar Espla's Sonate du Sud.
Pleasure: Boris Kochno's and Roland Petit's Les Ballets des Champs-Elysées performs Tchaikovsky's La Belle au bois dormant (Kœchlin's orchestrations and sets by Alexandre Benois and Petipa's choreography). Stravinsky's Jeu de cartes is premiered with Janine Charrat in the leading female role, and Sauguet's Les Forains (W25), with sets and costumes by Bérard, fills out the bill. André Girard conducts the orchestra for the evening.

S195. Mises au point d'orgue. 4, no. 48 (25 October, 1945): 6.
The critic complains to performers that French music, especially modern compositions, seems to be excluded from programs. Several soloists inform him that they prefer not to absorb the performance rights for such works, which can run from 8% to 42% for music by living French composers who are members of La Société des Auteurs, Compositeurs et Editeurs de Musique, or other performing rights' organizations.

S196. Concerts surprise. 4, no. 49 (1 November, 1945): 6.
A Black American conductor leads Concerts Pasdeloup in a suite from a ballet by Walter Piston, a symphony by Roy Harris, and a symphony (No. 2) by Virgil Thomson. La Société des concerts du Conservatoire, under Jean Martinon, performs Stravinsky's Jeu de cartes, Hindemith's Symphonie en mi bémol, and Georges Dandelot's Concerto romantique.

S197.   Les Ballets des Champs-Elysées. 4, no. 50 (8 Novem-
        ber, 1945): 6.
            Tcherepnine's Déjeuner sur l'herbe (with sets by
        Marie Laurencin) is performed. Roland Petit creates
        the choreography. Jean Babilée's performance in Le
        Spectre de la rose reminds Sauguet of the greatness
        of Diaghilev's Ballets russes.

S198.   Le Festin de la sagesse. 4, no. 51 (15 November,
        1945): 6.
            Manuel Rosenthal conducts l'Orchestre national in
        the public premier of Darius Milhaud's Le Festin de
        la sagesse (based on a scenario by Paul Claudel). Ida
        Rubinstein commissioned the work in 1935. Thomas Beec-
        ham conducts the Société des concerts du Conservatoire
        in a program which features the symphonic fragments
        from Benjamin Britten's Peter Grimes.

S199.   Semaine grasse. 4, no. 52 (22 November, 1945): 6.
            Highpoints of a week filled with music include
        Charles Munch leading the London Philharmonic Orches-
        tra in William Walton's Symphony, Manuel Rosenthal and
        Yvonne Loriod and the Orchestre national in a tribute
        to the memory of Béla Bartók, Chorale d'Yvonne Gouverné
        in a performance of André Caplet's Le Miroir de Jésus,
        Olivier Messiaen's L'Ascension, and Henri Barraud's
        Piano Concerto.

S200.   Semaine maigre. 4, no. 53 (29 November, 1945): 6.
            A thin week for music includes Benjamin Britten's
        Les Illuminations and his Suite for violin and piano.

S201.   Ariane et Barbe-bleue. 4, no. 54 (6 December, 1945):
        6.
            Paul Dukas' Ariane et Barbe-bleue is performed at
        the Opéra.

S202.   Deux concerts de musique anglaise. 4, no. 54 (13 De-
        cember, 1945): 7.
            The British Council organizes two concerts in
        Paris honoring the 250th anniversary of Henry Purcell's
        death. Dido and Æneas is featured at one of them.

S203.   Darius Milhaud. 4, no. 56 (20 December, 1945): 4.
            A Milhaud festival showcases several new works:
        Concerto for two pianos and orchestra, String Quartet
        No. 12, Sonata for viola and piano, La Cheminée du roi
        René, Poèmes juifs, and Pan et la Syrinx.

S204.   L'Accidentel et l'éternel. 4, no. 57 (27 December,
        1945): 6.
            Manuel Rosenthal conducts l'Orchestre national in
        a performance of Alban Berg's Violin Concerto and Stra-
        vinsky's Scènes de ballet.

WRITINGS AND SPEECHES FROM OTHER PUBLICATIONS AND EVENTS

S205.   A. M. Cassandre. In Weg zum Licht. Munich: Bayer-
        isches Staatstheater, 1952.

Program notes about a scenic designer in a play-
bill for a production for which he designed the sets.

S206.   Après la mort de Stravinsky. **Courrier musical de
France** no. 34 (1971): 68-69.
Tribute to a friend and colleague from the Paris
days of the 1920s.

S207.   Armade de Polignac. **Le Guide du concert** 44, no. 361
(28 September, 1962): 38.
Tribute to a patron and friend.

S208.   Attendez la mort des ballets et faites moi ministre.
Combat, 10 January, 1950, 2.
Sauguet's response to a question: What would you
do to promote a renewal in the lyric theater? ("Pour
une renaissance du théâtre lyrique") His solutions
are many, but he prefers to keep them secret until he
is made minister of education or of the lyric theater.

S209.   Avant-propos. In Poulenc, Francis. **Journal de mes
mélodies.** Paris: Les Société des amis de Francis
Poulenc, 1964.
Tribute to and introduction to a book by his late
friend and colleague.

S210.   Bébé Bérard. **Arts, lettres, spectacles** no. 763 (24
February-1 March, 1950): 1.
Memorial tribute to his friend and collaborator
in many stage works.

S211.   Christian Bérard. **Labyrinth**, 1950. Quoted in Kochno,
Boris: **Bérard.** Paris: Hachette, 1987
Tribute to the artist.

S212.   Le 50ème anniversaire de Pelléas. **Les Lettres françaises**, 4 September, 1952, 6.
A series of tributes by composers, authors, and
others involved in the lyric stage on the 50th anniversary of Debussy's <u>Pelléas</u> <u>et</u> <u>Mélisande</u>.

S213.   Claude Debussy: fransk tonsattre. **Musikrefy** 17, no.
6-7 (1962): 175-178.
Swedish translation of the following article.

S214.   Claude Debussy, Musicien français. **La Revue musicale**
no. 258 (1962): 41-56.
A tribute to one of the greatest influences on
Sauguet in his decision to become a composer.

S215.   Comme je me vois aujourd'hui. **La Revue musicale** no.
361-363 (1983): 251.
Self-analysis of his place in music as seen from
today's point of view.

S216.   Des divers sens de l'recherche. **La Revue musicale**
no. 317 (1978): 9-13.
An essay on the process of creativity.

S217.   **Difficultè d'être de la musique française.** Paris:
        Institut, 1985.
        Transcript of a speech delivered to the Institut
        on 4 December, 1985.

S218.   **1924** (i.e., Dix-neuf cent vingt-quatre) **Paris capitale
        des createurs.** (sound recording) Paris: Desalle,
        26 FT 64.
        An interview with Sauguet about the creative atmo-
        sphere in Paris during the year 1924. recorded at the
        composer's home in Coutras.

S219.   Un Enquête sur Schoenberg et sur ses théories. **Le
        Guide du concert** 32, no. 4 (16 November, 1951): 57.
        Sauguet's response to a series of interviews con-
        cerning Arnold Schoenberg and the twelve-tone school.

S220.   Erik Satie. **Courrier musical de france** no. 52 (1975):
        129.
        Brief biographical sketch about the composer's spi-
        ritual master.

S221.   Erik Satie. Eight page insert in **Erik Satie par Cic-
        colini.** Aldo Ciccolini, pianist. Paris: Columbia
        FCS 561.
        Biographical commentary about Satie with critical
        commentary about his piano music.

S222.   Extraits de ma mémoire. In **Au temps du "Bœuf sur le
        toit" 1918-1929.** Paris: Artcurial, 1981.
        A few reminiscences about Paris in the 1920s.

S223.   La Festival à Aix-en-Provence et la renaissance de
        l'Opéra in France. **Corps écrit** 20 (1986): 21-36.
        Sauguet's comments about his contributions to the
        Festival and his experiences in its support of new
        operas and new performances of opera in general. Others
        who contributed their observations are: Georges Auric,
        Yves Florenne, Roland-Manuel, and Francis Poulenc.

S224.   French song--Some notes. **Parnassus: Poetry in re-
        view** 10, no. 2 (1982): 251-255.
        Comments, in English translation, about the special
        qualities which make French song writing unique.

S225.   Georges Migot. **Courrier musical de france** no. 53
        (1976): 3.
        Brief biography of the composer Migot.

S226.   Groupe des Six. **Encyclopédie de la musique.** Paris:
        Fasquelle, 1961.
        Collective description of a group of French com-
        posers.

S227.   Hommage à Alfred Loewenguth. **La Revue musicale** no.
        347 (1981): 13-17.
        Tribute to Loewenguth.

S228.   Hommage à Darius Milhaud. **Courrier musical de France**
no. 38 (1972): 66-67.
Tribute to Sauguet's friend and colleague.

S229.   Hommage à Roger Désormière. **Les Lettres françaises**
no. 1,001 (31 October, 1963): 10.
Tribute to a fellow member of L'Ecole d'Arcueil.

S230.   Hommages et témoignages. **La Revue musicale** no. 340-
341 (1981): 10-21.
Sauguet's contribution to a series of memoirs and
tributes to the influential Charles Kœchlin.

S231.   Igor Markevitch. Der Weihergarten. In **Melos** 10, no.
3 (March, 1931): 17-18.
An early biographical sketch of the composer/con-
ductor who had been sponsored by Serge Diaghilev.

S232.   Introduction. **Catalogue des œuvres de Charles Kœchlin.** Paris: Eschig, 1975.
Brief tribute to Sauguet's only formal composition
teacher.

S233.   Maurice Ohana. **La Revue musicale** no. 391 (1986): 5.
Biographical sketch of the composer Ohana.

S234.   Max Jacob et la musique. **La Revue musicale** no. 210
(January, 1952): 151-159.
Commentary about Jacob's support of musical com-
position, followed by the libretto of **Un Amour du
Titien** (W2).

S235.   Un Musicien français en U.R.S.S. **Les Lettres françaises** no. 1,019 (11 March, 1964): 8.
Sauguet writes of his experiences and impressions
after a trip to Moscow in 1964.

S236.   Musique. **Dictionnaire du snobisme.** Paris: Plon,
1958.
Sauguet's contribution to a satirical dictionary
edited by Jullian Philippe. He writes under the nom
de plume Princesse Alexandra Poutoff, née Fleau de
Dieu.

S237.   Musique d'entre deux guerres. **Nouvelle revue fran-
caise** no. 324 (February, 1941): 370.
Brief account of musical life in Paris in the
1920s and 30s.

S238.   **La Musique, ma vie.** Paris: Librairie Segier, 1990.
Posthumus publication of Sauguet's memoirs which
he worked on for over half a century. His profound
sense of history makes this an important document to
study in connection with the history of creative life
in Paris between 1920 and 1950.

S239.   **Notice sur la vie et les travaux de Darius Milhaud.**
Paris: Institut de France, 1976.
Sauguet's tribute to Milhaud, whose chair he filled

at the Académie des Beaux-Arts after Milhaud died. The speech was delivered as part of his initiation.

S240. L'Œuvre lyrique de Francis Poulenc. **Avant scène opera operette musique** no. 52 (1983): 4-5.
The brief article about Poulenc and his songs is accompanied by a photograph of Sauguet with Poulenc and Piccaso.

S241. Ou va la musique française? **Le Guide du concert** 38, no. 200 (13 June, 1958): 1401.
Commentary about the current trends and direction of French music in the late 1950s.

S242. Petite histoire d'un concerto. **Musica** no. 122 (May, 1964): 32-33.
Narrative about the genesis of the **Mélodie concertante** (W80).

S243. Préface. In Henry, Hélène, and Jean Claude Roda. **Max Jacob à la bibliothèque municipale d'Orleans.** Orleans: Municipale, 1986.
Facsimile of Sauguet's handwritten tribute to his friend and collaborator from the 1920s.

S244. Quand j'écrivais un opérette avec Max Jacob. **Cahiers Max Jacob** 3 (March, 1953)
Brief account of the collaboration with Jacob, followed by the text for **Un Amour du Titien** (W2).

S245. Quelques extraits de Souvenirs. **La Revue musicale** no. 361-363 (1983): 225-249.
Unpublished memoirs concerning Erik Satie and musical life in Paris,1922-1925.

S246. Réflexions sur le musicien et le théâtre. In **Dictionnaire des hommes du théâtre.** Paris: Olivier Perrin, 1967.
Comments about what a composer can contribute to dramatic productions.

S247. Satie. **Encyclopédie de la musique.** Paris: Fasquelle, 1961.
Brief biographical sketch of Satie.

S248. **Séance solennelle du 18 décembre 1984 en l'honneur de Darius Milhaud.** Aix-en-Provence: Académie des sciences, agriculture, arts, et lettres, 1984.
Commemorative talk delivered by Sauguet upon the 10th anniversary of the death of Milhaud.

S249. **La Situation du théâtre lyrique en France.** Paris: Institut, 1971.
Transcript of a speech delivered at the Académie des Beaux-Arts.

S250. Le Snobisme de Bach. **La Revue musicale** no. 381 (1985): 11-14.
Concerning the popular infatuation with Bach.

S251.   Souvenirs d'en France. **Le Monde de la musique** no.
125 (September, 1989): 40-42.
Excerpts from the projected **La Musique, ma vie**
(See: S238) concerning Erik Satie, Darius Milhaud,
Charles Kœchlin, and the genesis of **Les Forains** (W25).
Printed here as part of Sauguet's obituary.

S252.   Souvenirs et réflexions autour d'Erik Satie. **La Revue
musicale** no. 386 (1986): 106-110.
Memoirs and a tribute to Satie.

S253.   Témoignages. **Toute la danse** no. 20-21 (May-June, 1954).
The two issues are dedicated as a "Hommage à
Diaghilev." Sauguet adds his tribute in the May issue.

Discography

The following compilation includes recordings of music by
Henri Sauguet, many of which are now available only in sound
archives. Some of them were never generally available since
they were made for private distribution. Recordings appear
in alphanumeric order by record label. Whenever possible
later releases of a specific recorded performance, even when
issued by another company, are noted under the label of original release. "See" references refer to citations in the
"Works and Performances" and "Writings about Henri Sauguet
and his Work" sections.

D1.   Adès COF 7084/87.   1980.

        Contents: **Trio.**
        Members of the Quintette à vent de Paris.
        Title on album: <u>Du duo au quintette à vent.</u>
        Includes works by Paul Taffanel, Gabriel Pierné,
           Vincent d'Indy, Guy Ropartz, Albert Roussel, Flo-
           rent Schmitt, Francis Poulenc, André Jolivet,
           Louis Durey, Georges Auric, Darius Milhaud, and
           Jean Françaix.
        <u>See</u>: W90.

D2.   Adès TS LA503. 196?

        Contents: "Quand j'étais petit" from **La Nuit des
           rois.**
        Performer unknown
        Album title and contents unknown
        Series title: <u>L'avant-scène.</u>
        <u>See</u>: W397.

D3.   AFA 20863.   Date of issue unknown.

        Contents: **Choral varié.**
        Alain Abott,   accordion.
        <u>See</u>: W176.

D4.   Angel 36405. 1967

> Contents: "Berceuse créole" from **La Plumet du Co-
> lonel.**
> Régine Crespin, soprano; John Wustman, piano.
> Title on album: A Régine Crespin song recital.
> Includes works by Robert Schumann, Gabriel Fauré,
> Joseph Canteloube, and Albert Roussel.
> Reissued on Pathé-Marconi as 290446, 1985.
> See: W1, B410.

D5.   Anthologie sonore. Florilège HP 1203.   194?

> Contents: **La Cigale et la fourmi.**
> Unnamed orchestra; Roger Désormière, conductor.
> See: W22.

D6.   Arion ARN 38272. 1974.

> Contents: **ballade** for violoncello and piano.
> Pierre Penassou, violoncello: Jacqueline Robin,
> piano.
> With works for violoncello and piano by Darius Mil-
> haud and Jean Wiener.
> See: W110.

D7.   Arion ARN 38720. 1983.

> Contents: **La Voyante.**
> Isabel Garcisanz, soprano; Ensemble Ars Nova; Alex-
> andre Siranossian, conductor.
> With: Trois opéras-minute by Darius Milhaud.
> See: W209.

D8.   Arion ARN 68071. 1989.

> Contents: **Garden's concerto** (arranged for oboe);
> **Sonate d'église; L'Oiseau a vu tout cela.**
> Jacques Vandeville, oboe (in the Concerto); Jean-
> Patrice Brosse, organ (in the Sonate); Michel
> Piguemal, baritone (in L'Oiseau); Ensemble in-
> strumental Jean-Walter Audoli; Jean-Walter Audoli,
> conductor.
> See: W81, W82, W209, respectively, B673.

D9.   Azergues Z0278. Date of issue unknown.

> Contents: **Six pièces facile.**
> Michel Roger, guitar, Michel Camus, flute.
> Album title and accompaning works unknown.
> See: W115.

D10.   BASF 215 0012-1. Date of issue unknown.

> Contents: **Ecce homo** (subtitled here La Passion de
> Jésus).
> Chorale Yvonne Gourverné.
> Album title and accompaning works unknown.
> See: W183.

D11.   Boîte à musique EX-241-242. 1959.

> Contents: **Aspect sentimental.**
> Realized by Le Group de Recherche Musicale de la R.
> T.F.
> Album title: Musique concrête 1959.
> With electronic music by Luc Ferrari, Michel Phili-
> pott, Pierre Schaeffer, and Iannis Xenakis.
> Also issued as BAM LD 070.
> See: W324.

D12.   Boîte à muisque LD 042. 1957.

> Contents: **Visions infernales.**
> Louis-Jacques Rondeleux, baritone; Henri Sauguet,
> piano.
> With: Chants populaires hébraîques by Darius Mil-
> haud.
> See: W250.

D13.   Bourg BG 3017. 1960.

> Contents: **Cinq poèmes de Max Jacob.**
> Paul Derenne, tenor; Henri Sauguet, piano.
> With: La Mort de Socrate by Erik Satie.
> Reissued on Orphée as LD OE 51-023.
> See: W246, B80, B89.

D14.   Calliope CLA 1866. 1979.

> Contents: **L'Oiseau a vu tout cela.**
> Jacques Herbillon, baritone; Orchestre de chambre
> Paul Kuentz; Jacques Murgier, conductor.
> With: Le Livre d'heurs; Sonate for solo flute, by
> Jacques Murgier.
> Reissued on Mixtur Schallplatten as MXT C 1868.
> See: W209.

D15.   Chant du Mond LCD 278300. 197?

> Contents: **Les Forains.**
> L'Orchestre de l'Association du Concerts Lamoureux;
> Henri Sauguet, conductor.
> With: Suite provençale by Darius Milhaud; Aubade
> by Francis Poulenc.
> Reissued on Helikon as CM 278 300.
> See; W25, B739.

D16.   Chant du Monde LCD 278 330. 1989.

> Contents: **Concerto no. 1.**
> Vasso Devezzi, piano; U.S.S.R. Radio Symphony Or-
> Orchestra; Gennady Rozhedstvensky, conductor.
> With: Piano solo, and piano and orchestra composi-
> tions by Gabriel Fauré.
> See: W75, B11.

D17.   Chant du Monde LDX A 8300. 1964.

Contents: **Concerto no. 1; Les Forains.**
Vasso Devetzi, piano; U.S.S.R. Radio Symphony Orchestra; Gennady Rozhdestvensky, conductor (in the Concerto); L'Orchestre de la Société du Concerts Lamoureux; Henri Sauguet, conductor (in Les Forains).
Reissued on Chant du Monde as LDX 78300; on Polydor as 540 003; and on Philips as A 02298 L and S 05800 R.
See; W75, W25, respectively, B81, B216, B326, B553, B632.

D18.   Chant du Monde/Melodia DX 78435.   1971.

Contents: **Mélodie concertante; Quatuor à cordes no. 2.**
Mstislav Rostropovich, violoncello; Moscow Radio Symphony Orchestra; Henri Sauguet, conductor (in the Mélodie); Quatuor Parrenin (in the Quartet).
See: W80, W91, respectively.

D19.   Charlin CCPE 2.   1963, 1985.

Contents: **Les Animaux et leurs hommes; Divertissement de chambre; Neiges; Trois duos.**
Suzanne Lafaye, soprano (in Les Animaux, Duos); Paul Derenne, tenor (in Neiges, Duos); Henri Sauguet, piano or conductor throughout; Robert Heriche, flute; Henri Dioset, clarinet; Roger Lebauw, viola; Maurice Allard, bassoon; Raoul Gola, piano (in the Divertissement).
See: W224, W85, W242, W240, respectively, B215.

D20.   Christophorus SCGLX 73975.   Date of issue unknown.

Contents: **Six pièces facile.**
Duo Geminiani (Hermut Schaarschmidt, Bernhard Hebb).
With: Duets by Falla, Geminiani, Selma y Selmaverdi, Sor, Telemann, Villa-Lobos, and anonymous.
See: W115.

D21.   Columbia DSJF 6 A.   Date of issue unknown.

Contents: **Concerto no. 1.**
Arnaud de Gontau-Brion, piano; L'Orchestre de la Concerts du Conservatoire; Roger Désormière, conductor.
Reissued on Columbia as LFX 648/649.
See: W75, B317, B318.

D22.   Columbia ML 2147.   196?

Contents: **Valse brève.**
Arthur Gold, Robert Fizdale, pianos.
Title of Album: Modern waltzes for two pianos.
With: Waltzes for two pianos by Auric, Rieti, Thomson, Tailleferre, and Bowles.
See: W128, B315.

D23.   Columbia WL 138.   1958.

> Contents: **Valse des si.**
> Juliette Greco.
> Album title: <u>Juliette.</u>
> With: Various other popular songs.
> <u>See</u>: W305.

D24.   Cybelia CY 711.   1985.

> Contents: **Quatuor à cordes no. 2; Quatuor à cordes
> no. 3.**
> Quatuor national d'Aquitaine.
> <u>See</u>: W91, W100, respectively, B74, B674.

D25.   Cybelia CY 811.   1986.

> Contents: **Cadence; Musiques pour Claudel 1, 2;
> Soliloque; Trois préludes.**
> Alain Prévost, guitar
> With: <u>Pour hommage à Claude</u> Debussy; <u>Sonate (Nov.,
> 1960)</u> by Georges Migot.
> Also issued on Cybelia as DS 813.
> <u>See</u>: W180, W178, W174, W175, respectively.

D26.   Cybelia CY 832.   1985.

> Contents: **La Chanson du soir; Feuillets d'album;
> Nuit coloniale sur les bords de la Seine; Pièces
> poétiques 1, 2; Romance en ut; Sonate en ré ma-
> jeur; Trois françaises; Trois nouvelles françaises.**
> Billy Eidi, piano.
> Also issued on E.M.S. as SB-032.
> <u>See</u>: W162, W148, W153, W151, W147, W145, W141,
> W143, respectively, B84, B461.

D27.   D.D.L.S. 115 D.S.   Date of issue unknown.

> Contents: **Les Forains** (arranged for band).
> Garde Republicaine Band; Roger Boutry, conductor.
> <u>See</u>: W25.

D28.   Decca DL 10108.   1962.

> Contents: **Suite royale.**
> Sylvia Marlowe, harpsichord.
> With works by: Elliott Carter, Ned Rorem, and Man-
> uel de Falla.
> Also issued on Decca as DL 710 108; and on Serenus
> as SRS 12056.
> <u>See</u>: W159, B133, B262, B409, B689.

D29.   EMI Pathé-Marconi 2C 069 16 220.   1978.

> Contents: **Les Forains; Tableaux de Paris.**
> L'Orchestre du Capitole de Toulouse; Michel Plasson,
> conductor.
> <u>See</u>: W25, W58, respectively.

D30.   Etcetera KTC 1061. 1988.

> Contents: **Nuit coloniale sur les bords de la Seine.**
> Bennett Lerner, piano.
> Title on album: Exposition Paris, 1937.
> See: W153, B624, B738.

D31.   Fanfare DFL 9024. 1964.

> Contents: "Berceuse créole" from **Le Plumet du Co-
> lonel.**
> Maureen Forrester, soprano; Andrew Davis, piano.
> Title on album: An Evening with Maureen Forester
> and Andrew Davis.
> With: Songs and arias by Handel, Dvorak, Reger,
> Paladilhe, Strauss, Schubert, Niles, Brockway,
> Dougherty, and traditional.
> Reissued as DFCD 9024.
> See: W1, B13.

D32.   Festival du son YPARTK 82083. 1976.

> Contents: **Le Retour de l'enfant prodigue.**
> Unnamed ensemble; Henri Sauguet, conductor.
> Private release.
> See: W362.

D33.   Guilde international du disque SMS 5227. 1972.

> Contents: **La Chatte.**
> L'Orchestre national de l'Opéra de Monte-Carlo; Igor
> Markevitch, conductor.
> Originally issued privately as part of 125e anniver-
> saire SACEM.
> Single disc commercial release with Les Biches by
> Francis Poulenc.
> Released as such on Varèse Sarabande as VC 81096,
> and on Le Connaisseur as Con VC 81096.
> Two-disc commercial issue as Musiciens français des
> Ballets russes on Concert Hall 5227-5228. Reis-
> sued as Diaghilev at Monte-Carlo on Pearle as
> SHE 554/555.
> With: Le Train bleu by Darius Milhaud; Jack-in-the-
> box by Erik Satie; Les Fascheux by Georges Auric,
> and Les Biches by Francis Poulenc.
> See: S14, B25, B625.

D34.   Harmonia Mundi HMC 201219. 1987.

> Contents: "Le Chat" from **Six mélodies sur des poèmes
> symbolistes.**
> Felicity Lott, soprano; Graham Johnson piano.
> Title on album: Mélodies sur des poèmes de Baude-
> laire.
> See: W239.

D35.   Heugel D.H. 1. Date of issue unknown.

> Contents: **Rêverie symphonique.**

Orchestre pro musica; Henri Sauguet, conductor.
Publisher's private release for promotional purposes.
See: W66.

D36.   Inédit O.R.T.F. 995021.   1971.

Contents: **Deux mouvements pour archets; Garden's concerto.**
Claude Garden, harmonica (in the Concerto); L'Orchestre de chambre de l'O.R.T.F.; Henri Sauguet, conductor.
See: W68, W81, respectively, B239.

D37.   Louisville First Edition Recordings LOU-545-10.   1955.

Contents: **Les Trois lys.**
Louisville Symphony Orchestra; Robert Whitney, conductor.
With: Pampeana no. 3 by Alberto Ginastera; A Carol on twelfth night by William Bergsma; Euphony by Robert Ward.
See: W61, B133.

D38.   Magellan 23 503 T.   1972.

Contents: **Les Thibault.**
L'Orchestre national de l'O.R.T.F.; unnamed conductor.
See: W448.

D39.   Melodiya/Angel SR 40180.   1971.

Contents: **Mélodie concertante.**
Mstislav Rostrovich, violoncello; Grand Orchestre de la Radio et Télévision de l'U.R.S.S.; Henri Sauguet, conductor
With: Concerto no. 1 by Vladimir Vlasov.
Reissued on Musical Heritage Society as MHS 444.
See: W80, B82, B83, B133, B331, B411, B722.

D40.   Musical Heritage Society MHS 1916.   1974.

Contents: **Soliloque.**
Turibio Santos, guitar.
Title on album: Five centuries of French guitar music.
With music by Delphin, Alard, Jolivet, Le Roy, Milhaud, Poulenc, Roussel, Sor, and Visée.
See: W174, B133.

D41.   Oiseau-Lyre O.L. 137/138.   1932.

Contents: **La Voyante.**
Unnamed chamber group; Roger Désormière, conductor.
See: W201, B317, B318.

D42.   Oiseau-Lyre O.L. 219/220.   Date of issue unknown.

Contents: **Trio.**

René Daraux Trio.
See: W90, W340.

D43.   Ophélia OP 67103. 1985.

Contents: **Sonate crépusculaire.**
Aurelio Perez, violin; Janis Vakerelis, piano.
With: <u>Sonate</u> for violin and piano by Francis Poulenc.
See: W119, B79.

D44.   Pathé PA 2551. 194?

Contents: "Valse" from **Les Amoureux sont seuls au mond.**
C. Robin, baritone; E. Warner Orchestra.
See: W295.

D45.   Pathé-Marconi ESRF 1036. 195?

Contents: **Le Chemin des forains.**
Edith Piaf.
Reissued numerous times. Currently available on
<u>Edith Piaf</u>, EMI Pathé-Marconi as 2519284.
See: W297.

D46.   Le Petit Ménestrel ALB 6045. 1981.

Contents: **Tistou-les-pouces-verts.**
Jacques Bocquillon; Martine Masquelin; Lionel Erpelding; Jean-Claude Pennetier, conductor.
See: W10.

D47.   Philips P370/179 F.   Date of issue unknown.

Contents: **Valse des si.**
Juliette Gréco.
Album title and accompaning works unknown.
See: W305.

D48.   Polydor (number unknown). 1934.

Contents: **Aria d'Eduardo poeta.**
Hugues Cuenod, tenor; Henri Sauguet, piano.
See: W287.

D49.   Polydor 566245/6. 1948.

Contents: **Les Forains.**
L'Orchestre de la Société des Concerts Lamoureux;
Henri Sauguet, conductor.
Reissued on long-playing album as Polydor 54003
with **Concerto no. 1** (D15).
See: W25. B318, B450, B555.

D50.   Radio Canada International RCI 365. 1973.

Contents: **Mouvements du cœur; Visions infernales.**
Joseph Rouleau, bass; Claude Savard, piano.

With: <u>Saisons canadiennes</u> by Rudolphe Mathieu.
<u>See</u>: W251, W250, respectively.

D51.   R.E.B. REB 2. 1949.

Contents: **Mouvements du cœur; Visions infernales.**
Doda Conrad, bass; David Garvey, piano.
<u>See</u>: W251, W250, respectively, B287, B318, B511,
B548.

D52.   REM 10 852. Date of issue unknown.

Contents: **Suite royale.**
Denise Balanche, harpsichord.
Album title and accompaning works unknown.
<u>See</u>: W159.

D53.   René Gailly CD 87 008. 1986.

Contents: **Nuit coloniale sur les bords de la Seine.**
Daniel Blumenthal, piano.
Title on album: <u>Souvenirs de l'Exposition Paris,</u>
<u>1937</u>.
<u>See</u>: W153, B626.

D54.   RPART 57 80 L. 1966.

Contents: **Symphonie de marches.**
L'Orchestre de la S.N.C.F.; Robert Blot, conductor.
Private recording reserved for attendants at XIXe
Congrès International des Chemins de Fer.
<u>See</u>: W70.

D55.   Vega C 30 A98. 195?

Contents: **Farrebique.**
Unnamed orchestra; Serge Baudo, conductor.
Title on album: <u>Vingt-cinq ans de cinéma</u>.
With: Film music by Maurice Jaubert, Georges Auric,
Maurice Jarre, Maurice Le Roux, Joseph Kosma, and
Darius Milhaud.
<u>See</u>: W337, B563.

D56.   Vega C35 A171. 1957.

Contents: **Quatuor à cordes no. 2.**
Quatuor Parrenin.
Later combined with Mélodie concertante for Chant
du Monde/Melodia for reissue as DX 78435; and
LCS A 78.435 (See: D29).
<u>See</u>: W91, B449, B554.

D57.   Verseau M 10.050. 1979.

Contents: **Clochemerle** (arranged for band)
L'Orchestre d'Harmonie de la Musique Municipal de
Bordeaux, Lucien Mora, conductor.
With: <u>Mouvements faunesques</u> and <u>Vision de Pan</u> by
Gilles Cagnard; <u>Overture pour un conte gai</u> by

Maurice Emmanuel; and Rapsodie d'Auvergne by Camille Saint-Saëns.
See: W339.

D58.   Vogue VG 671.   1987.

Contents: "Berceuse créole" from Le Plumet du Co-
lonel.
Gabriel Bacquier, tenor; Claudie Martinet, piano
Title on album: Récital de mélodies.
With songs by Gounod, Duparc, Fauré, Hahn, Bonde-
ville, Ravel, Satie, Milhaud, Poulenc, and Yvain.

D59.   Le Voix de son maître 2C 065-12.805.   1974.

Contents: Sonatine bucolique.
Jean-Marie Londeix, saxophone; Pierre Pontier, piano.
Title on album: Œuvres pour saxophone et piano.
With: Sonata for saxophone and piano by Paul Cres-
ton; Sonate for saxophone and piano by Jean Absil;
Sonata for saxophone and piano by Edison Denisov;
and Improvisation I by Ryo Noda.
See: W111.

D60.   Private tape.   Boston University.   School of Music.
1980.

Contents: La Voyante.
Performers unidentified.
Title of program: Three centuries of French master-
works, presented 13 November, 1980.
With music by Debussy, Fauré, Poulenc and Milhaud.
See: W201

D61.   Private tape.   Indiana University.   1985.

Contents: Trois chants de contemplation.
Program no. 262.   Contemporary Vocal Ensemble.
Performers unidentified.
With music by Schoenberg, Webern, Cage, Hindemith,
and Penderecki.
See: W211.

D62.   Private tape.   Robert Orchard.

Robert Orchard recorded a number of works by Henri
Sauguet, along with those of other composers.   The
recordings were made under a variety of conditions:
live performances; off the air of recorded perfor-
mances; and off the air from live performances.
Copies of these tapes have been deposited at many
universities in the United States.
Contents: Le Plumet du Colonel; La Contrebasse; La
Gageure imprévue; Les Caprices de Marianne; and
La Voyante.
See: W1, W3, W5, W5, W201, respectively.

Bibliography

Writings about Henri Sauguet and his works are listed alphabetically by author or title if anonymous. For the reader's convenience reference to the "Works and Performances" section, indicated by "W" numbers, and to the "Discography" section, indicated by "D" numbers, are included in parentheses.

B1.   "A Bruxelles." **L'Information musicale** nos. 96-97 (22 December, 1942): 157.
     Brussels, like Paris, has a renewed interest in music. The spring and fall seasons at the Palais des Beaux-Arts is announced. Among the "jeunes Français" represented are Poulenc and Sauguet. Sauguet's contribution, while not specifically mentioned, was probably **Ombres du jardin** (W203).

B2.   "A l'Empire--Les Ballets Cuevas ouvrent leur saison." **Le Monde**, 24 October, 1952, 9.
     Brief article about the opening of the Ballets Cuevas' season which included **Cordélia** (W29).

B3.   A., R. "Reception chez Heugel." **Le Guide du concert** no. 184 (14 February, 1958): 765.
     Henri Sauguet and Darius Milhaud sign publishing contracts with Heugel who hold a welcoming reception on 3 February, 1958.

B4.   Abel, Jean. "Nos correspondents nous écrivent de Marseilles." **Le Guide du concert** no. 271 (15-21 May, 1960): 623.
     The Corps de Ballet of l'Opéra municipal de Marseilles performs **Les Forains** (W25) with choreography by Géo Stone.

B5.   Achères, Victoria. "Le Ballet neerlandais." **Les Lettres françaises** no. 936 (19 July, 1962): 9.
     The performance of **La Rencontre** (W26) features Sonja van Beers and Billy Wilson in roles created by Leslie Caron and Jean Babilée.

B6.   Achères, Victoria. "Ballets des Champs-Elysées." **Les
       Lettres françaises** no. 235 (25 November, 1948): 6.
       Comments about the dance and staging of **La Ren-
       contre** (W26).

B7.   -----. "Les Ballets des Champs-Elysées." **Les Lettres
       françaises** no. 259 (12 May, 1949): 6.
       Commentary about the dance aspects of **La Nuit** (W17)
       performed in memory of Christian Bérard.

B8.   -----. "La Dame aux Camélias à L'Opéra." **Les Lettres
       françaises** no. 811 (11 February, 1960): 6.
       Review of the dance aspects of **La Dame aux camélias**
       (W35).

B9.   Ackere, Jules van. **L'Age d'or de la musique française,
       1870-1950**. Brussels: Meddens, 1966.
       Brief biographical references to Sauguet.

B10.   Adri. "Faudra-t-il transcribe J.-S. Bach pour les
       guitaristes?" **La Vie musicale et théâtrale** 2, no.
       6 (December, 1959): 102-103
       In response to a series of interviews subtitled,
       "Une grande enquête de la Vie Musicale et théâtrale,"
       Sauguet replies that he has no objection to transcrip-
       tions of Bach's music for guitar, but he suspects that
       there is already enough contemporary music for guitar
       without transcribing older compositions.

B11.   Aguettant, R. "Sauguet: Nouvelle versions des For-
       ains et du 1er Concerto par Vasso Devetzi." **Disques**
       no. 130 (November/December, 1962): 331.
       Review of the new Chant du Monde recording of **Les
       Forains** with Sauguet conducting, and the **Concerto no.
       1**. (See: D17)

B12.   Alden, Robert. "Beaton costumes a hit at Comédie."
       New York Times, 18 May, 1962, 34.
       Cecil Beaton designed the costumes for **L'Ecole de
       médisance** (W399) and Sauguet composed the incidental
       music. After the first half of the play many of the
       audience started to leave. Sauguet tried to assure
       them that the second half was funnier.

B13.   Alfano, Vincent. "An evening with Maureen Forester
       and Andrew Davis." **Fanfare** 10, no. 3 (January/Feb-
       ruary, 1967): 231.
       Review of a recording which included the "Berceuse
       créole." See: D31.

B14.   Amberg, Georges. **Art in modern ballet**. New York:
       Pantheon, 1946.
       Amberg includes illustrations for the set and cos-
       tume sketches (plates 57, 58) for **Fastes** (W19). He
       also cites **La Chatte** (W14), **Les Forains** (W25), **Les
       Mirages** (W24), and a mysterious "Les Nuages."

B15.   Ancelin, Pierre. "Entretiens sur l'art actuel--Henri

Sauguet." **Les Lettres françaises** no. 1,044 (3-9 September, 1964): 1f.
   Ancelin interviewed a number of people active in the creative arts. Henri Sauguet was the first composer. Sauguet explains his creative philosophy, his attitudes to audiences and public performances, and to his contemporaries.

B16.   Ancelin, Pierre, ed. **Henri Sauguet.** Paris: Richard Masse, 1983 (Special triple number of **La Revue musicale**)
   Ancelin organized this lengthy work into six sections: "L'homme," "Hommages," "L'œuvres," "Ecrits," "Catalogue" (compiled by Christine Steinmetz), and "Iconographie" (organized by Raphaël Cluzel). "L'homme" contains character sketches by Marcel Schneider, Daniel-Lesur, Raymond Lyon, Marcel Mihalovici, Pierre Gaxotte, Paul Collaer, Maurice Schumann, Paul Guth, Henri Troyat, Boris Kochno, Jean Matthyssens, Odette Joyeux, Pierre Schaeffer, Maurice Ohana, André Fraigneau, Doda Conrad, René de Obaldia, and Virgil Thomson. Janine Charrat, Georges-Emmanuel Clancier, Paul Derenne, Vasso Devetzi, Gabriel Dussurget, Serge Lifar, Madeleine Milhaud, Florence Mothe, Gaston Palewski, Manuel Rosenthal, and Claude Aveline contributed "Hommages." "L'œuvre" contains more analytical essays by Raphaël Cluzel, Jean Roy, Pierrette Mari, France-Yvonne Bril, André Hofmann, Frédéric Robert, Jean-Paul Holstein, Jacques Chailley, Roger Delage, and Pierre Ancelin, along with extracts from reviews which are cited in full elsewhere in the "Writings about Henri Sauguet and his Works" section. Sauguet contributed material for "Ecrits," and they are cited individually in the "Writings by Henri Sauguet" section.

B17.   -----. "Manifestations chorégraphiques à l'opéra de Marseilles." **Les Lettres françaises** no. 1,028 (13 March, 1964): 9.
   Ancelin interviews Sauguet in connection with a performance of **Les Forains** (W25). Sauguet's intention was for the music to function as a scenario. A melodic motive may connect a dramatic or story block. One motive in particular characterises the tragedy in their lives and unites them in the final Pas de quatre.

B18.   Andreu, Pierre. **Vie et mort de Jax Jacob.** Paris: La Table ronde, 1982.
   After Max Jacob's arrest by the Germans, Pierre Colle and Sauguet tried to intervene with the authorities, but to no avail. Sauguet contributed a speech when Jacob's body was transfered to a new grave in 1949.

B19.   Andrieux, Françoise. "Présence du concerto pour piano dans la musique française contemporaine." **Revue d'information musicale français** no. 15 (November, 1984): 113-122.
   Andrieux presents an overview of piano concertos

written between 1946 and 1981. In response to a question about his philosophy Sauguet acknowledges that
writing a concerto these days is difficult. One is
torn between writing something monumental like Tchaikovsky or Rachmaninoff or writing something flashy and
pushy like Prokofiev or Bartók. Sauguet has tried to
arrive at a middle ground with a balance between the
orchestra and the soloist. **Concerto no. 2** (W76) and
Concerto no. 3 (W79) are cited.

B20. **Les Années 50.** Paris: Editions du Centre Pompidou,
      1988.
      Aspect sentimental (W324) was performed as part of
      the exhibition.

B21. **Les Années 40 d'Anne Bony.** Paris: Editions du Regard,
      1985.
      Contains brief citations to **Les Mirages** (W24),
      Ondine (W364), **La Folle de Chaillot** (W375), and **Les
      Amoureux sont seuls au monde** (W340) in articles by
      Paul-Louis Mignon ("Théâtre"), Claude-Jean Philippe
      ("Cinéma"), and William Mahder ("Musique").

B22. **Les Années 30 d'Anne Bony.** Paris: Editions du Regard,
      1987.
      Contains brief citations to **Concerto no. 1** (W75)
      and **La Chartreuse de Parme** (W4), as well as a group
      photography of the founders of "La Sérénade" in the
      article "Musique" by William Mahder.

B23. **Les Années 20 d'Anne Bony.** Paris: Editions du Regard,
      1989.
      Contains citations to **La Chatte** (W14) and valua-
      ble articles by Paul-Louis Mignon ("Théâtre"), Marie-
      Françoise Christout ("Opéra, Ballets"), Francis Paud-
      ras ("Musique, Jazz"), and Anne-Marie Deschodt ("Var-
      iétés").

B24. "L'Anniversaire d'Henri Sauguet." **Musica** no. 95 (Feb-
      ruary, 1962): 10.
      L'Orchestre national presents a concert at the
      Théâtre des Champs-Elysées in honor of Sauguet's 60th
      birthday. Many society people attended and heard the
      Concerto d'Orphée (W77) and Erik Satie's Parade in
      which Sauguet played one of the typewriters. The com-
      mentator questions why Sauguet's best known piece,
      Les Forains (W25), was not performed.

B25. Aprahamian, Felix. "Diaghilev at Monte Carlo." **Sun-
      day Times,** 10 August, 1980, 30.
      Review of a recording which contains **La Chatte.**
      See: D33.

B26. Ardoin, John. "Aspen 1962." **Musical America** 82
      (September, 1962): 106-107.
      American premiers of the **Symphony no. 3** (W62), **La
      Contrebasse** (W3), and **La Voyante** (W201) are cited.
      Jennie Tourel sings **La Voyante** which Walter Susskind

conducts. Madeleine Milhaud's staging of **La Contre-basse** makes it great fun. Wolfgang Vacano conducts the opera.

B27. Armes, Roy. "Farrebique." In **The International dictionary of films and filmmakers**, edited by Christopher Lyon. Chicago: St. James, 1984.
Description, bibliography and assessment of **Farrebique** (W337).

B28. "Au profit de 'Revivre' Hommage à André Gide." **Le Figaro**, 7 June, 1949, 4.
Brief citation of an evening which included **Le Retour de l'enfant prodigue** (W362).

B29. "Au théâtre." **Nouvelle revue musicale** 22 (April, 1924): 166-167.
Brief review of Mme. Beriza's presentation of three short works which included the Paris premiere of Stravinsky's L'Histoire du Soldat, Lord Berners' La Carrosse du Saint-Sacrement, and **Le Plumet du Colonel** (W1). Of the last-named the critic merely says it was "without pretension."

B30. "Au Théâtre Louis Jouvet-Athénée 'Avant l'Ondine.'" **L'Œuvre**, 24 April, 1939, 9.
Brief citation to Sauguet's contribution as "important." See: W364.

B31. Auric, Georges. "Au la Cigal." **Les Nouvelles littéraires, artistiques et scientifiques** no. 88 (21 June, 1924): 7.
Auric is acquainted with the young composer of **Les Roses** (W13) and finds it easy to speak frankly about the little adaptation of Olivier Metra's celebrated waltz. He finds it perfectly useless with no personal investment on the part of the composer. Happily there are other things like the **Françaises** (W141) or the flute **Sonatine** (W102) upon which to base a judgement of Sauguet.

B32. -----. "Au Théâtre des Champs-Elysées--Ballets Suédois." **Les Nouvelles littéraires, artistiques et scientifiques** no. 56 (10 November, 1923): 3.
Henri Sauguet is incontestably full of gifts of the most fortunate kind. His **Nocturne** and **Danse des matelots** (W12) are artlessly fresh and, in the case of the **Rapsodie nègre** (W123), like the early works of Francis Poulenc.

B33. -----. "La Chatte." **Annales politique et littéraire** no. 2,287 (1 June, 1927): 552.
The music is fluent but not trite; the themes are spontaneous and continually developed into something new. There is a melodic outpouring in Sauguet's work which is rich and, with the exception of Poulenc's music, is very rare these days.

B34.   Auric, Georges. "Les Concerts." **Les Nouvelles lit-
        téraires, artistiques et scientifiques** no. 37 (30
        June, 1923): 5.
            Sauguet's songs, full of invention and charming
        detail, seem somewhat badly balanced and a bit long.
        His **Françaises** (W141) are completely successful pieces.
        They contain vivacious writing and are in perfect
        taste.

B35.   -----. "Les Concerts." **Les Nouvelles littéraires,
        artistiques et scientifiques** no. 80 (26 April, 1924):
        7.
            The **Françaises** (W141) and **Danse** (W12) of Sauguet
        affirm a very strongly formed personality, spontaneous
        without artificiality or false peculiarities. Listen
        at the end of this month to his little opéra-bouffe
        Le Plumet du Colonel (W1) when the full scope of his
        artistry and his gift of taste will be made manifest.

B36.   -----. "Les Forains." **Lettres françaises** no. 100
        (22 March, 1946): 7.
            Sauguet's score for **Les Forains** (W25) is exquisite
        throughout. There is no useless padding, and it seems
        effortless. It is clearly orchestrated and very rhyth-
        mic; nicely balanced throughout. It is one of those
        successes that one rarely meets.

B37.   -----. "Francuzskaiā muzyka vyzila." **Sovetskaiā Mu-
        zyka** no. 9 (September, 1975): 140-141.
            Russian translation of his article which appeared
        in **Modern music**, 1945. <u>See</u>: B39.

B38.   -----. "Paris resurgent." **Modern music** 22, no. 4
        (May/June, 1945): 247-250.
            Concerning **Les Forains** (W25), it is in every note
        a "ballet" score. There is no useless turgidity. His
        music has a facility of a kind that few possess right
        now.

B39.   -----. "Paris--The survival of French music." **Modern
        music** 22, no. 2 (March/April, 1945): 157-160.
            La Chatte (W14) produced with remarkable success.
        La Chartreuse (W4) was rare with attractive qualities.
        La Gageure imprévue (W5) confirmed all our expecta-
        tions. Without once trying to shock or surprise, the
        compositions, delicate and of a keen and ingenious
        wit, happily carried on in one of the better veins of
        our national art.

B40.   -----. "Reception de Henri Sauguet à l'Institut, le
        14 janvier, 1976, par Georges Auric, de l'Institut."
        **Bulletin de la Société des auteurs et compositeurs
        dramatiques** 60 (April, 1976): 9-13.
            A description of Sauguet's election to and initia-
        tion speech as he took his chair in the Académie des
        Beaux-Arts.

B41.   Baigneres, Claude. **Ballets d'hier et d'aujourd'hui.**

Paris: Le Bon Plasir, 1954.
Sauguet is characterized as a sensitive and refined
musician, full of grace, level-headedness and elegance.
Les forains (W25) and **Les Mirages** (W24) described in
detail.   Emphasis is placed on how appropriate the
music is to the dance and the scenario.

B42.   Baigneres, Claude.   "Les Ballets Jean Babilée." **Le
        Figaro**, 23-24 June, 1945, 8.
        Jacques Noël's set for **Le Caméléopard** (W33) seems
to absorb all the attention of the dance.   It is curiously designed to alter the prespective and proportion
of the dancers.   The music has a quality of enchantment.

B43.   -----. "'Chemin de lumière' a l'Opéra." **Le Figaro**,
        1 November, 1957, 8.
        Cassandre's set and Lifar's choreography is so
similar to their efforts on behalf of **Les Mirages** (W24)
that one wonders why this ballet was created.   Auric's
music is no better than Sauguet's.

B44.   -----. "La Dame aux camélias." **Le Figaro**, 5 February,
        1960, 12.
        A memorable opening line refers to the Lady of the
camelias: <u>Verdi la faisait chanter, Sauguet la fait
danser.</u> (Verdi made her sing, Sauguet makes her dance).
The rhythmic quality of Sauguet's music will, no doubt,
help the dancers who seem excessively distracted.   The
ballet will probably succeed, but there seems to be
too much emphasis on display over pure art.   <u>See</u>:   W35.

B45.   -----. **Yvette Chauviré**.   Paris: Lafont, 1956.
        Contains numerous references to **Les Mirages** (W24).

B46.   "Les Ballets Russes de Serge de Diaghilev." **La Revue
        musicale** no. 110 (December, 1930)
        La Chatte (W14) is cited in this special number of
the **Revue**.

B47.   Barazov, Konstantin.   "Diaghilev and the radical years
        of modrn art." **Art and Artists** 10 (July, 1975): 6-
        15.
        Illustration on page 14 from **La Chatte** (W14) mis-
labeled as Alice "Nikitiva" and Serge "Lefer" in "La
Notte."

B48.   Barnes, Clive.   "'La Guirlande de Campra' by John
        Taras." **New York Times**, 2 December, 1966, 4.
        Sauguet's contribution is "not half bad." <u>See</u>:
W41.

B49.   Bathori, Jane.   "Les Musiciens que j'ai connus." **Re-
        corded Sound** no. 15 (July, 1964): 238-245.
        Portion of a transcribed lecture presented 17
October, 1961, for Radiodiffusion télévision française.
The lecture is translated and annotated by Felix
Aprahamian.   Bathori cites Sauguet as a great song

writer with a real gift for vocal writing. She illustrates this by accompaning Louis-Jacques Rondeleux on
"Le petit paysan" and "Exhortation" from **Visions infernales** (W250).

B50.   Bauer, Marion. "The composer's plight; An interview
       with Arthur Honegger." **Modern msuic** 1, no. 2 (Sep-
       tember/October, 1924): 23.
           Satie's influence is a reaction against experimen-
       tation which is out of place today. The Arcueil School
       is representative of this.

B51.   Beaton, Cecil. **The Restless years. Diaries, 1955-1963.**
       London: Weidenfeld and Nicolson, 1978.
           Until Sauguet came over from Paris to record the
       music for **Landscape with figures** (W394) Beaton's will
       to remount The Gainsborough Girls flagged.

B52.   Beaumont, Cyril. **Ballets of today.** London: Putnam,
       1954.
           La Nuit (W17) described.

B53.   -----. "Christian Bérard." **Studio** no. 798 (October,
       1959): 75-80.
           Bérard creates the appropriate atmosphere for
       Sauguet's bitter-sweet melodies. Music was often a
       source of inspiration for Bérard and acted upon his
       imagination like a drug.

B54.   -----. "Designs for Ballets des Etoiles de Paris."
       Studio no. 792 (March, 1959): 72-77.
           Beaumont recalls being impressed by the delightful
       simplicity of **Les Forains** (W25).

B55.   Beauvert, Thierry. "Les Enfants d'abord! Voix d'eau
       cristalline dans la Vaisseau lyrique." **Avant scène
       opéra** no. 104 (1987): 96-99.
           With **Tistou-les-pouces-verts** (W10) Sauguet's ban-
       ner floats on the side of the traditionalists.

B56.   Bernard, Robert. **Les Tendances de la musique française
       moderne.** Paris: Durand, 1930.
           The simplicity, austerity and youthful freedom of
       Maxime Jacob, Sauguet, and some others cited.

B57.   Bessy, Maurice, and Jean-Louis Cardane. **Dictionnaire
       du cinéma et de la télévision.** Paris: Jean-Jacques
       Pauvert, 1971.
           Biographical sketch and selected list of film music.

B58.   Bex, Maurice. "Le Dernière saison des Ballets russes
       de Serge de Diaghilew." **La Revue hebdomadaire** 36,
       no. 32 (6 August, 1927): 109-115.
           Sauguet's music for **La Chatte** (W14) contributes
       little to, and has far to go before it matches, the au-
       dacious set and costumes. It is more like Délibes or
       Gounod in his conservative and consonant vocabulary.

B59.   Blitzstein, Marc. "Coming--the mass audience!"
       Modern music 13, no. 4 (May/June, 1936): 23-29.
           Blitzstein condemns members of Les Six, Ecole
       d'Arcueil and Satie. He characterizes La Sérénade as
       a snobish clique which promotes effete pieces like
       those written by Sauguet and Massimo.

B60.   -----. "Popular music--an invasion, 1923-33." **Modern
       music** 10, no. 2 (January/February, 1933): 96-102.
           Milhaud, Auric and Poulenc merely accept the ready-
       made boulevard music of Satie. Sauguet uses it more
       to advantage by accepting it for what it is.

B61.   -----. "Theatre music in Paris." **Modern music** 12,
       no. 3 (March/April, 1935): 128-134.
           Sauguet's music for **Le Sicilien** (W363) simply fol-
       lowed an old court music pattern. The pieces were
       small and thin; Wattausian, rather than Mozartian, and
       lift an uneasy and indefinite impression. He suggests
       that Sauguet select less "phoney masters" than Gounod
       and Ambroise Thomas.

B62.   Boas, Robert. "Bordeaux--Sauguet revival." **Opera**
       (London) 21 (Autumn, 1981): 73.
           Sauguet's music for **Le Contrebasse** (W3) has back-
       ward-looking amiability which suggests the subtle
       melodic indirectness of Messager. The instrumental
       pieces were the most effective.

B63.   Boireau, Gérard. Correspondence. 14 June, 1990.
           M. Boireau informed the author of a performance on
       14 May, 1990, in the Salle Jacques Thibaud, as part
       of the Mai musical de Bordeaux of "Quatre images des
       saisons," "Ballet d'un grand amour" and **La Chatte**
       choreographed and directed by Joseph Lazzini. See:
       W14, W28, W35.

B64.   "Bon anniversaire, M. Sauguet! au Centre culturel
       suédois." **Le Monde**, 26 March, 1981, 20.
           Sauguet speaks about his experiences of the last
       twenty years at the Swedish Cultural Center in Paris.

B65.   Bonte, Hans Georg. "Musik im Rundfunk." **Zeitschrift
       für Musik** 115, no. 8 (August, 1954): 478-482.
           Sauguet has everything--everything that a French-
       man can have. **Les Caprices de Marianne** (W6) is a pure
       incarnation of the romantic spirit.

B66.   Bouchot, Alphonse. "Ballets russes." **L'Echo de Paris**,
       30 May, 1927, 4.
           For **La Chatte** (W14) Sauguet has written a score
       which affirms the lively and rhythmic openness of the
       dance. Bouchot comments: <u>C'est</u> <u>amusant</u>. (It's amus-
       ing.)

B67.   Bourdet, Denise. **Pris sur le vif**. Paris: Plon, 1957.
           Bourdet compiled several volumes of casual, de-
       lightful biographical sketches of important creative
       people in Paris. In her chapter here on Sauguet, she

recounts, among other things, the composer's career as
an actor, beginning with the role of Baron Méduse in
Satie's Le Piège de Méduse, his appearance in Edouard
Bourdet's Le Fleur des Pois, and as Mme Pernelle in
Marcel Herrand's production of Tartuffe.

B68. Boziwick, George. "Henri Sauguet. Cantilène pastorale." Notes 39, no. 3 (1983): 696-697.
The Cantilène pastorale (W117) is a charming vig-
nette suitable for even a moderately accomplished o-
boist. It is not terribly challenging for the advanced
performer, but makes a welcome addition to the peda-
gogical repertoire.

B69. Bradley, Lionel. "Ten ballets of 1946--one man's
choice." Ballet today 1, no. 4 (January/February,
1947): 4.
Les Forains (W25), while perhaps not a masterpiece,
is a completely satisfying work of art.

B70. Brahms, Caryl. Footnotes to the ballet. London:
Lovat Dickson, 1936.
Sauguet's music for La Chatte (W14) is designed
like a divan upon which the ballet could lie until the
next idea arrives.

B71. -----. "Sheer tights and diamante." Ballet today 1,
no. 2 (July, 1946): 13-16.
Les Forains (W25) with its evocative score by
Sauguet is the best ballet that the company presents
and, simply, one of the best ballets.

B72. Bril, France-Yvonne. Henri Sauguet. Paris: Seghers,
1967.
A good early biography, in French, for the general
reader, with a works list, selected bibliography, and
discography.

B73. -----. "Sauguet." Dizionario enciclopedio univer-
sale della musica e dei musicisti. Turin: Utet,
1988.
Biographical sketch with a works list.

B74. -----. Sauguet: Quatuor à cordes no. 2; Quatuor à
cordes no. 3. (Program notes). Paris: Cybélia,
1986.
Three short essays by Bril, in French with an Eng-
lish translation, accompany the recording. "La Mémoire
chèrie," "Les couleurs et les sons se repondent," and
"Un sixième sens" are worthy poetic descriptions of
Sauguet's work. See: D24.

B75. Brillat, Maurice. "Deux visages de la danse." Con-
trepoints no. 4 (May/June, 1946): 82.
Sauguet's score for Les Forains (W25) is lively,
clear, colorful, rhythmic, charming, and, overall, is
one of the happiest pieces of music for the dance that
has been heard in years.

B76.   Brown, Frederick. **An impersonation of angels; a bio-
       graphy of Jean Cocteau.** New York: Viking, 1968.
       Sauguet, Roger Désormière, and Vittorio Rieti are
       cited as part of groups gravitating around Cocteau and
       Christian Bérard. The Hôtel Nollet, whose tenants in-
       cluded Sauguet, Max Jacob, and Rieti, is cited as a
       gathering place for creative young men.

B77.   -----. **Theater and revolution; the culture of the
       French stage.** New York: Viking Press, 1980.
       Irma (W361) was staged as a pure burlesque with
       appropriate music by Sauguet.

B78.   Brown, Royal S. "French music since Debussy and Ravel."
       High Fidelity 23 (19 September, 1973): 50-65.
       Sauguet is the true inheritor of Satie's philosophy.
       Les Forains (W25), **Mélodie concertante** (W80), and **Les
       Caprices de Marianne** (W6) are cited in particular. A
       brief, selected discography follows.

B79.   -----. "Poulenc: Sonata for violin and piano. Sau-
       guet: Sonate crépusculaire." **Fanfare** 10, no. 6
       (July/August, 1987): 161.
       An understated work which alternates between line-
       against-line asceticism and a more opulent Gallic
       style. <u>See</u>: W119, D43.

B80.   -----. "Satie: La mort de Socrate. Sauguet: Les
       Penitents en maillots roses." **Fanfare** 11, no. 6
       (July/August, 1988): 240.
       The work has grace, charm, tenderness and even
       sadness which matches Jacob's mixture of surrealism
       and religious awe. <u>See</u>: W246, D13.

B81.   -----. "Sauguet: Les Forains. Concerto no. 1 in A
       for piano and orchestra." **Fanfare** 6, no. 3 (January/
       February, 1983): 247-248.
       Forains is situated within the anti-serious tra-
       ditions which produced <u>Les</u> <u>Six</u>. Debussy is not for-
       gotten in the second movement of the **Concerto**. <u>See</u>:
       W25, W75, D17.

B82.   -----. "Sauguet: Mélodie concertante in C minor for
       Cello and Orchestra." **Fanfare** 6, no. 3 (January/
       February, 1983): 247-248.
       Mélodie concertante is pervaded with an almost
       Slavic melancholia with its dark-hued lyricism.
       <u>See</u>: W80, D39.

B83.   -----. "Sauguet: Mélodie concertante for cello and
       orchestra." **High Fidelity Magazine** 22, no.1 (Jan-
       uary, 1972): 97-98.
       Sauguet's haunting and rhapsodic **Mélodie** stands
       as one of the most strikingly beautiful works for cello
       in the twentieth century. <u>See</u>: W80, D39.

B84.   -----. "Sauguet: Trois Françaises . . . ." **Fanfare**
       12,no. 2 (November/December, 1988): 268.
       The highly tonal harmonies bear the faintest tinge

of acidity. <u>See</u>:   W141, W143, S145, W147, W148, W151, W153, W162, D26.

B85.   Brunel, Raoul.   "A l'Opéra."   **L'Œuvre**, 27 March, 1939, 9.
The costumes and sets for **La Chartreuse de Parme** (W4) are praiseworthy, but the score is long, monotonous, and the instrumentation is often thin and badly handled.   The criticism may be too strong, the critic feels, because the composer knows how to make the best of certain effects and has constructed the opera in the classic style of a light operetta.

B86.   Bruyr, José.   **La Belle histoire de la musique.**   Paris: Corrêa, 1946.
The author cites Jean Cocteau's couplet:
<u>Désormière</u>, <u>Jacob</u>, <u>Cliquet-Pleyel</u>, <u>Sauguet</u>,
<u>De vos quatre ou cinq noms, je fais un seul</u> bouquet
(Désormière, Jacob, Cliquet-Pleyel, Sauguet,
Of your four or five names I make a single bouquet.)
He believes, however, that four or five names refers to Cliquet-Pleyel's hyphenated name.   It refers, rather, to Jacques Benoist-Méchain who, for the briefest period of time, was considered a fifth member of L'Ecole d'Arcueil.

B87.   -----.   **L'Ecran des musiciens.**   Paris: Les Cahiers de France, 1930.
Interviewed as a composer active in film music, Sauguet relates events of his early career and Milhaud's important influence in helping him to become established.   Major influences in his music are Chopin and Debussy.   A brief works list follows.

B88.   -----.   "Un Entretien avec Henri Sauguet."   **Le Guide du concert** no. 23 (7 March, 1930): 631-634.
"He sings with his heart," according to Bruyr.

B89.   -----.   "Henri Sauguet, Les Pénitents in maillots rose."   **Disques** no. 126 (January, 1962): 69.
The composition is a sort of melodic declamation in the voice over a supple and profound motion which nearly constitutes a true "morceau de piano."   <u>See</u>: W246, D13.

B90.   -----.   **L'Operette.**   Paris: Presses universitaires de France, 1962.
Brief citations concerning **Le Plumet du Colonel** (W1), **Un Amour du Titien** (W2), and **La Contrebasse** (W3), and a general evaluation of Sauguet.

B91.   -----.   "Quatuor Lespine."   **L'Information musicale** (13 June, 1942): 650-651.
The **String Quartet no. 1** (W87) incorporates techniques similar to those used by Gounod.   There is much in it like a master-piece which an apprentice turns out in preparation for entering a build.   The music by Henri Sauguet promises much for the future.

B92.   Bruyr, José. "Trio Jacques Canet." **L'Information
        musicale** (5 December, 1941): 446.
        The most favorable judgement is reserved for the
        Madrigal (W204) which is infused with a melancholy
        atmosphere. The simplicity of the setting creates
        the most poetic climate for the presentation of the
        musical poems.

B93.   Buckle, Richard. **Buckle at the ballet.** New York:
        Atheneum, 1980.
        The 15 October, 1949 **Observer** review of **La Ren-
        contre** (W26) at Prince's Theatre in London is rather
        bland and noncommittal about the music.

B94.   -----. **Diaghilev.** New York: Atheneum, 1979.
        The discussion of **La Chatte** (W14) is based on
        interviews with many of the participants. Also cited
        are performances in London (Prince's Theatre, 14 June,
        1927), Budapest, and Vienna.

B95.   -----. **In search of Diaghilev.** New York: Thomas
        Nelson, 1956.
        La Chatte (W14) performed at King's Theatre,
        Edinburgh, 25 November - 9 December, 1928.

B96.   -----. **In the wake of Diaghilev.** New York: Holt,
        Rinehart and Winston, 1982.
        Sauguet relates his relationship with Diaghilev.
        The origin of Edward James' Les Ballets 1933, for
        which Sauguet wrote **Fastes** W19) is also recounted.

B97.   Caby, Robert. "Les Caprices de Marianne." **L'Age
        nouveau** (November, 1955): 6.
        The melodic continuity which is constantly sup-
        ported by the orchestra, blends recitative and aria
        and also connects the scenes. It is subtle and pro-
        foundly innovative which will last longer than other
        spectacular inventions which attract audiences. See:
        W6.

B98.   Cadieu, Martine. "Quelques instants avec Iakov Zak."
        Les Lettrers françaises 7 (November, 1963): 8.
        When asked if he know of French composers, Zak
        replied that he had played a Ravel Concerto before
        Sauguet in Moscow.

B99.   Capron, Marcelle. "Au Vieux-Colombier 'La Nuit des
        Rois' de Shakespeare." **Combat**, 2 March, 1961, 8.
        Henri Sauguet's music underlines the comedy and
        the character of the roles so well and connects the
        scenes so smoothly that it whould always be used with
        the play in the future. See: W397.

B100.   Carmichael, John. "Henri Sauguet." **Music and musi-
        cians** 9 (June, 1961): 28.
        The performance of **La Voyante** (W201) clearly
        stated the humor and grace of the work. **L'Oiseau a vu
        tout cela** (W209) which was written only last year, shows
        that the composer has been evolving toward a refinement

of texture and a concentration on line and harmonic
austerity.

B101.   Chamfray, Claude. "Avant Première 'La Dame aux camélias.'" **La Vie musicale et théâtrale**, 2, no. 7
(January, 1960): 173.
Sauguet describes the changes that he made in the
score after the Berlin performance and explains why
he revised the work. See: W35.

B102.   -----. "Entretien avec Henri Sauguet à propos de
Cantate pour le Festival de Bordeaux." **Le Guide du
concert** no. 310 (21 April, 1961): 999.
Sauguet describes **Le Plus longue que la nuit et
le jour** (W38) which is to be premiered at the Mai musical de Bordeaux.

B103.   -----. "Henri Sauguet." **Courrier musical de France**
no. 57 (1977): 37-42.
Chamfray establishes a chronology for Sauguet's
life and works.

B104.   -----. "Henri Sauguet: Mélodie concertante pour
violoncelle et orchestre." **Courrier musical de
France** no. 37 (1972): 116.
The **Second Quartet** (W91), so well known since its
appearance, is paired with **Mélodie concertante** (W80),
a recent work. One is as good and attractive as the
other, and the match provides a way to judge the evolution of Sauguet's development. See: D19.

B105.   -----. "Musique de films." **Le Guide du concert** no.
257/258 (29 January-15 February, 1960): 366.
Sauguet's music for **Tu es Pierre** (W352) is almost
a symphonic work. The first half of the film is the
best and gives the composer the most freedom of creativity. He even includes a kind of divertissement
during the scene of the marriage at Cana. The second
half relates the period between the death of Pius XII
and the election of John XXIII.

B106.   -----. "Ou va la musique française?" **Le Guide du
concert** no. 213 (5 December, 1958): 410-412.
It seems that in certain musical circles there is
a panic to join the serial or dodecaphonic wave which
is new and truly international. This wave has, up to
now only inundated the unfortunates who were at first
drowned in the teachings of the Conservatoire or the
Scholars.

B107.   Champigneulle, Bernard. "Concert de plein air à Aix-
en-Provence." **France illustration** no. 402 (September, 1953): 101.
The audience seemed to enjoy the more conservative
works. Even the **Concert d'Orphée** (W77) by Sauguet
seemed to irritate the audience a little. The role
of the festival should be, however, to expose young
musicians and the public to creations of its own
time.

B108.   Chantevoine, Jean.   **Petite guide de l'auditeur de mu-
        sique.** Paris: Plon, 1947.
        Concert no. 1 (W75) is described.

B109.   Chantevoine, Jean, and Jean Gaudefroy-Demombyues.
        Romantisme dans la musique europeéene. Paris:
        Albin Michel, 1955.
        La Chartreuse de Parme (W4) is compared to earlier
        operas because of its use of ballet.

B110.   Chauviré, Yvette. "La Musique intérieure; A conver-
        sation with Yvette Chauviré by Otis Stuart." **Ballet
        international** 7, no. 6/7 (June/July, 1984):   24-27.
        When Chauviré premiered **Les Mirages** (W24) she gave
        her best effort because it was such a special work with
        complete balance between choreography, music, and de-
        cor.

B111.   Chion, Michel, and Guy Reibel. **Les Musiques electro-
        acoustiques.** Aix-en-Provence: C. Y. Chaudoreille,
        1976.
        References to **Aspect sentimental** (W324).

B112.   "Chronique musicale--En matinée." **Le Figaro,** 30 March,
        1930, 8.
        Pierre Monteux and L'Orchestre symphonique de Paris
        premiere the suite from **La Nuit** (W47).

B113.   Chujoy, Anatole. **The New York City Ballet.** New York:
        A. A. Knopf, 1953.
        Sauguet, **La Chatte** (W14), and **Fastes** (W19) cited
        in connection with possible commission by NYC Ballet
        of **Cordélia** (W29). The commission came to nought,
        and it was accomplished for the Grand Ballet du Marquis
        de Cuevas.

B114.   Chujoy, Anatole, and P. W. Manchester. **The Dance
        encyclopedia.** Rev. and enlarged ed. New York:
        Simon & Schuster, 1967.
        Contains references to Sauguet, Les Ballets 1933,
        and Serge Diaghilev and his Ballets russe.

B115.   "La Cigale, Soirées de Paris." **L'Annuaire des artistes**
        34 (1925): 319.
        In Metra's celebrated waltz there was a theme which
        inspired **Les roses** (W13).

B116.   Clarendon. "Un 'Cantate' de Sauguet." **Le Figaro,** 6
        September, 1960, 18.
        It was dangerous to program **L'Oiseau a vu tout
        cela** (W209) so closely to Bach's <u>Cantata</u> <u>202</u> at the
        Festival de Besançon, but it was a great success. The
        poem departs radically from Sauguet's usual style and
        opens with a twelve note theme which gives it a do-
        decaphonic effect. All the verses were used in a man-
        ner somewhat like Gregorian chant. The voice perfect-
        ly decried all the realism of the horrors of the poem.
        It is rich in highly colored pages, and has sincere
        images of pathos which does Sauguet honor.

B117.   Clarendon. "Le Mai artistique de Bordeaux a debute
        sous le signe de l'Espagne." **Le Figaro**, 18 May,
        1951, 6.
        This year, at least, the concerts will recognize
        a Bordelais composer and offer the premiere of Henri
        Sauguet's **Les Saisons** (W28).

B118.   -----. "Marseilles au Théâtre des Champs-Elysées--
        Triptyque d'opéras bouffes." **Le Figaro**, 1 october,
        1957, 14.
        As for **La Contrebasse** (W3) the work stretches to
        excess a situation which otherwise would have been
        amusing.

B119.   -----. "Musique 'moderne' au Conservatoire." **Le
        Figaro**, 8 April, 1960, 20.
        What better and more charming image can there be
        than Henri Sauguet's suite from **Les Forains** (W52)?
        As for the **Guirlande** (W63) I prefer not to comment on
        the individual contributions.

B120.   -----. "'La Nuit,' d'Henri Sauguet--Ellabelle Davis."
        Le Figaro, 26 April, 1949, 4.
        His music is agreeable and charming by itself, but
        it does not seem to give body to the ballet, nor ex-
        actly reflect the ambiance suggested by Bérard in **La
        Nuit** (W17).

B121.   -----. "L'Orchestre de la reine de Belgique." **Le
        Figaro**, 12 November, 1948, 18.
        Among other items the orchestra, conducted by
        Franz André, performed Sauguet's **Rêverie symphonique**
        (W66).

B122.   -----. "La Symphonie d'Henri Sauguet." **Le Figaro**,
        10 February, 1948, 4.
        A lengthy review of **Symphony no. 1** (W53) which
        concludes: The faults of the vast work are visible.
        Sauguet is not a born symphonist. He doesn't develop
        ideas, he juxtaposes and repeats them. All this is
        not to ridicule the musician. He is an essayist, and
        this is his first novel. It is necessary to try some-
        thing for the first time to see what is necessary to
        make it better.

B123.   Clarke, Mary. "Obituary." **Dancing times** no. 948
        (1989): 1124.

B124.   Clarke, Mary, and Clement Crisp. **Ballet art from the
        renaissance to the present.** New York: Clarkson N.
        Potter, 1978.
        Citations for **La Chatte** (W14) and **La Nuit** (W17)
        along with acknowledgement of Sauguet's work for Les
        Ballets 1933, but no mention of **Les Roses** (W13).

B125.   Cliquet-Pleyel, Henri. "Témoignages et souvenirs.
        L'Ecole d'Arcueil." **Combat**, 1 June, 1953, 8.
        An article by another member of L'Ecole d'Arcueil
        who considers Sauguet the closest inheritor of Satie's

philosophy. He cites **Les Forains** (W25) and the **Sonnets de Louise Labé** (W230) as outstanding.

B126.   Clouzot, Marie-Rose. "Sauguet." **Musik in Geschichte
und Gegenwart.** Wiesbaden: Bärenreiter Verlag,
1949-1986.
Biographical sketch with bibliography and works
list.

B127.   -----. "Sonatine aux Bois." **Guide musical,** 8 January,
1972, 4.
The most recent work, full of freshness and poetry.
See: W112.

B128.   Cœuroy, André. "Ballets russes." **Revue universelle**
30, no. 10 (15 August, 1927): 487-490.
Sauguet seems to have escaped the worst of Satie
and appears to be a sensible musician. **La Chatte** (W14)
confirms the fine and clear poetry of his earlier
works like the **Françaises** (W141, W143).

B129.   -----. "La Chartreuse de Parme." **Gringoire,** 19 March,
1939, 7.
There is a certain tenderness held together by refined irony in the opera (W4). Some of the music
seems to exist in the shadow of Mozart, Rossini, Verdi
or Chabrier; some of it is good Sauguet, like the ballet music, the berceuse, or the vocal quintet.

B130.   -----. "a Musique--Ballets." **Gringoire,** 16 June,
1933, 11.
Refers to the "vacuity of Sauguet in **Fastes** (W19)."

B131.   -----. "'Œdipus' and other music heard in Paris."
Modern music 5, no. 1 (November/December, 1927):
39-42.
The composer of **La Chatte** (W14) is a Satie pupil
who revealed a well defined personality. He still
leans on Auric and Poulenc, though he lacks the Gallic
bite of the former and the sensuous grace of the latter. He commands a bright and limpid poetry and knows
how to handle his orchestra to suit his temperament.

B132.   Cogniat, Raymond. **Cinquante ans de spectacles en
France. Les Décorateurs de théâtre.** Paris: Lib-
rarie Théâtrale, 1959.
Numerous citations of stage productions in which
Sauguet was a participant, including sketches of stage
designs for **Les Mirages** (W24), **Cordélia** (W29), **Les
Caprices de Marianne** (W6), **Ondine** (W364), **M. et Mme.
Roméo** (W374), **Dom Juan** (W379), **Les Fourberies de
Scapin** (W381), and **Comme il vous plaira** (W386).

B133.   Cohn, Arthur. **Recorded classical music; a critical
guide.** New York: Schirmer Books, 1981.
Contains citations and brief comments on **Les Trois
lys** (W61), **Mélodie concertante** (W80), **Soliloque** (W174),
and **Suite royale** (W159). See: D37, D39, D40, D28.

B134.   Collaer, Paul. "La Chartreuse de Parme, d'Henri Sau-
        guet." **La Revue internationale de musique** 2, no. 7
        (January, 1940): 47-48.
        The opera (W4) is reminiscent in a sense of the
        grand operas of Berlioz, Gounod, and Verdi. Like
        their work this one contains a high degree of dramatic
        and melodic invention which is so precious and so rare.
        You will be convinced of this when you hear it for the
        first time because of the music's beauty and dramatic
        appropriateness.

B135.   -----.   "L'Edition musicale--Musiques moderne. Œuvres
        de la Renaissance." **L'Europe nouvelle** no. 654 (23
        August, 1930): 1217-1218.
        La Nuit (W17), how blue and transparent, how
        Sauguet makes us love it. He paints it for us with
        rare delicacy of tone. His melodic traits are solid
        but very refined and bear the imprint of an authentic
        personality.

B136.   -----   **La Musique moderne, 1905-1955.** Paris ; Brussels:
        Elsevier, 1955.
        Collaer's volume is worth reading for the non-Ger-
        manic bias survey of early twentieth century music.
        The chronology is also quite interesting. "La musique
        française après les 'Six'" suggests that Sauguet is
        the only member of the Arcueil School worth discussing
        as a composer. In particular **La Chartreuse de Parme**
        (W4) is cited for its anticipation of a return to real
        operatic composition which is confirmed, in Collaer's
        opinion, by Britten's Peter Grimes.

B137.   -----.   "'Wozzek' d'Alban Berg; 'Suite' D'Arnold
        Schœnberg; œuvres de Satie, Milhaud, Poulenc, Sau-
        guet." **L'Europe nouvelle** no. 595 (6 July, 1929):
        935-936.
        Among the new collections by Henri Sauguet, **Quatre
        poèmes de Schiller** (W231), "L'Apparition" and "Le Sou-
        venir" are especially appealing. These two pages are
        great and beautiful music, simple and strong, sober
        and moving. They are among the most beautiful songs
        of modern literature.

B138.   Colpi, Henri. **Defense et illustration de la musique
        dans le film.** Lyon: Société d'édition, de recher-
        ches et de documentaire cinématographique, 1962.
        Brief biographical citation and discography con-
        concerning the appearance of the music to **Farrebique**
        (W337) on the recording Vingt-cinq ans de cinéma (D55).
        André Cluytens conducted a program of film scores on
        a Concerts Colonne program in 1951 which featured an
        unnamed work by Sauguet. This may have been **Symphonies
        de la montagne** (W50) from **Premier de cordée** (W336).

B139.   Comité national pour la celebration du centennaire de
        Claude Debussy. **Claude Debussy, 1862-1962, Livre
        d'or.** Paris: Richard-Masse, 1962. (Special number
        of **La Revue musicale**)
        The document of the Debussy centennial year. On

24 October, 1962, Sauguet spoke on "Debussy, révolu-
tion permanente" as part of the conference entitled
"Debussy et l'évolution de la musique au XXe siècle."
Sauguet also contributed an article to the issue.
(See: S214)

B140.   Core, Philip. **The Original eye; arbiters of 20th
century taste.** Englewood Cliffs: Prentice-Hall,
1984.
Among the plates in the volume is one which depicts
"The rehearsing of a concert under the conductor Roger
Désormière, in the rococo ballroom of the Place des
Etats-Unis mansion." It shows Sauguet standing next
to the shirt-sleeved Désormières on the podium. Also
in the photograph are Francis Poulenc and Georges Auric
in the ensemble. The instrumentation seems to be that
of **La Voyante** (W201).

B141.   Cossart, Michel de. **The Food of love: Princess Edmond
de Polignac (1865-1943) and her salon.** London: Ham-
mish Hammilton, 1979.
A good narration concerning Sauguet and his participation in the salon of Winnaretta Singer for whom
he wrote **Les Jeux de l'amour et du hassard** (W127).
The two-piano piece was later transformed into **Le
Dompteur dompte** (W20).

B142.   "La Couronne de Marguerite Long." **Le Figaro,** 18 December, 1957, 14.
To celebrate in music the birthday of Marguerite
Long composers have woven a crown for her braids,
taking letters from her name and matching them to the
scale degrees according to German notation. To my
taste the pearls of the crown are . . . Henri Sauguet,
his **Berceuse** (W63) is a success.

B143.   "Courrier musical." **Le Figaro,** 26 June, 1932, 7.
During the course of the dance gala given by the
great artist of the Théâtre des Champs-Elysées on
Tuesday evening, 29 June, Mlle. Nikitina will present
new creations. The group of scenic artists and composers who will aid Mlle. Nikitina to mount her spectacle includes names of the most celebrated artists
alive. See: W18.

B144.   Covington, Kate R. "Non Morietur in Aeternum, for
trumpet and organ." **Notes** 41, no. 2 (1984): 374-
375.
Characteristics of Satie's music are evident in
the piece (W118). Harmonies are often ambiguous and
varied. There is no traditional tonal return sig-
naling the return of a section; they are, rather, sig-
nified by a return of tempo, rhythm and melodic con-
tour. It is a good student piece, but there are no
registrations for the organ.

B145.   Crosland, Margaret C. **Piaf.** London: Hodder & Stough-
ton, 1985.
Interesting but undocumented information about the

creation of **Le Chemin des forains** (W297) which impli-
cates Christian Bérard as an intercessor between Sauguet and Piaf.

B146.   Cuneo-Laurent, Linda. "The Performer as catalyst.
The role of the singer Jane Bathori (1877-1970) in
the careers of Debussy, Ravel, 'Les Six,' and their
contemporaries in Paris, 1904-1926." Ph.D. diss.,
New York University, 1982.
The work contains considerable information about
the interaction between Sauguet and Bathori, especially
during his early days in Paris.

B147.   Daguerre, Pierre. **Le Marquis de Cuevas.** Paris:
Denoel, 1954.
Descriptions of **Les Saisons** (W28) and **Cordélia**
(W29).

B148.   Dale, R. C. **The Films of René Clair.** New York: Scare-
crow Press, 1986.
In October, 1968, the Société nouvelle des Acacias
released a sound version of <u>Entr'acte</u> for which Sauguet
conducted Satie's score.

B149.   Dale, S. S. "Contemporary cello concerti; 22: Henri
Sauguet and Bohuslav Martinu." **The Strad** 85 (November, 1974): 413.
The **Mélodie concertante** (W80) is akin to the Schumann piano concerto. The material is shared rather
than fought over by the orchestra and the soloist.

B150.   Dalí, Salvador. **Journal d'une génie.** Paris: La
Table ronde, 1964.
Entry for 23 August, 1953, notes a meeting between
Dalí, Sauguet, Serge Lifar, and Baron Philippe de
Rothschild concerning work on a ballet. This was prob-
ably an abortive attempt on **Le Sacre de l'automne** (W32).

B151.   "Danse." **Le Monde,** 23 May, 1951, 9.
Gustave Cloez originally conducted L'Orchestre de
la radiodiffusion nationale in a radio broadcast of
the **Symphonie allégorique** (W57) which, with the aid
of Jacques Dupont, has been transformed into **Les Saisons** (W28)

B152.   **Danse à Paris.** Paris: Editions Dell'arte, 1983.
The collection of pieces by Boris Kochno ("Preface"), Marcel Schneider ("Ballets des Champs-Elysées"),
and Marcelle Michel ("Festival International de Danse
de Paris") contains information on **Les Forains** W25),
La Rencontre (W26), and **La Dame aux camélias** (W35).

B153.   "Dansé plus cent fois, en trois années." **Le Guide du
concert** no. 17 (25 January, 1935): 441.
Preparatory to a performance of the orchestral
suite from **La Chatte** (W45) the announcement describes
the ballet (W14) as having been presented more than
100 times during three years.

B154.   "David." **Nouvelle revue musicale** 26, no. 2 (December
         1928): 52.
            David (W15) is infantile in comparison to **La Chatte**
         (W14).

B155.   Davies, Lawrence. **The Gallic muse.** London: Dent,
         1967.
            Les Forains (W25) is compared to Satie's Parade.
         The British author grants begrudging praise to Sauguet
         as a song writer of some repute.

B156.   "De Marc-Antoine Charpentier à Henri Sauguet." **Le**
         Monde, 11 March, 1964, 16.
            Brief notice of a performance of **La Voyante** (W201)
         at "Studio d'Arlequin," Théâtre Grévin.

B157.   Decharnes, Robert. **Salvador Dalí, the work, the man.**
         New York: Harry N. Abrams, 1984.
            The author states that only the cartoons for **Le**
         Sacre de l'automne (W32) were left of the unfulfilled
         project. He implies that "The Grape pickers" (also
         entitled "The Chariot of Dionysus") is a sketch for
         the stage design.

B158.   Delannoy, Marcel. "La Gageure imprévue." **Les Nouveaux**
         temps, 24 April, 1944, 3.
            Only between the lightness of the vocal parts in
         the opera (W5) and the weight of the orchestra is
         there a contradiction. The composer is at the height
         of his career but does not show overconfidence. He
         still retains a mixture of naturalness and a lack of
         pretense which this critic finds desirable although
         some others may not.

B159.   Demarquez, Suzanne. "A. M. C." **L'Information musi-**
         cale, 14 March, 1941, 494-495.
            Three songs, "Le Printemps," "Pardon," "L'Hiver,"
         and **Trois françaises** (W141) (one brisk and lively,
         another languid, the third frantic) are excellent pro-
         ductions from his pen.

B160.   -----. "Aix-en-Provence." **Musical courrier** no. 150
         (September, 1954): 25.
            Sauguet's music is charming from beginning to end.
         The work is more like a lyric conversation with con-
         tinuous melodic dialogue. The **Caprices** (W6) is filled
         with fantasy, nostalgia and emotional tenderness which
         combine beautifully in the ravishing monologue sung
         at the window by Marianne.

B161.   -----. "Boulez dirige Mozart." **Les Lettres françaises**
         no. 1,056 (26 November-2 December, 1964): 4.
            Over time the **Concerto no. 1** (W75) has proven its
         charm. Such care in writing has always been one of
         the qualities of our race. Why do the so-called young
         turks form factions at the concerts and set themselves
         against it and embarrass themselves?

B162.   -----. "Concerts symphoniques." **Les Lettres fran-**

çaises no. 1,022 (26-31 March, 1964): 11.
The years have robbed nothing from **Les Forains**
(W25). It is still completely charming, refined, and
filled with sweet melancolic sensitivity.

B163.   Demarquez, Suzanne. "Dimitri Markevitch." **Le Guide
du concert** no. 131 (16 November, 1956): 261.
The cascading arpeggios of the **Sonate** (W172) pre-
cede the theme which exhibits intimate poetry. The
work seems to fall spontaneously from the tip of his
pen.

B164.   -----. "Festival Henri Sauguet." **Les Lettres françaises** no. 904 (7 December, 1961): 7.
In the **Concerto d'Orphée** (W77) the violin rises
little by little over the organized chaos of the orchestra and proclaims, one more time, the victory of
melody. The **Third Symphony** (W62) is a symphonic poem
but organized into three sections: Impetuous, Noble,
and Resolute, the first letter of each expressing the
symbol of Radio Belgium. Finally, in **La Mort de la
Dame aux camélias** (W65) the motive of two notes des-
cending slowly within the murmur of the orchestra is
sufficient for Sauguet to recreate the ambiance of
the drama and to sustain the emotion.

B165.   -----. "Festival Henri Sauguet à l'occasion de son
soixantième anniversaire." **Le Guide du concert**
no. 332 (1 December, 1961): 477-478.
In the **Concerto d'Orphée** (W77) it is the violin
which sings madly a melody of infinite beauty which
moves from the depths of a passionate orchestra which
attemps to subsume it or at least to combat it. It
seems as if the entire art of Sauguet has been written
into the last page of the **Symphony no. 3** (W62). **La
Mort de la dame aux camélias** (W65) is so expressive
that it seems to recreate before your very eyes the
entire last scene of the ballet.

B166.   -----. "Gala Debussy at la S.A.C.E.M." **Les Lettres
françaises** no. 949 (25 October, 1962): 7.
How can one put a value on the spiritual vivacity
of the "allegro moderato" and the tender revery of
the "Lento quasi adagio" in the **Concerto no. 1** (W75)?

B167.   -----. "Hommage à Mme. Beriza." **L'Information musicale**, 11 June, 1943, 353.
La Plumet du Colonel (W1) expresses the witty and
clever side of Sauguet.

B168.   -----. "Le Mai de Versailles." **Les Lettres françaises**
no. 879 (8 June, 1961): 6.
The art of Sauguet, expressed in **Le Cornette** (W208)
has a subtle and personal poetry, but it does not ex-
clude forceful writing when necessary.

B169.   -----. "Le Micropéra." **Les Lettres françaises** no.
1,021 (18-24 March, 1964): 11.
Brief notice of a performance of **La Voyante** (W201).

B170.   Demarquez, Suzanne. "Mises en scène à Aix-en-Provence."
        Les Lettres françaises no. 943 (13 September, 1962):
        8.
            Brief mention of the premier of **Les Caprices de
        Marianne** (W6).

B171.   -----. "Musiques contemporaines et autres." **Les Let-
        tres françaises** no. 921 (5 April, 1962): 7.
            Sauguet, along with Milhaud, Barraud, Françaix,
        and Dutilleux endorse a newly formed chamber orchestra
        for contemporary music.

B172.   -----. "Orchestre de la Reine Elisabeth de Belgique."
        Le Guide du concert no. 213 (5 December, 1958): 423.
            Henri Sauguet's **Solitude** (W66) precisely suggests
        a rêverie symphonique. It depicts a road which his
        muse has shown him and which calmly traverses a pretty
        countryside.

B173.   -----. "Paris." **Musical courrier** no. 161 (April,
        1960): 31.
            Brief mention of **La Dame aux camélias** (W35).

B174.   -----. "Paris and Bordeaux stage novelties." **Musical
        courrier** no. 57 (August, 1951): 8.
            Brief mention of the premier of **Les Saisons** (W28).

B175.   -----. "Pierre Bernac et Francis Poulenc." **L'Infor-
        mation musicale**, 26 June, 1942, 999-1000.
            Henri Sauguet's **Deux poèmes de Tagore** (W237) under-
        lines the concentrated emotion beneath the simple de-
        cor of inspiration.

B176.   -----. "Premier Audition--Symphonie allégorique."
        Le Guide du concert no. 249/250 (20 November-6 De-
        cember, 1959): 184.
            The critique is primarily descriptive of the pro-
        gram of the symphony (W57) rather than an appraisal
        of the music. "I think that the music of Sauguet, so
        direct, and animated by a sincere emotion, truly cor-
        responds to the philosophical thoughts he wanted to
        transmit.

B177.   -----. "Rostropovitch." **Les Lettres françaises** no.
        1,060 (24-30 December, 1964): 7.
            Is this a bet that the composer made with himself?
        In any case he has launched into a particularly dif-
        ficult enterprise which requires him to construct a
        compact melody that can be transformed and lend it-
        self to fantasy. The great lyric spirit of the **Mélo-
        die concertante** (W80) perfectly lends itself to the
        virtuosity displayed here.

B178.   -----. "Les semaines musicales internationales." **Les
        Lettres françaises** no. 1,047 (24-30 September, 1964):
        11.
            An announcement of the festival's events which in-
        cludes Rostropovitch's performance of Sauguet's **Mélo-
        die concertante** (W80).

B179.   Demarquez, Suzanne. "Le Triptyque." **L'Information**
        musicale 12 June, 1942, 973.
        The **Trois Duos** (W240) carry the impulsive, witty,
        and fresh mark of their composer.

B180.   Demuth, Norman. **Musical trends in the twentieth cen-**
        tury. London: Rockliff, 1952.
        The **Second Quartet** (W91) is square, but it is a
        useful work and an indication of the Gallic concept
        of classicism.

B181.   "Deux réprésentations supplémentaires des Ballets
        russes." **Le Figaro,** 9 June, 1927, 6.
        Unprecented success creates a need for additional
        performances at the Théâtre Sarah-Bernhardt. **La Chatte**
        (W14) was on the bill for the extra performances.

B182.   Devay, Jean-François. "Un Festival International de
        Musique se déroulera à Aix-en-Provence du 16 au 31
        juillet." **Combat,** 9 June, 1949, 2.
        Announcement of the season at Aix-en-Provence
        which includes the **Second String Quartet** (W91).

B183.   ------. "La Saison des ballets prend fin ce soir à
        l'Opéra où Jean Vilar et Claude Nollier vont créer
        prochainement 'Jeanne au bucher.'" **Combat,** 28 July,
        1950, 2.
        Among the attractions in the season to come **Le**
        Sacre de l'Automne (W32) by Henri Sauguet with sets
        by Salvador Dalí is listed.

B184.   Didier, Béatrice. "Hommage à Henri Sauguet." **Europe:**
        Revue littéraire mensuelle 59, no. 631 (1981): 226-
        228.
        An eightieth birthday salute to Sauguet, the Gi-
        ronde, and to the Mai musical de Bordeaux which will
        feature a concert of his music.

B185.   ------. "Musique à quatre." **Europe: Revue littéraire**
        mensuelle 64, no. 690 (1986): 200-202.
        The **Second String Quartet** (W91) which received its
        premier at the Festival d'Aix by the Calvet Quartet,
        was written during the period after Sauguet had lost
        his mother. It is charged with anguish, but a sub-
        lime anguish, in which the movements are balanced like
        those of a classic quartet. The work is attractive
        because of its flowing melodic line and its richness
        of harmony. The **Third Quartet** (W100) is equally as
        good.

B186.   ------. "Requiem pour Henri Sauguet." **Europe: Revue**
        littéraire mensuelle 66, no. 724 (1989): 178-180.
        Obituary.

B187.   Dior, Christian. **Christian Dior et moi.** Paris: Amiot-
        Dumont, 1956.
        Dior describes Sauguet of the late twenties as a
        real cut-up with lively eyes, sparkling with malice
        behind his spectacles. He possessed immense mobility

in his face and intelligence and humor in his talk. At Max Jacob's apartment in the Hôtel Nollet Sauguet and Christian Bérard, costumed in lampshades, bedspreads and curtains, would turn themselves into all the characters of history.

B188.   Downes, Olin. "Doda Conrad, bass, presents recital." **New York Times**, 26 January, 1953, 16.
The **Mouvements du cœur** (W251) is on the satirical side.

B189.   -----. "Doda Conrad gives original program." **New York Times**, 29 December, 1949, 16.
The **Visions infernales** (W250) are songs of death, somewhat fantastical and morbid, but songs of real individuality of idiom and expression.

B190.   -----. "French composer Henri Sauguet, visiting America, talks about his life, art, and philosophy." **New York Times**, 19 April, 1953, sec. 2, 7.
The **Cardinal aux chats** (W31) is described. Sauguet plays the part of Richelieu in the ballet.

B191.   -----. "Music by Sauguet heard at Museum." **New York Times**, 24 April, 1953, 18.
La Voyante (W201) is a very amusing and original song cycle, not only very diverting but distinguished in its verbal manipulation.

B192.   Drew, David. "Modern French music." In **European music in the twentieth century**, edited by Howard Hartog. New York: Praeger, 1957.
Drew considers Sauguet better than Françaix. Although Satie is said to have been his master, Gounod is his true spiritual forebear. An interesting comparison of Sauguet to his contemporaries is made with emphasis placed on **La Voyante** (W201), **Bocages** (W92), **Concerto d'Orphée** (W77), **Symphonie no. 3** (W62), and the **Caprices de Marianne** (W6).

B193.   Drummond, John. **Diaghilev**. London: BBC-TV, 1967?
Reel II contains photographs from **La Chatte** (W14) and an interview with Sauguet.

B194.   Dufourcq, Norbert. **La Musique des origines à nos jours**. Paris: Larousse, 1946.
Brief biographical sketches of members of L'Ecole d'Arcueil. **La Chartreuse de Parme** (W4) contains some excellent pages, and **La Voyante** (W201) and **Concerto no. 1** (W75) attain real mastery.

B195.   Du Gard, Maurice-Martin. "Spectacle du Rideau, Théâtre de l'Avenue." **Les Nouvelles littéraires, artistiques et scientifiques**, 18 March, 1933, 8.
The excellent music of Henri Sauguet for **Le Retour de l'enfant prodigue** (W362) once again made the shepherd king sing.

B196.   Duke, Vernon. **Passport to Paris**. Boston: Little,

Brown & Co., 1955.
Comment on an unnamed composition by Sauguet on a High-Low Concert in 1938.

B197.   Dumesnil, René. "Aix-en-Provence aux Champs-Elysées --Les Caprices de Marianne." **Le Monde**, 9 June, 1956, 9.
Henri Sauguet has surrendered himself in the **Caprices** (W6) to the light atmosphere of Naples from the chiming of the bells when one arises until the last notes have faded away in the evening. Everything here is happy, fresh, like the voice of the birds, like the Mlle. Graziella Sciutti.

B198.   -----. "L'Année chorégraphique." **Le Monde**, 8-9 August, 1948, 3.
The combination of all the elements in **Les Mirages** (W24) made it an assured part of the repertoire.

B199.   -----. "Ballets des Champs-Elysées." **Le Monde**, 11 November, 1948, 6.
Sauguet's music for **La Rencontre** (W26) is one of his best scores. Expressive, rhythmic and colorfully orchestrated, it allows the themes to express themselves. It transposes the sets of Bérard and the choreography of Lichine successfully into a harmonious spectacle.

B200.   -----. "Ballets des Champs-Elysées--La Nuit." **Le Monde**, 21 April, 1949, 6.
Sauguet's music for **La Nuit** (W17) contributes to the melancholy note of the ballet in a way that the composer most happily was able to obtain in his **Les Forains** (W25).

B201.   -----. "Ballets des Champs-Elysées 'La Nuit.'" **Le Monde. Section hebdomadaire**, 22-28 April, 1949, 6.
Essentially a repeat of B200. <u>See</u>: W17

B202.   -----. "Ballets des Champs-Elysées--La Rencontre ou Œdipe et le Sphinx." **Le Monde. Section hebdomadaire**, 13-19 November, 1948, 4.
The music for **La Rencontre** (W26) by M. Henri Sauguet is one of his best scores. Expressive and very rhythmical, colorfully orchestrated with thematic material of value, it transposes the sets into sound.

B203.   -----. "Les Concerts." **Le Monde**, 10 February, 1948, 6.
The beginning of the **Symphony no. 1** (W53) seemed hesitant, sometimes feeble. In the finale at last the writing firms up and is better balanced in its development. The ability to handle the contrasts and the dissonances is happily at odds with this lack in the preceding parts.

B204.   -----. "Les Concerts--Jean-Fery Rebel--Henri Sauguet." **Le Monde**, 2 January, 1952, 9.
Le Cornette (W208) is conceived in the manner of

a troubadour chanson; the orchestra score is rhapsodic, and the voice recites the epic of Rilke. Sauguet's music is in complete, intimate agreement with the text.

B205.   Dumesnil, René. "Les Concerts--Lorin Maazel et Sauguet." **Le Monde**, 25 November, 1964, 19.
　　　　Maazel stands aside to let Sauguet conduct his **Concert no. 1** (W75).

B206.   -----. "Les Concerts--Société des concerts: Quatuor Champeil." **Le Monde**, 12 December, 1950, 8.
　　　　The Quatuor Champeil was formed to be at the service of contemporary music. It has a fervor which allows them to play impeccably. Brief mention of the **Quartet no. 2** (W91).

B207.   -----. "Les Concerts--La Symphonie allégorique." **Le Monde**, 2 November, 1949, 6.
　　　　A lengthy and somewhat analytic review that comments that the **Symphony** (W57) contains six movements and lasts one hour and fifteen minutes. This is a tremendous undertaking in this day and age.

B208.   -----. "Les Concerts--R. Boutry, P. Sancan, H. Sauguet, J. Ibert." **Le Monde**, 25 March, 1964, 12.
　　　　Les Forains (W52) is a faithful depiction of the precarious condition of the humble traveling circus whose life depends on the caprice of the masses.

B209.   -----. "Créations et reprises en 1951 à l'Opéra." **Le Monde**, 1 February, 1951, 9.
　　　　Among the projects is a ballet by Henri Sauguet with sets by Salvador Dalí. See: W32.

B210.   -----. "La Dame aux camélias--Les partitions." **Le Monde**, 5 February, 1960, 12.
　　　　To write the music for **La Dame aux camélias** (W35) and deprive it of the support of the warmth and passion of the human voice reduces its role to something that only provides rhythm for the dances which comment on the story in the same way as does the mime theater. This explains why the new work appears uneven.

B211.   -----. "La Danse--Les Ballets du Théâtre Sarah-Bernhardt." **Le Monde**, 19 June, 1945, 7.
　　　　The music for **Les Forains** (W25), by the obstinate repetition of the same phrase, creates an atmosphere of discouragement.

B212.   -----. "Dernier concert de la Société." **Le Monde**, 8 April, 1960, 13.
　　　　At a concert honoring Marguerite Long Jean Gittou conducts the **Variations sur le nom de Marguerite Long** (W63) and **Les Forains Suite** (W52).

B213.   -----. "Deux premières auditions d'Henri Sauguet aux Champs-Elysées." **Le Monde**, 8 June, 1963, 18.
　　　　The text of **Le Cornette** (W208) finds in Sauguet a musician whose temperament is in perfect accord with

the poetry. The **Concert no.** 3 (W79) was suggested to
the composer by Baudelaire's exploration and description of a subterranean grotto. All the elements are
organized in a fashion which allows for surprise, but
never gives the impression of incoherence.

B214.   Demesnil, René. "Les Disques--H. Sauguet: Les Fo-
        rains." **Le Monde,** 1 March, 1956, 13.
        Rarely have artists found themselves in better a-
        greement than Sauguet, Bérard, Kochno, and Petit when
        they created **Les Forains** (W25). Sauguet's music seems
        like a transposition into sound of Bérard's sets and
        costumes. See: D49.

B215.   -----. "Les Disques: Henri Sauguet--Jean Langlais."
        Le Monde, 18-19 August, 1962, 11.
        The scope of the recording which contains **Les an-**
        imaux et leurs maîtres (W224), **Divertissement de**
        chambre (W85), **Neiges** (W242) and **Trois duos** (W240) is
        nearly biographical. The music displays a richness
        of inspiration and a facility to reuse the common ele-
        ments in a new way. See: D19.

B216.   -----. "Les Disques--Musique instrumentale." **Le Monde,**
        20 December, 1962, 19.
        Brief review of Chant du Monde (LCX 8 300) release
        of **Concerto no.** 1 (W75) and **Les Forains** (W25). See:
        D17.

B217.   -----. "Les Disques. Musique lyrique." **Le Monde,** 17
        October, 1962, 14.
        Brief review of Chant du Monde (LCS A 8 292) which
        contains Satie's Socrate and has extensive program
        notes by Sauguet. The same information was repeated
        in the 8 November, 1962, issue of **Le Monde** on p.13.

B218.   -----. "Les Mirages." **Le Monde,** 20 December, 1947,
        6.
        M. Henri Sauguet has written music for **Les Mirages**
        (W24) which has a texture that easily offers abundant
        material for the choreographer.

B219.   -----. "La Musique." **Mercure de France** no. 291 (1
        May, 1939): 677-679.
        An extensive analysis of **La Chartreuse de Parme**
        (W4) which suggests the impossibility of setting such
        a huge novel as an opera, but Sauguet has done so with
        rare perfection.

B220.   -----. "La Musique." **Le Monde,** 29 May, 1927, 9.
        Brief mention of a performance by the American
        Ellabelle Davis performing the "Berceuse créole" from
        Le Plumet du Colonel (W1).

B221.   -----. "La Musique." **Le Monde,** 11 November, 1958,
        13.
        France was represented by **La Solitude** (W66), a
        rêverie symphonique by Henri Sauguet, which was given
        its premier. It is a dialogue with ones self. A

single motive undulates throughout the rather long
development and returns throughout the work to create
unity. The work is of good proportions and instru-
mented with skill.

B222.   Dumesnil, René. "La Musique--L'Année chorégraphique."
        Le Monde, 12 August, 1945, 5.
            With Les Forains (W25), which is already known,
        the true originality resides in more than the inven-
        tion of the set designer.

B223.   -----. "La Musique--Lamoureux: J.-B. Mari, Mme Vasso
        Devetzi." Le Monde, 16 October, 1962, 19.
            The Concerto no. 1 (W75) is a work which lightly
        carries the weight of time since its creation thirty
        years ago. It still contains the freshness and sin-
        cerity which was expressed in the care of its compo-
        sition due to the variety of its three movements and
        the briskness of the tarentella finale of the rondo.

B224.   -----. "La Musique--Nouveaux ballets à l'Opéra et à
        l'Opéra-Comique." Mercure de France no. 1,014 (1
        February, 1948): 334-337.
            The score for Les Mirages (W24) is all that one
        can wish for. Its principle merit is that it can be
        danced, something which is not at all as ordinary a
        quality that one may imagine.

B225.   -----. "La Musique--Société des concerts." Le Monde,
        20 March, 1956, 12.
            Brief mention of the performance of Variations sur
        un thème de Campra (W60) directed by Georges Tzipine.

B226.   -----. "Musiques de film." Le Monde, 23 October,
        1951, 8.
            Concerts Colonne, under Richard Blareau, presents
        a program of excerpts from film scores. Sauguet is
        among those represented on the bill. This could have
        been either Les Saisons et le jours (W54) or Sympho-
        nies de la montagne (W50).

B227.   -----. "Opéra--'Les Mirages.'" Le Monde, 17 Decem-
        ber, 1947, 5.
            Sauguet has written music for Les Mirages (W24)
        which has a rather light texture and offers abundant
        material for the choreographer to develop.

B228.   -----. "Les Spectacles--'La Gageure imprévue' à
        l'Opéra-Comique." Le Monde, 26 April, 1945, 3.
            The score reveals some real gifts and some draw-
        backs which may be less important. The orchestra,
        which is treated symphonically, imposes a barrier o-
        ver which the voices are never able to rise. See: W5.

B229.   -----. "'Variations pour Marguerite Long' au Chate-
        let." Le Monde, 22-23 December, 1957, 14.
            Brief notice of the Variations (W63) performed in
        honor of Marguerite Long in the Salle Gaveau.

B230.   Dumolin, Henri. "Aux Célestins une comédie musical
        'Boule de suifs' d'après Guy de Maupassant." **Le
        Progrès** (Lyon), 14 December, 1978, 12.
        The music for **Boule de suif** (W9) is elegant and
        heady like yesterday's perfume.

B231.   -----. "Création de 'Boule de Suif.'" **Le Progrès**
        (Lyon), 16 December, 1978, 13.
        Henri Sauguet has written light music which is
        ironic or tender. It is in the tradition of Massager
        or Hahn and never importunes or intrudes itself. He
        finds his true inspiration as a composer of ballets in
        the two imaginary intermezzos of the caf-conc' scene.

B232.   -----. "Des 13 au 21 decembre aux Célestins 'Boule
        de Suif.'" **Le Progrès** (Lyon), 13 December, 1978, 1.
        An interview with the creators of **Boule de suif**
        (W9) during which Sauguet describes his score as a
        work of our time which suggests poetry of an epoch
        and molds it so that the music and the poetry are in
        accord and make the text speak.

B233.   Dunoyer, Jean-Marie. "Paul Claudel chez Silvia Mon-
        fort 'Conversation dans le Loir-et-Cher.'" **Le Monde**,
        13 September, 1973, 15.
        Brief citation concerning the incidental music
        which Sauguet wrote and Raphaël Andia played on his
        guitar. <u>See</u>: W404.

B234.   "Duo concertante for clarinet and piano." **Music Jour-
        nal** 31 (February, 1973): 31-32.
        Brief citation noting a Town hall performance by
        Annie Kafavian, clarinet, and Warren Wilson, piano, in
        November, 1973, of the **Sonatine** (W114) for clarinet
        and piano.

B235.   Dupêchez, Charles. **Histoire de l'Opéra de Paris**.
        Paris: Perrin, 1984.
        Citations for **Les Mirages** (W24) and **La Dame aux
        camélias** (W35).

B236.   Duteurtre, Benoit. "Henri Sauguet." **Diapason-harmonie**
        no 351 (September, 1989): 24.
        Obituary.

B237.   Eaton, Quaintance. "Reports: U.S.--New York." **Opera
        news** 32, no. 14 (3 February, 1968): 30.
        Gageure imprévue (W5) performed at the Lincoln
        Center with staging by Jean-Louis Barrault and sets
        by Jacques Dupont. The production, which was accom-
        panied at the piano by George Schick, contained agree-
        able and melodious writing. Karen Altman also per-
        formed some songs, and Virgil Thomson paid Sauguet a
        tribute.

B238.   Ehinger, Hans. "Henri Sauguets Ballet 'Die fünf Eta-
        gen.'" **Neue Zeitschrift für Musik** 121 (April, 1950):
        138-139.
        He shuns experimental effects and only occasionally

includes sharp accents, in a masterly fashion, mind
you, to illustrate or underscore dramatic events.
See: W34.

B239.   Ellis, Stephen W. "Sauguet: The Garden's Concerto.
        Deux mouvements pour archets." **Fanfare** 5, no. 6
        (July/August, 1982): 98-100.
        The **Garden's concerto** (W81) is an engaging concer-
        to in the top ranks of works for that genre. It con-
        tains atonal elements and a general capriciousness
        that add variety to the requisite instrumental vir-
        tuosity. The **Deux mouvements** (W68) reflects a poetic
        structure which mirrors the dedicatee, Paul Gilson.
        The tension of the first movement resolves into a
        quick-step waltz in the second before fading off into
        silence. See: D36.

B240.   Emié, Louis. **Dialogues avec Max jacob.** Paris: Cor-
        rêa, Buchet et Chastel, 1954.
        Contains quotations from Sauguet concerning his
        work with Jacob on **Un Amour du Titien** (W2)

B241.   -----. **Louis Emié.** Paris: Seghers, 1961.
        Contains citations about the joint projects of
        Complaint (W200), **Les Trois cygnes** (W222), and **Uriel**
        (W434).

B242.   Erickson, Franck. "Le Cinéma redonne vie à l'opéra."
        L'Avant scènes opèra no. 98 (1987): 181.
        During an interview with Henri Sauguet the compo-
        ser expresses hope that film will reinstate and popu-
        larize opera with a wider audience. An example pointed
        out is Ingmar Bergman's Magic Flute. Concerning the
        power of music, Sauguet relates: "One day Salvador
        Dalí said to me: 'I do not like music because it is
        not able to describe an egg sitting flat on a chair.'
        I responded, 'Yes, but it may be able to describe the
        nausea felt in seeing that egg.'"

B243.   "Etudes musicales analytiques." **Le Guide du concert**
        no. 23 (March, 1930): 650.
        Descriptive analysis of **David** (W46), noting its
        performance as an orchestral suite by Concerts Pasde-
        loup and D.-E. Inghelbrecht. The ballet (W15) was
        performed in Milan, Vienna, Monte-Carlo and Brussels,
        besides its premier in Paris.

B244.   "Etudes musicales analytiques." **Le Guide du concert**
        no. 26 (29 March, 1930): 746-747.
        Descriptive analysis of **La Nuit** (W17) and an-
        nouncement of its performance in concert version (W47).

B245.   "Etudes musicales analytiques." **Le Guide du concert**
        19, no. 17 (27 January, 1933): 435)
        Brief notice of the premier of **Les Jeux de l'amour
        et du hasard** (W127) on 4 February, 1933, at Salle Ga-
        veau.

B246.   "Etudes musicales analytiques." **Le Guide du concert**

21, no. 7 (25 January, 1935): 441.
Descriptive analysis of **La Chatte** (W14) and announcement of its performance in concert version (W45).

B247.   "Etudes musicales analytiques." **Le Guide du concert**
21, no. 20 (15 February, 1935): 530.
Descriptive analysis of the **Suite** for clarinet
and piano (W105) and announcement of its premier at
Concerts de La Sérénade.

B248.   "Etudes musicales analytiques." **Le Guide du concert**
25, no. 23 (10 March, 1939): 597-598.
Descriptive analysis of **Petite messe pastorale**
(W185). It was written in a simple style for two e-
qual voices and intended for liturgical use.

B249.   "Etudes musicales analytiques." **le Guide du concert**
27, no. 11 (13 December, 1946): 12.
Descriptive analysis of **Concerto no. 1** (W75). The
solo piano begins the piece. There is no departure
or alteration of the rhythm except that it is performed
either lightly or lyrically, brilliantly or expressive-
ly. The concerto was played in Brussels, New York,
London, Geneva, Lausanne, Strasbourg, Bordeaux, and
Lyon.

B250.   "Etudes musicales analytiques." **Le Guide du concert**
28, no. 17/18 (30 January/6 February, 1948): 202.
Descriptive analysis and preview of **Symphonie no.
1** (W53) which indicates that the movements center a-
round E minor.

B251.   "Etudes musicales analytiques." **Le Guide du concert**
30, no. 6 (13 January, 1950): 108.
Descriptive analysis of **Symphonie no. 1** (W53).

B252.   "Etudes musicales analytiques." **Le Guide du concert**
37, no. 160 (14 June, 1957): 1216.
Analytic description of the **Concerto no. 1** (W75)
and notice of its performance at the Théâtre des
Champs-Elysées, 20 June, 1957.

B253.   "Etudes musicales analytiques." **Le Guide du concert**
38, no. 182 (31 January, 1958): 702.
Descriptive analysis of **La Chartreuse de Parme**
(W4) and notice that fragments from the opera will be
performed on the radio on 6 February, 1958.

B254.   "Etudes musicales analytiques." **Le Guide du concert**
39, no. 209 (7 November, 1958): 239.
The suite from **La Dame aux camélias** (W65) is a
collection of states of the soul, feelings and sentiments, which the composer attemps to transmit. It
possesses a romantic and lyric character and reflects
the style and language of the grand ballet (W35)
which Henri Sauguet wrote the past year and which was
premiered by Yvette Chauviré at the Festival of Berlin.

B255.   "Etudes musicales analytiques." **Le Guide du concert,**

39, no. 209 (7 November, 1958): 239.
Solitude (W66), which is dedicated to La Comtesse
Jean de Polignac, is sort of a grand reverie on the
theme of solitude.

B256.   "Etudes musicales analytiques." **Le Guide du concert**
42, no. 316 (2 June, 1961): 1204.
Heroic, amorous, tender, dramatic, and intense
emotions occupy a very special place in the score for
Le Cornette (W208) by Henri Sauguet. These rather un-
commonly combined elements succeed in wedding the text
and the music throughout the fifty minute work.

B257.   "Etudes musicales analytiques." **Le Guide du concert**
43, no. 330 (17 November, 1961): 404-405.
Three works will be heard on the concert honoring
Henri Sauguet's sixtieth birthday. In the **Concerto
d'Orphée** (W77) the voice of the violin pacifies the
block of orchestral sound and establishes a sort of
equilibrium and order, and opens up in an extremely
expressive and sentimental berceuse. The **Symphonie
no.** 3 (W62) is made up of tensions and contrasts which
give the work a life of nervous gaiety and melancholy
reverie and juxtaposes tragic and moving sentiments.
The music for **La Mort de la dame aux camèlias** (W65)
very nearly follows the same route as that found in a
symphonic poem by Liszt.

B258.   "Events of the week. Ballets de Paris tonight--con-
certs and recitals." **New York Times**, 8 october,
1950, sec. 2, 6.
Les Forains (W25) receives its New York premier.

B259.   Ewen, David. **European composers today**. New York: H.
W. Wilson, 1954.
Biographical sketch, photo, brief works list, and
Ewen's usual misinformation.

B260.   Eymieux, Paul. "Les Soirées de Paris à La Cigale."
Le Théâtre et comœdia illustrée, 27, no. 33 (May,
1924): unpaged.
Brief mention of **Les Roses** (W13).

B261.   F., P. "Le retour à la danse classique. Mlle. Alice
Nikitina estime que la vraie technique du ballet se
perd. . . ." **Le Monde. Section hebdomadaire**, 5-11
May, 1950, 5.
An interview with Nikitina in which she cites her
experiences in **La Chatte** (W14).

B262.   F., W. "Carter: Sonata for flute, oboe, ..."
HiFi/Stereo Review 15, no. 1 (July, 1965): 68.
Sauguet's **Suite royale** (W159) is a product of the
Franco-Russian neo-Romantic school. The super-refined
lyricism is cast in a somewhat rigid eighteenth century mold. There is much that is essentially songlike
in the work, but the stylistic dichotomy imposed upon
it adds a stiffness. See: D28.

B263.   Ferchault, Guy. "Récitals Touraine, Blanc-Audra et
        Lœwenguth." **L'Information musicale** , 12 March, 1943,
        245.
            Neiges (W242) is a new triumph for this friendly
        artist, for whom delicacy, grace and charm are pro-
        perties of his sure talent.

B264.   "Les Festivals." **Le Monde**, 5 September, 1969, 3.
            On Sunday, 7 September, 1969, in Saint-Emilion
        Sauguet will present music by Les Six. **Six fanfares**
        W94) was probably written for this occasion.

B265.   "Les Festivals--A Bordeaux. **Le Monde**, 21-22 May,
        1961, 15.
            An announcement of the program of the Mai musical
        for the year which included **Plus loin que la nuit et
        le jour** (W38).

B266.   Feuilly, Jacques. "Danse et télévision." **Les Saisons
        de la danse** no. 61 (February, 1974): 8-9.
            It seems that the greatest part of the success of
        Les Forains (W25) derived from the score by Sauguet,
        a masterwork of the genre.

B267.   Florenne, Yves. "A Aix-en-Provence--Premières audi-
        tions: Maurice Jarre, M. Le Roux, H. Sauguet, D.
        Milhaud. **Le Monde**, 5 August, 1953, 9.
            The charming (in both senses of the word) **Orphée**
        (W77) of Sauguet, and the Concertino d'été of Milhaud
        seem to casually wander backward in music. Neither
        one nor the other seem to be in bad taste to me except
        that they are stuck in the past of their youths.

B268.   -----. "Le Festival d'Aix-en-Provence, et 'Mireille.'"
        Le Monde, 7 May, 1954, 12.
            Announcement of the season which included **Les
        Caprices de Marianne** (W6).

B269.   -----. "Au Festival d'Aix-en-Provence--Nocturne sur
        un terrasse." **Le Monde**, 29 July, 1952, 8.
            Announcement of the season which included **Trésor
        et magie** (W30).

B270.   -----. "Œuvres nouvelles à Six--La 'Symphonie' de
        Dutilleux et la 'Guirlande' de sept." **Le Monde**, 5
        August, 1952, 8.
            Finally, in the Menuet and the Moderato, there is
        the poetry of Provence, completely inward looking
        which one hears as dancing and shimmering in the mu-
        sic of Sauguet. See: W60.

B271.   Fracasse, Le Captaine. "Dans le théâtre--Les Ballets
        de Mme Ida Rubinstein." **L'Echo de Paris**, 2 December,
        1928, 5.
            David (W15) is announced on the same bill with
        Stravinsky's Le Baiser de la fée.

B272.   -----. "Dans le théâtre--Les Ballets de Mme Ida
        Rubinstein." **L'Echo de Paris**, 8 December, 1928, 5.

David (W15) exhibits an extraordinary impression of biblical poetry.

B273.   François, Lucien. "Le peintre costumier de ballet." **La Revue musicale** no. 219 (1952/53): 83-99.
References to **Les Mirages** (W24), **Les Forains** (W25), and **La Rencontre** (W26).

B274.   Friskin, James, and Irwin Freundlich. **Music for the piano**. New York: Holt, Rinehart & Winston, 1954.
The **Concerto in A minor** (W75) has vitality and liveliness without great depth of feeling.

B275.   Fuller, Donald. "Airborne over New York." **Modern music** 23, no. 2 (Spring, 1946): 116-123.
The **String Quartet in D** (W87) is spontaneous music, distinguished more for its honest directness and natural sentiment than for any striking qualities of invention. It seems strangely related, even stylistically, to Schumannesque romanticism.

B276.   G.-H., P. "Les Pénitents en Maillots Roses." **Musical America** 70 (15 January, 1950): 90.
The **Pénitents** (W246) leans heavily on attitudes and styles already explored, but they possess a great deal of charm in spite of the composer's rather irritating habit of implanting nineteenth-century cliches here and there in a twentieth-century idiom.

B277.   Gadan, Frances, and Robert Maillard, eds. **Dictionnaire du ballet moderne**. Paris: Fernand Hazan, 1957.
Biographical sketch with references to individual ballets: **La Chatte** (W14), **La Nuit** (W17), **Fastes** (W19), **Les Mirages** (W24), **Les Forains** (W25), **La Rencontre** (W26), and **La Caméléopard** (W33) along with sketches of people important to the creation of the ballets.

B278.   Gaillard, Pol. "Textes et musiques." **Les Lettres françaises**, 10 May, 1946, 7.
Brief mention of Sauguet's music for **La Voiture versée** (W376).

B279.   "Les Galas du Théâtre Beriza au Théâtre des Champs-Elysées." **Le Figaro**, 23 April, 1924, 4.
La Plumet du Colonel (W1) is a modernized return to the style of true French operetta.

B280.   Gandrey-Rety, Jean. "Du ballet à Berlioz." **Les Lettres françaises**, 19 November, 1953, 6.
The Ballet of the Opéra remains able to perform a diverse and flexible repertoire which includes **Les Mirages** (W24).

B281.   Garafola, Lynn. **Diaghilev's Ballets russes**. New York: Oxford University Press, 1989.
La Chatte (W14) is discussed.

B282.   Gautier, Jean-Jacques. "'La Nuit des rois' de Nicole

et Jean Anouilh, d'après Shakespeare." **Le Figaro,** 2 March, 1961, 22.
I would have preferred less learned music. The excessively refined and distinguished music of Sauguet left me wanting lighter melodies which were more singable.

B283.   Gautier, Jean-Jacques.   "'Robinson' de Jules Supervielle." **Le Figaro,** 12 November, 1952, 6.
Sauguet's music created an atmosphere proper to the revelation of this insular dream. See: W387.

B284.   Gavoty, Bernard.   "Douze heures au festival de Bordeaux." **Le Figaro,** 23 May, 1951, 6.
A lengthy review which describes **Les Saisons** (W28) in great detail.   The work is long but never monotonous, and finely orchestrated.   The children's chorus signals the change of seasons and the change of scene and movement in the six-movement work.   Massine's choreography reflects his taste for constant movement. Dupont's costumes are beautiful.

B285.   Gavoty, Bernard, and Daniel Lesur.   **Pour ou contre la musique moderne?**   Paris: Flammarion, 1957.
After the editor's brief biographical sketch, Sauguet replies, in sum, that composers of modern music must not forget that they are composing for real people if they wish their work to be heard and appreciated.

B286.   Gaxotte, Pierre.   "Morte subite de Christian Dior à Montecatini."   **Le Figaro,** 25 October, 1957, 1.
Dior, along with Gaxotte, Jean Ozenne, Sauguet, and a few others had been close friends in the twenties and remained so thereafter.

B287.   Gelatt, Roland.   "French grab-bag."   **Saturday review** 33, no. 25 (29 April, 1950): 49.
In the review of REB 2 the author says that **Mouvements du cœur** (W251) and **Visions infernales** (W250) show Sauguet to be a musician of lofty sentiments who writes in an urbane and rather complicated language. See: D51.

B288.   George, André.   "De Mozart à Poulenc."   **Les Nouvelles littéraires, artistiques et scientifiques,** 27 February, 1929, 10.
The **Polymètres** (W234) of Sauguet are charming, easy, with a melodic grace in the style of Gounod which is particularly expressed in the second, "Le Muguet."

B289.   -----.   "La Musique."   **Les Nouvelles littéraires, artistiques et scientifiques,** 26 December, 1931, 10.
The **Divertissement à chambre** (W85), performed at the Concerts de "La Sérénade," is charming and clean.

B290.   -----.   "La Musique--Autour de l'Ecole d'Arcueil."
Les Nouvelles littéraires, artistiques et scientif-

iques, 4 April, 1925, 7.
  The **Françaises** (W141) are full of personal, poetic sentiment, craftsmanlike or playfully fantastic,
or melancholy in turn. The **Suite** for violin and piano
(W103) is less happy, especially in the "Andante"
which is ordinary and thin. The "Finale," however is
characterized once again with beautiful, healthy
attraction with its clear and sweeping rhythm.

B291. George, André. "La Musique--Les Ballets russes." **Les**
      Nouvelles littéraires, artistiques et scientifiques,
      4 June, 1927, 9.
        The music for **La Chatte** (W14) is charming and cer-
      tain. The author seems to voluntarily limit himself
      and does not try for scandal or excess like some other
      young French composers. It has a simplicity and clear-
      ness that is fresh and lively. The diverse numbers
      of the suite are full of movement and rhythmic life.
      The orchestra is, in itself, bright and sonorous.
      When it is put together with the choreography it is
      very danceable, direct, melodic, and a happy success.

B292. -----. "La Musique--Les Ballets de Mme. Rubinstein."
      Les Nouvelles littéraires, artistiques et scienti-
      fiques, 18 December, 1928, 11.
        "But, what did you think of **David** (W15) and <u>La</u>
      <u>Baiser</u> <u>de</u> <u>la</u> <u>fée</u>? My apologies to the reader, to
      Sauguet and to Stravinsky. I was not invited, so I
      did not attend.

B293. -----. "La Musique--Une 'Exposition de mélodies.'"
      Les nouvelles littéraires, artistiques et scienti-
      fiques, 16 March, 1929, 12.
        Henri Sauguet, always gifted, curious, individual,
      seriously translates the inspiration of Schiller and
      the memories of Schumann into French. <u>See</u>: W231.

B294. -----. "La Musique--Les Galas Beriza aux Champs-
      Elysées." **Les Nouvelles littéraires, artistiques**
      et scientifiques, 3 May, 1924, 7.
        His score for **Le Plumet du Colonel** (W1) reveals a
      very spontaneous musical personality with a melodic
      gift which flows from a fresh source. This is his
      first important attempt, and there are some short-
      comings, but we will do well to attend to the original
      qualities of M. Sauguet, which are none too rare.

B295. -----. "La Musique--La Sérénade." **Les Nouvelles lit-**
      téraires, artistiques et scientifiques, 16 March,
      1935, 12.
        The **Suite** for clarinet and piano (W105) is very
      flexible and slight.

B296. Gere, Charlotte. **Marie Laurencin.** New York: Rizzoli,
      1977.
        Brief mention of **Les Roses** (W13).

B297. Giroud, Françoise. **Dior.** New York: Rizzoli, 1987.
        Dior wanted to become a composer and developed a

passion for the works of <u>Les Six</u> and <u>L'Ecole d'Arcueil</u>.
He gave up the idea but became one of the mainstays
of the Hôtel Nollet "gang" to which Sauguet belonged.
Their friendship remained fast, and Sauguet composed
the **Pie Jésus** (W189) which was performed at Dior's
funeral in October, 1957.

B298.   Goldbeck, Fred. "Mélodies de Maxime Jacob, Massimo,
Nabokoff, Sauguet, etc." **La Revue musicale** no. 124
(March, 1932): 221-222.
Brief mention of songs by Sauguet which were pos-
sibly **Cirque** (W228).

B299.   -----. "La Musique--Au Festival de Berlin--Ballets."
Preuves no. 81 (November, 1957): 66.
La Dame aux camélias (W35) is an excellent classical ballet score full of inspired orchestration and
an experiment in the nostalgic heritage of Ravel's
<u>Valses</u> <u>nobles</u> <u>et</u> <u>sentimentales</u>.

B300.   Golea, Antoine. "Les Caprices d'Euterpe." **Musica**
no. 113 (August, 1963): 29.
Le Cornette (W208) would be a rather moving work
if it were less monotonous and better orchestrated.
Monotony derives from a true absence of harmonic fantasy.   I also find this blunder in the **Concerto for
piano** (W79).   How can one explain these faults in a
composer who has enchanted us with scores like **Les
Forains** (W25), **La Rencontre** (W26), **Les Mirages** (W24),
and **La Dame aux camélias** (W35)?

B301.   -----. "Festival Sauguet." **Le Guide du concert** 44,
no. 393 (22 June, 1963): 28.
In **Le Cornette** (W208) the emotion is disclaimed
by a curious monotony in lack of changes in rhythm
and tempo.   I believe that this monotony comes from
the harmonic language.   In the **Concerto for piano no.
3** (W79) the orchestra constantly pounds out its sound.
The piano nearly always plays in the same register as
the orchestra.

B302.   -----. "Les Festivals de musique en 1949." **Almanach
de la musique**, 1950, 53-62.
For my part, I want to add to the activities of
the Festival of Aix the premier of a work of remarkable inspiration and sensitivity by a contemporary
French musician who is attaining the most beautiful
maturity: The **Second Quartet** (W91) by Henri Sauguet.

B303.   -----. "Quatrième Symphonie." **Carrefour**, 8 December,
1971, 12.
The rhythm is very nearly immutable in the three
movements of the **Fourth Symphony** (W71) which is domi-
nated by a single, craftily varied theme.   I envision
a ballet without a specific subject, but which expresses all the sadness experienced by a man who arrives at 70 and regards his life as a tale told by
someone else and welcomes death as a dolorous friend.
It is orchestrated with skill, if not always with

B304.   Greene, David Mason. **Greene's biographical encyclo-
pedia of composers.** Garden City: Doubleday, 1985.
Biographical sketch of Sauguet with a selected
discography.

B305.   Gregory, James. "Made in Paris." **The Strad** 70 (April, 1960): 471.
The score of **La Dame aux camélias** (W35) begins
with great vivacity in a mixture of atonality and
polyphony. Sauguet produced some of his most beautiful music for the ballroom scene of the first movement, the mazurka of the second, and the poignant
moments of the second and fourth tableaux, where one
finds the composer producing music of such distinc-
tive character as that found in **Les forains** (W25).

B306.   Grout, Donald Jay. **A Short history of opera.** 2nd ed.
New York: Columbia University Press, 1965.
Brief references to **Le Plumet du Colonel** (W1) and
La Gageure imprévue (W5). Special mention of **La Chartreuse de Parme** (W4) as a work which conforms in every
external detail to traditional nineteenth century
opera, but is couched in simple, though far from un-
sophisticated, musical idiom which might have traced
its lineage back to Satie.

B307.   Grovlez, Charles. "Ce qu'on a joué dans les Lyriques
--La Chartreuse de Parme." **L'Art musical** 4, no. 119
(31 March, 1939): 789.
Grovlez reserves his final judgement on the opera
(W4) until he sees the score, but to him the work
seems to have deficiencies in its qualities. The author certainly has a sense of the theater, but lyric
spirit exists side by side with pedestrianism. Some
parts, like the superb Nurse's aria, possess freshness, simplicity and charm. The last tableau, the
sermon in the light, is particularly well wrought.
The composer is, without contradiction, a man of the
theater.

B308.   Guest, Ivor. **Le Ballet de l'Opéra de Paris. Trois
siècles d'histoire et de tradition.** Paris: Théâtre
National de l'Opéra, 1976.
Citations concerning the importance of **Les Mirages**
(W24) and **La Dame aux camélias** (W35).

B309.   -----. "An introduction to the Paris Opéra Ballet."
The Ballet Annual 9 (1955): 64-70.
Les Mirages (W24) contains profundity in its con-
ception and interpretation.

B310.   Guilly, René. "Les ballets des Champs-Elysées font
hommage à Christian Bérard de leur saison de printemps." **Combat,** 15 April, 1949, 4.
Description of **La Nuit** (W17) to be performed 30
April.

B311.   -----. "Pour leur quatrième saison les Ballets des
Champs-Elysées créeront quatre œuvres de Boris
Kochno sur des musiques de Sauguet, Stravinsky et

Bizet." **Combat**, 3 November, 1948, 2.

In **La Rencontre** (W26) Sauguet allows an innovation of five minutes wherein dance continues without music. This permits Kochno, the author of the scenario, to play with the lighting. The ballet was conceived for Danielle Darmance, but she became ill and the sixteen year old Leslie Caron took her part opposite Jean Babilée.

B312. Guth, Paul. **Quarante contre un.** Paris: Librairie Générale Française, 1973.
Biographical sketch of Sauguet, subtitled "Fils de Carmen."

B313. H., F. "Heureux anniversaire Henri Sauguet." **Le Guide du concert** 43, no. 331 (24 November, 1961): 443.
Birthday wishes to the composer and an announcement of a concert featuring his music.

B314. H., F. "London season closes." **New York Times**, 24 July, 1927, sec. 7, 4.
The music of Henri Sauguet no longer follows the posings of Les Six, but has reverted to the old type of French stage music and might be a page of Godard or Thomas slightly flavored with more modern spice.

B315. Haggin, B. H. "Records." **The Nation**, 16 June, 1951, 273-274.
Short review of the Gold and Fizdale recording (D22). Predictably, Haggin doesn't like the **Valse brève** (W128) or the works by Auric, Tailleferre and Bowles.

B316. Hainaux, René. **Stage design throughout the world since 1935.** London: George G. Harrap, 1957.
Citations for **Les Forains** (W25), **La Rencontre** (W26), **Les Saisons** (W28), **La Folle de Chaillot** (W375), **Dom Juan** (W379), and **Les Fourberies de Scapin** (W381).

B317. Hall, David. **The Record book.** International ed. New York: Oliver Durrell, 1948).
Cites a recording of the **Piano Concerto** (D21) and says of **La Voyante** (W201) that it is a most effective bit of vocal writing on the subject of astrology and its allied fields. See: D41.

B318. -----. **Records.** New York: Alfred A. knopf, 1950.
Cites recordings of **Les Forains** (D49), **Mouvements du cœur** and **Visions infernales** (D51), the **Trio** (D42), **Piano concerto in A** (D21), and **La Voyante** (D41) which he considers pleasant music in a theatrical sort of way. He considers Sauguet one of the most successful contemporary composers among his own countrymen.

B319. Hammond, Richard. "Ballets russes, 1928." **Modern music** 6, no. 1 (November/December, 1928): 25-28.
Revivals from the recent years, **La Chatte** (W14) by Henri Sauguet and Rieti's Barabau prove diverting on the lighter side.

B320.   Hammond, Richard.   "Paris notes." **Modern music** 7,
        no. 2 (January/February, 1932): 88-89.
                Sauguet's **Divertissement** (W85) "manifested un-
        deniable talent and musicality, nevertheless, erred
        seriously on the side of cheapness and harmonic ba-
        nality."

B321.   Hamnett, Nina.   **Laughing torso.**   London: Constable,
        1932.
                Hamnett meets Sauguet at Satie's funeral. He had
        attended Satie's estate sale and bought fifteen of the
        twenty umbrellas which were on sale.

B322.   Hamon, Jean.   "Henri Sauguet à l'honneur."   **Combat**, 7
        June, 1963, 10.
                A rather lengthy tribute to Sauguet on his sixtieth
        birthday. "He is a musician of heart and light. A
        poet before all else, a musician for whom music is,
        above all else, a melody which one sings to himself
        to enchant his interior universe. Sometimes Sauguet,
        before this tide which currently diverts young French
        musicians, becomes doubtful with some disenchantment.
        We know that he will survive. He may be eclipsed,
        perhaps, but he will be rediscovered."

B323.   -----.   "Nouvelles musicales."   **Combat**, 13 April,
        1962, 8.
                Brief notice that Sauguet will participate with
        other composers in a conference at Le Centre français
        d'humanisme musical in a centennial discussion of
        Claude Debussy's music.

B324.   Harding, James.   **Erik Satie.**   New York: Praeger, 1975.
                The author clearly relates details concerning
        Satie's introduction of Sauguet to Diaghilev and the
        reason for the introduction. It was Satie's way of
        making amends for his rudeness with Sauguet who had
        earlier turned pages for Satie during a performance
        of the latter's Socrate.

B325.   Harewood, Earl of.   "Summer Festivals: II--Aix-en-
        Provence."   **Opera** (London) 5 (September, 1954): 532-
        534.
                The audience clearly demonstrated its approval of
        Les Caprices de Marianne (W6). It is probably a work
        for the Comique rather than for the Opéra, as, though
        it is anything but precious, it is undeniably fragile.
        The light orchestration is a marvel of subtlety and
        suggestiveness. The Aix theatre made it seem as
        though there were too little dynamic contrast. Above
        it we heard romantic vocal music of great charm, di-
        vided, for the most part, into set pieces.

B326.   Harrison, Max.   "Sauguet. Piano concerto no. 1 in A
        minor. Les Forains--ballet."   **Gramophone** 59, no.
        699 (August, 1981): 278.
                Review of Le Chant du Monde LCS 78300 (D17). There
        is a lot of conventional piano rhetoric in the **Concer-
        to** (W75), yet no memorable ideas. **Les Forains** (W25)

is dedicated to the memory of Satie, yet, even though
Parade is in a sense the model, Sauguet's music is
really very different.

B327.   Hastings, Baird. **Christian Bérard, painter, decora-
        tor, designer.** Boston: Institute of Contemporary
        Art, 1950.
        Brief comments about **La Nuit** (W17), **Les Forains**
        (W25), and **La Folle de Chaillot** (W375). Concerning
        the first named he says that Sauguet's wonderful mu-
        sical score serves as a base, an aural décor, while
        Bérard's visual creation suggests everything, and the
        dances have only to portray the story which Kochno
        has invented.

B328.   ------. "The designer" In "Aspects of French ballet
        since the liberation." **Dance magazine** 25, no. 5
        (May, 1951): 24.
        Brief comment concerning **La Nuit** (W17). He be-
        lieves that it is due to works like **Les Forains** (W25)
        and its creators that Paris and France are still
        great centers for theater.

B329.   Hell, Henri. "Bilan musical." **La Table ronde** no. 22
        (October, 1949): 1624-1628.
        I very much like the music for **La Rencontre** (W26).
        Incontestably Henri Sauguet is a musician of the bal-
        let. **Visions infernales** (W250) seems to me less ac-
        complished than **La Rencontre**, but it is a work of
        great interest and importance to the evolution of its
        composer. These melodies do not have the easy charm,
        elegance and sensitivity of the previous songs.

B330.   ------. "Le Cornette de Henri Sauguet." **La Revue mu-
        sical** no. 24 (February 1952): 10-12.
        With **L'Amour et la mort du Cornette Christopher
        Rilke** (W208) it gets much worse, when M. Henri Sauguet
        comes to give us his most important and finished work.
        Each time M. Sauguet undertakes a task above his means,
        each time he forces his talent. Even so, **Le Cornette**
        remains a lyric and poetic work, deeply moving, which
        is not afraid of being heard from the heart. That
        voice is one which one hears rarely in contemporary
        music, nor is it met with the welcome it deserves.

B331.   Henahan, Donald. "Records." **New York Times**, 14 Nov-
        ember, 1971, sec.4, 30.
        The **Mélodie concertante** (W80) is a "sensuous 25
        minute rhapsody, improvisatory in feeling, in the na-
        ture of variations on a mood from Debussy's String
        quartet, rather than on a theme. The melodic in-
        vention holds up quite well, it is an excellent piece
        as well as an effective one." See: D39.

B332.   Hennesy, Jossleyn. "Ballet Olympic in London." **Mod-
        ern music** 23, no. 4 (Fall, 1946): 285-287.
        Les Forains (W25) has "captivating music by Henri
        Sauguet and gay décors by Christian Bérard."

B333. "Henri Sauguet." **Encyclopédie de la musique** 1,70-71.
       Paris: Fasquelle, 1961.
       A two page spread in a section subtitled <u>Livre</u>
       <u>d'or</u> which features photographs, facsimiles of manu-
       scripts and other pictorial material about prominent
       musicians of the time.

B334. "Henri Sauguet: composer for ballets, theater." **Los**
       Angeles Times, 25 June, 1989, 32.
       Obituary.

B335. "Henri Sauguet, président de la S.A.C.D." **Courrier**
       musical de France no. 26 (1969): 131.
       Announcement in the section "Nouvelles diverses"
       that Sauguet was elected president of the Société des
       Auteurs et Compositeurs Dramatiques. He was at that
       time first vice-president of the Comité national de
       la Musique.

B336. "Henri Sauguet; wrote musical scores for ballets."
       Chicago Tribune, 23 June, 1989, sec. 2, p. 6.
       Obituary.

B337. Hering, Doris. "Presstime News." **Dance magazine** 40,
       no. 5 (May, 1966): p.A.
       Notice that a new ballet **La Guirlande de Campra**
       (W41) was included in a gala benefit program program
       19 April.

B338. -----. "Reviews." **Dance magazine** 41, no. 1 (January,
       1967): 32.
       Concerning **La Guirlande de Campra** (W41), "rarely
       was the music a help."

B339. Hersin, André-Philippe. "Hommage à Lifar." **Les Sai-**
       sons de la danse 10, no. 99 (10 December, 1977): 4.
       Brief reference to **Les Mirages** (W24) which was in-
       cluded in a homage to Serge Lifar, held in November,
       1977, and sponsored by Rolf Liebermann.

B340. Hiégel, Pierre. **Edith Piaf.** Paris: Editions de
       l'Heure, 1962.
       Discography cites Piaf's recording of **Le Chemin**
       des forains (D45).

B341. Hinson, Maurice. **Guide to the pianist's repertoire.**
       2nd ed. Bloomington: Indiana University Press,
       1987.
       Brief references to the **Sonata in D** (W145),
       Feuillets d'album (W148), and **Romance in C** (W147).

B342. -----. **Music for more than one piano.** Bloomington:
       Indiana University Press, 1983.
       Brief references to **Les Jeux de l'amour et du**
       hasard (W127) "which possesses wit and a certain
       charm," and **Valse brève** (W128) which is "graceful,
       flowing and effective."

B343. -----. **Music for piano and orchestra.** Bloomington:

Indiana University Press, 1981.
Sauguet's style contains subtle ostinato, ambiguous harmonies, simplicity, and refined popular elements found in Satie. Brief references to the **Concerto in A** (W75) and the **Concerto no.** 3 (W79) which he
considers highly chromatic, almost atonal.

B344. Hoérée, Arthur. "Sauguet." **New Groves dictionary of
music and musicians.** New York: Macmillan, 1980.
Brief biographical sketch with works list.

B345. Holland, Bernard. "Henri Sauguet, French composer on
the Satie model, is dead at 88. **New York Times,** 23
June, 1989, 24.
Obituary.

B346. "Hommage à André Gide." **Le Monde,** 11 June, 1949, 8.
Announcement of an evening of tributes to Gide
which included a performance of **Le Retour de l'enfant
prodigue** (W362) with music by Sauguet.

B347. "Hommage à Henri Sauguet." **Le Monde,** 29 January,
1981, 24.
Announcement of a performance of **Concert d'Orphée**
(W77) sponsored by La Société française de musique
contemporaine in honor of its president (Sauguet) on
his 80th birthday.

B348. "Hommage à Louis Jouvet." **Le Monde,** 15 February,
1952, 12.
Announcement of a soirée on 20 February, 1952, in
memory of Louis Jouvet. Sauguet delivevered a speech
in honor of the director and actor.

B349. Honegger, Marc. "Sauguet." **Dictionnaire de la musique.** Paris: Bordas, 1986.
Biographical sketch with a works list.

B350. Honolka, Kurt, "Einakter-Spässe aus Frankreich."
Musica 21, no. 5 (September/October, 1967): 235-236.
This and the following two reviews by Honolka
basically relate, concerning **Le Plumet du Colonel** (W1),
that the libretto contained too many situations in too
short a period of time, and that the musical contribution, while basically harmless, was nice.

B351. -----. "Pforzheim." **Opera** (London), 18 (July, 1967):
582.
Concerning **Le Plumet du Colonel** (W1). See: B350.

B352. -----. "Pforzheim: Einakter-Spässe aus Frankreich."
Opernwelt 8 (August, 1967): 48.
Concerning **Le Plumet du Colonel** (W1). See: B350.

B353. Horowicz, Bronislaw. **Musiques et paroles souvenirs.**
Paris: France-Empire, 1979.
Brief reference to **La Voyante** (W201) and its per-
formance August, 1954, at Canne as part of the first
Festival International de la Radio et de la Télévision.

Also cited is the 195-7 radio broadcast honoring Jane
Bathori in which Sauguet took part.

B354.   Hughes, Allen. "Festival in Provence." **New York
Times**, 22 August, 1954, sec. 2, 7.
The composer has set a number of graceful arias
and ensemble pieces in **Les Caprices de Marianne** (W6)
within a framework of what he himself calls "lyric
conversation," a more or less continuous melody as
opposed to a chain of recitatives and arias. This
reduces the impact of the set-pieces they surround
and deprives the work of variety. Rhythmic and harmonic ingredients in the score leven the resulting
monotony. The inherent piquancies of irregular
stresses and sharp dissonances are all but neutralized
by the limpid and genteel orchestration.

B355.   Hurard-Viltard, Eveline. **Le Groupe des Six ou le
matin d'un jour de fête.** Paris: Meridiens Klinck-
sieck, 1987.
Material transcribed from a radio broadcast by
Pierre Minet entitled "Emission sur Satie." Includes
Sauguet's comments on the influence of Les Six on him
and especially the catalytic times in Paris when he
first arrived.

B356.   Huré, Jean. "Gageure imprévue." **La Guide du concert**
26, no. 17 (8 March, 1946): 239.
Concerning the opera (W5), it is representative
of the admirable work of our young school, and it
especially shows how conscientious the effort is.
One must not submit to the worrysome oppression of
Wagnerianism, second rate Franckists, or impression-
ism to comprehend the sensation of deliverance in
reading a work of this young school, even when this
work is awkward and hesitating. Mr. Sauguet is
neither hesitant nor awkward.

B357.   Hussey, Eyneley. "Some new French ballets." **The
Dancing times** no. 429 (June, 1946): 445-446.
In **Les Forains** (W25) Sauguet has taken the kind
of tunes that may be heard upon the steam organs of
roundabouts and constructed of them a charming and
evocative score. The music does not copy the glare
and vulgarity of the original; it suggests it. I defy
anyone who is not incurably high-brow and humorless,
not to be captivated by that enchanting, nostalgic
waltz.

B358.   Huth, Arno. "Postwar European revival." **Modern music** 23, no. 1 (Winter, 1946): 36-39.
Reference to Paul Collaer, director of the Belgian
Radio Orchestra mounting performances during the War
which featured **Les Ombres du jardin** (W203), and his
efforts to revive it.

B359.   ------. "Where nations still meet." **Modern music** 21,
no. 1 (November/December, 1943): 39-41.
Radio Geneva broadcasts a performance of the **Con-
concerto no.1** (W75).

B360. "The International scene." **Musical courrier** 150
(August, 1954): 33.
Concerto d'Orphée (W77) was broadcast with the
American violinist Louis Kaufmann. Its technical dif-
ficulties are considerable, but were surmounted with
ease and eloquence.

B361. J., N. "Tribune de la musique vivante." **Le Figaro**,
30 November, 1961, 16.
Announcement for a radio series which featured
artists critiquing their own work entitled Je m'accuse,
one of which featured Henri Sauguet and Marcel Schneider.

B362. Jacob, Maxime. "Le plumet du colonel." **L'Information**
universitaire, 20 June, 1924, 4.
Libretto of the opera (W1) is a farce in the tone
of Cocteau's Les Mariés de la tour Eiffel. The light
moments are compared to works by Offenbach of Milhaud
with particular praise for the "Berceuse créole."

B363. Jacobin, Bernard. "Vlasov: Cello concerto no. 1 in
C major. Sauguet: Mélodie concertante." **Stereo**
review 28, no. 4 (April, 1972): 84-85.
The **Mélodie** (W80) is essentially nostalgic in manner; it has the feeling of a greatly expanded Sibelius
Valse triste. Though a bit directionless as a dreamy
romantic effusion this is a thoroughly genuine, imaginative and individually felt composition. See: D39.

B364. Jacobson, R. "The annual appearance of soprano Alice
Esty." **Musical America** 83 (July, 1963): 28.
Non-committal on the vocal content of **Vie des**
compagnes (W259), but it contains expert pictorial
piano writing.

B365. Jeanson, Henri. "Les Amoureux sont seuls au monde--
Scenario dialogue." **Paris théâtre** no. 18, n.d.
Dialogue for the film (W340) and cast list which
includes Sauguet who not only composed the music for
the film but also played the role of the orchestra
conductor.

B366. Jeener, J.-B. "Avant leur depart pour l'Amérique du
Sud Les Ballets des Champs-Elysées preparent une
semain parisienne." Le Figaro, 18 April, 1949, 4.
Description of Irène Skorik and Youly Algaroff
rehearsing **La Nuit** (W17) in preparation for a farewell
recital before the Ballet tours South America.

B367. Jolly, Cynthia. "Neapolitan Caprices." **Opera news**
20 (20 February, 1956): 12-13.
In the opera house Sauguet's score for **Les Cap-**
rices de Marianne (W6), is "subtle, but it lacks vigor
and contrast; it is beautifully written and orchestrated but fails to grip."

B368. Jourdan-Morhange, Hélène. "Un Apostolat." **Les Lettres**
françaises no. 616 (19 April, 1956): 7.

Sauguet and Paul Derenne perform **Cinq poèmes de Max Jacob** (W246) at Les Amis de la musique de chambre. "Under the simple melody in the voice it is the piano which creates the atmosphere with its undulating arabesques and varied rhythm. Sauguet, the pianist, astonishes me. I did not believe he was a virtuoso."

B369. Jourdan-Morhange, Hélène. "Cantate." **Le Guide du concert** 42, no. 307 (24 March, 1961): 871.
The scene is situated during the occupation and describes the martyrdom of a man chained to a tree as he is tortued. Sauguet was especially distressed by this frightful period as can be seen in his **Symphonie expiatoire** (W53). Here, in **L'Oiseau a vu tout cela** (W209) Cayrol's very beautiful poem has inspired the work, and not one note of this Cantata is written to interfere with it. At first one is surprised by the presentation of a "series," but Sauguet has used this device to create an atmosphere of strangeness, the tone is somber from the beginning despite several chirpings of the bird to mark its presence.

B370. -----. "Les Caprices de Marianne." **Les Lettres françaises** no. 619 (10 May, 1956): 5.
Under the melody of the opera (W6) which flows like a spring, the orchestra is extremely diverse and lively. Inspite of the apparent simplicity, the complexity of its rhythm contributes to its richness, but as Sauguet has said, "It is not necessary for the listener to perceive this; above all, conceal art for art (Cachez l'art pour l'art) as Rameau said."

B371. -----. Concert des premiers Prix 1960 du Conservatoire." **Les Lettres françaises** no. 834 (21 July, 1960): 7.
Nicole Chouret wins the prize in dance for women. One of her selections is from **Les Forains** (W25).

B372. -----. "La Dame aux camélias à l'Opéra--La Partition." **Les Lettres françaises** no. 811 (11 February, 1960): 6.
"This was written in 1960?!" exclaimed a listener outside. Evidently Sauguet's score (W35) does not resemble closely enough the mathematic imaginings of today. But why reject the charm and tenderness of his music? Would he have preferred **La Dame aux camélias** if it had been written with "Tcha-tcha-tcha" or electronic music? Moreover, he does not have an ear finely enough attuned to certain "Very Sauguet" harmonies such as those in **Les Forains** (W25) or the **Symphonie allégorique** (W57) which always mark his characteristics.

B373. -----. "Deux jours au Festival de Bordeaux: Concert en hommage à Diaghilev. **Les Lettres francaises** no. 776 (4 June, 1959): 7.
Igor Markevitch requested Sauguet, both as a Bordelaise and as the composer of **La Chatte**(W14) to sanction the event and lend it some authenticity.

B374. Jourdan-Morhange, Hélène. "Doda Conrad." **Le Guide du concert** 40, no. 255-256 (15-31 January, 1960): 331.
Concerning **Visions infernales** (W250) there are subtle suggestions. "This is great Sauguet." Concerning **Mouvements du cœur** (W251) despite its hommage to Chopin the personality of each composer is asserted.

B375. -----. "Un élan qui rejoint celui du poète." **Les Lettres françaises** no. 462 (23 April, 1953): 7.
Force et faiblesse (W244) and **Les Animaux et leurs hommes** (W224) are performed at a concert given in homage to Paul Eluard.

B376. -----. "Entretiens avec Henri Sauguet." **Les Lettres francaises** no. 507 (11 March, 1954): 9.
An interview with Sauguet who previews **Les Caprices de Marianne** (W6) which will be performed at the Festival d'Aix-en-Provence.

B377. -----. "Le Festival d'Aix-en-Provence--Le Journal d'Hélène Jourdan-Morhange." **Les Lettres françaises** no. 507 (11 March, 1954): 9.
To hear the paper given by one of our most distinguished colleages against **Les Caprices de Marianne** (W6) by Sauguet and especially against the construction of the the plot, the audience would have been astonished by the success of the opera accorded by them at the second performance. As for me, I understand that this direct, very humaine music can be understood by all people.

B378. -----. "'Le Fou' un opéra de philosophe." **Les Lettres francaises** no. 690 (3 October, 1957): 7.
It may be noted that the public of 1957 is better prepared for the spirit of **Le Contrebasse** (W3) than it was when it was first presented.

B379. -----. "Hommage à Marguerite Long." **Le Guide du concert** 36, no. 119 (15 June, 1956): 1225.
Sauguet's delicious "Berceuse" in the **Variations sur le nom de Marguerite Long** (W63) gives the key to the theme.

B380. -----. "Hommage à Satie." **Les Lettres françaises** no. 617 (26 April, 1956): 7.
Sauguet and Cliquet-Pleyel present a concert of Satie's music at the Maison de la pensée française. Sauguet reminisces about his experiences with Satie.

B381. -----. "Journal d'Aix-en-Provence (II)--Harmonies Mozartiennes et dissonances modernes." **Les Lettres françaises** no. 477 (7 August, 1953): 6.
Its title, **Concerto d'Orphée** (W77), indicates a struggle of wills. It is characteristic of the work that the violin is always heard in tender lyricism while the orchestra offers some atonal passages (something which is astonishing in Sauguet). The theme at the beginning is excellent, always very important when

the solo violin incorporates it with infinite supple-
ness, sort of a very pleasant meditation. Perhaps it
may be regretted that it is repeated a little too often in the development. The orchestration is often
sparce and sometimes reminds us of Roussel. The work
reveals a new Sauguet.

B382. Jourdan-Morhange, Hélène. **Mes amis musiciens.** Paris:
Les Editeurs Française Rénuis, 1955.
An extended biographical sketch by a critic who
was aware of and sympathetic to musical life in the
1940s and 1950s.

B383. -----. "'Les Noces d'ombre' de Nikiproventzky et
Serge Moreux." **Les Lettres françaises** no. 703 (2
January, 1958): 8.
The pretty **Concerto** (W75) by Sauguet is rather
old-fashioned but full of music. It is agreeable to
listen to without having to try to imagine the equa-
tions applied by the composer. Vasso Devetzi and
Sauguet obtained a very great success.

B384. -----. "Présence de la musique contemporaine au T.
N. P." **Les Lettres françaises** no. 805 (31 December,
1959): 5.
Sauguet, in one charming symphonic page of **Les
Trois lys** (W61), depicts France; a France where fantasy never exceeds good taste. Sauguet confessed to
me that this music, which was supposed to be abstract,
is, nevertheless, haunted by the daily lives of his
cats! The fights, the tenderness, the felines at
play and repose. One can recognize all the supple-
ness of the sinewy music and the personal caprice of
Sauguet.

B385. -----. "Rescapés d'Aix-en-Provence." **Les Lettres
françaises** no. 409 (24 April, 1952): 6.
In the **Variations sur un thème de Campra** (W60)
Sauguet's contribution has charm and poetry. His
"Menuet" is worthy of his best pages.

B386. -----. "Symphonique allégorique d'Henri Sauguet."
Les Lettres françaises no. 796 (29 October, 1959):
6.
The **Symphonie** (W57) was originally premiered under
the baton of Désormières. It was thereafter transformed into the ballet **Les Saisons** (W28). Now it returns, ten years later, in a radio broadcast under
Manuel Rosenthal. Some people consider the music too
simple for the times. On the contrary, this is what
attracts me to Sauguet. He allows himself to speak
his heart and does not worry about the world. He does
not know what it means to become "strange;" this is
very courageous in a time when they speak of elderly
people becoming obsolete.

B387. K., H. "La Reprise d'Ondine." **Le Monde. Section
hebdomadaire,** 29 April-5 May, 1949, 4.
Notice of the reopening of **Ondine** (W364) with

music by Sauguet and sets by Tchelitchev, which remarkably have survived the war.

B388.   K.-M., N.   "Musica da Concerto."   **Musica d'oggi**, 7,
no. 3 (1964): 84.
Brief notice of the Moscow premiere of **Mélodie
concertante** (W80).

B389.   Kaldor, Pierre.   "Musique."   **Commune** no. 42 (February,
1937): 757.
The **Barcarolle** (W106) is marked by a fine, child-
like quality.   In order to preserve this the bassoon
must always play lightly which is not always easy to
do.

B390.   Keller, Hans.   "First performances."   **Music review**
11 (May, 1950): 146-150.
An extensive review which concludes that the **Symphonie expiatoire** (W53) is surprisingly impressive.
It is not a great work, but an original one.

B391.   Kemp, Robert.   "A l'Œuvre 'Robinson.'"   **Le Monde**, 12
November, 1952, 9.
The music by Henri Sauguet (W387) is a ravishing
little detail.

B392.   -----.   "Les Caprices de Marianne à Aix-en-Provence."
Le Monde, 23 July, 1954, 12.
The score for the opera (W6) is riddled with dis-
organization, but it is interspersed with sweetness.

B393.   Kerman, Joseph.   "Henri Sauguet: Les Caprices de
Marianne."   **Notes** 16, no. 3 (March, 1959): 320-321.
"Sauguet works with closed forms and almost no
recitative proper.   Qualities of extreme neatness and
extremely quiet lyricism--blended out of Satie, Milhaud and Stravinsky--make Sauguet's individual mood;
but the mood is sustained too long for this flimsy
dramatic material.   The polytonality, the pages of
diatonic dissonance, the scurrying motor pages in 5/8
and 6/8, the clipped neoclassic phraseology--these
grow sad and empty after a time."   Review of the
printed score (W6).

B394.   Kirk, Elise K.   Review of Catalogue des œuvres de
Charles Kœchlin.   Introduction by Henri Sauguet.
Notes 34, no. 3 (March, 1978): 613-614.
"At a minimum, the catalog opens the door into a
world of "unexplored, multifarious elements," as the
composer's distinguished pupil, Henri Sauguet, poetically expresses in his short introduction."

B395.   Kirsten, Lincoln.   **Ballet, bias and belief**.   New York:
Dance Horizons, 1983.
Reprint of a review from The Hound and Horn (3,
no. 4, 468-501) suggests that the music for **La Chatte**
(W14) is more like acrid Offenbach.

B396.   Knapp, Bettina L. **French theatre 1918-1939.** Hound-
        mills, Basingstoke, Hampshire: Macmillan, 1985.
        Brief reference to Sauguet's music for **Victor**
        (W377) and mention that his music for **Ondine** (W364)
        was lauded for its lively cadences, its harsh and
        strident notes, which replicated Giraudoux's own
        rhythms and sonorities. It reinforced the atmosphere
        of myth and magic.

B397.   -----. **Louis Jouvet, man of the theatre.** New York:
        Columbia University Press, 1957.
        Brief references to Sauguet's music for **Ondine**
        (W364), **La Folle de Chaillot** (W375), **Dom Juan** (W379),
        Les Fourberies de Scapin (W381), and **Tartuffe** (W382).

B398.   Kniesner, Virginia. "Tonality and form in selected
        French piano sonatas, 1900-1950." Ph.D. diss. The
        Ohio State University, 1977.
        A comparison of the **Sonate en ré** (W145) to other
        works of the time.

B399.   Knowles, Dorothy. **French drama of the inter-war
        years, 1918-1939.** London: Harrap, 1967.
        Brief references to **Le Retour de l'enfant** (W362),
        Ondine (W364), **La Folle de Chaillot** (W375), and **Robin-
        son Crusoë** (W378).

B400.   Kochnitzky, Léon. "Chronique et notes--Les Concerts."
        La Revue musicale no. 112 (February, 1931): 165.
        In reference to **La Nuit** (W17) it is lacking in
        originality, power and style. One can discover in
        the recent work a certain urban grace, a working class
        affection or tenderness.

B401.   -----. "Polymètres de Henri Sauguet--Poèmes de Francis
        Poulenc." **La Revue musicale** no. 124 (March, 1932):
        220-221.
        The natural gifts of M. Sauguet are no longer lost
        in easy shapeless lyricism. In **Polymètres** (W234) the
        vocal lines, always gracious, are surrounded by clev-
        erly constructed accompaniments where nothing is left
        to chance, where even the harmonization declares that
        all is full of taste and sensibility.

B402.   -----. "Sérénades, de Leone Massimo, Igor Markévitch,
        Vittorio Rieti--Divertissement de chambre de Henri
        Sauguet." **La Revue musicale** no. 122 (January, 1932):
        62-64.
        This **Divertissement de chambre** (W85) is nothing
        more than a salon amusement.

B403.   Kochno, Boris. **Le Ballet.** Paris: Hachette, 1954.
        Important references, including illustrations, for
        La Chatte (W14), **La Nuit** (W17), **Les Forains** (W25) and
        La Rencontre (W26) by an artistic collaborator.

B404.   -----. **Christian Bérard.** Paris: Herscher, 1987.
        Translated by Philippe Core. London: Thames and
        Hudson, 1988.

Important references, including illustrations, for **La Chatte** (W14), for which Sauguet wanted Bérard to design the set and costumes, **La Nuit** (W17), **Les Forains** (W25), the music for which Sauguet wrote in seventeen days, **La Rencontre** (W26), **La Folle de Chaillot** (W375), and **Dom Juan** W379).

B405.   Kochno, Boris. **Diaghilev and the Ballets russes.** Translated by Adrienne Foulke. New York: Harper and Row, 1970.
References to the production of **La Chatte** (W14) and an interesting photo of Sauguet, Poulenc and Vittorio Rietti and his wife at a carnaval.

B406.   Kœchlin, Charles. "La Chartreuse de Parme." **Commune** no. 69 (May, 1939): 641-643.
What is most appealing to this former teacher of Sauguet in the opera (W4) is the thought and the musical language which he considers natural, simple and sincere.

B407.   -----. "Correspondance." **La Revue musicale** no. 348-350, 1983.
Sauguet and Kœchlin corresponded between 1922 and 1945. The collection includes Darius Milhaud's introductory letter recommending the young composer to Kœchlin and Sauguet's letter which requests a meeting with Kœchlin when he returns to Paris later in the year (1922).

B408.   Koegler, Horst. **The Concise Oxford dictionary of ballet.** 2nd ed. London: Oxford University Press, 1982.
Numerous references to Sauguet and his ballets and to other people involved in their productions.

B409.   Kolodin, Irving. "Carter for harpsichord." **Saturday Review** 48 (26 June, 1965): 56.
Review of Decca DL 10.108, DL 710.108 (D28). The **Suite royale** (W159) "is the only work for solo harpsichord on the record and is appropriately austere. Its personality is more of the instrument than of the composer."

B410.   -----. "Recordings reports II: Miscellaneous LPS." **Saturday review** 50 (25 March, 1967): 70.
Review of "A Regine Crespin song recital (Angel 36405 (D4). "The Roussel and Sauguet songs bring a little happier conclusion to the session."

B411.   -----. "Vlasov: Concerto no. 1. Sauguet: Mélodie concertante." **Saturday Review** 54 (27 November, 1971): 76.
Review of Melodiya/Angel SR 40180 (D39). "General musical interest is much better served by Sauguet, if no flaming masterpiece, shows the composer of Chout[!] at the point of compositional development associated with 1964. The composer has identified its motivation as the old memory of a young girl playing Debussy on

the cello--a character that is quite consistent
the content.

B412.   Kotschenreuther, Helmut. "The World's music--Ber-
lin." **Musical Courrier** 164, no. 6 (July, 1962): 30.
The choreography contained too much acrobatics
and motion and not enough real dancing. The music for
La Rencontre (W26) is incidental.

B413.   Kremenliev, Boris. "Beifall für Carlos Chavez und
Aurelio de la Vega in Los Angeles." **Melos** 33 (February, 1966): 64-65.
Review of Los Angeles Percussion Ensemble, directed by William Kraft, which performed **L'Espace du dedans** (W195). The poetry of Michaux is neither verse
nor prose, and the composer takes this into consideration. The composer's attention seemed to wander from
the text, and thus did the listeners.

B414.   Krenek, Ernst. "Henri Sauguet; Zur geistigen Haltung
jüngerer französischer Musik." **Anbruch** 15, no. 9/10
(November/December, 1933): 137-140.
A discussion of Sauguet's style with emphasis on
Le Plumet du Colonel (W1).

B415.   -----. "Opera between the wars." **Modern music** 20,
no. 2 (1943): 102-111.
Krenek considers Sauguet's **Le Plumet du Colonel**
(W1) "Gounodized."

B416.   Lade, John. "Henri Sauguet. Lente valse d'Amour
inquiet." **Musical times** 201, no. 1,421 (July, 1961):
445.
Brief review of an excerpt from **La Dame aux camélias** (W35) arranged for piano solo.

B417.   Lajoinie, Vincent. **Erik Satie**. Lausanne: L'Age
d'homme, 1985.
Brief character sketch of Sauguet with emphasis
on Satie's influence.

B418.   Laloy, Louis. "Revue musicale." **Revue des deux
mondes** no. 852 (1 August, 1939): 708-109.
La Chartreuse de Parme (W4) illustrates that the
composer has learned little since **La Chatte** (W14).
He still sounds like a beginner.

B419.   Lambert, Constant. **Music ho!** New York: October
House, 1967.
Lambert considers Sauguet directly opposed to
Webern. His music is a deliberate return to its most
sentimental and least valuable elements. It is ad-
mired because it is in the true tradition of Gounod.

B420.   Landormy, Paul. **La Musique française après Debussy.**
Paris: Gallimard, 1943.
Brief biographical sketch, including a works list
which is flavored by Landormy's likes and dislikes.
"He insists on the traditional merits of French music,

made up of clarity, reserve, grace, sobriety and
elegance.

B421.   Lausanne (City).   **Serge Lifar.   Un Vie pour la danse.**
Lausanne: Musée historique de l'ancien-evêché,
1986.
Concert on 8 June, 1986, included a performance
of **La Chatte** (W14).   Exhibition also included a poster
for **Symphonie en blanc** (W331).

B422.   Lazarus, Daniel.   "At the Olympic games."   **Modern music** 1, no. 3 (November, 1924): 29-31.
Le Plumet du Colonel (W1) was not without freshness and charm.   "It is a pity that the very young
composer did not feel the necessity of a little further study before presenting himself to the public.
I cannot believe that the new spirit and the youngest
musical expression of France are revealed in Salade
by Milhaud, in Mercure of Satie, or **Les Roses** (W13)
by Sauguet."

B423.   Leblé. Christian.   "Sauguet rejoint ses 'Mondes souterrains.'"   **La Liberation,** 23 June, 1989, 45.
Obituary.

B424.   Leibowitz, René.   "A propos de critique musicale."
L'Arche 7, no. 25 (January, 1947): 118-126.
An important, damning criticism of conservative
music critics like Auric and Sauguet (in Leibowitz's
opinion).   In particular he criticizes Sauguet and
an article entitled "Les Voies dangereuses." which
the author has not been able to find.

B425.   -----.   "La Musique."   **L'Arche** 2, no. 8 (August, 1945):
114-118.
French critics are against any music that doesn't
contain a galant style.   Despite the gifts of composers such as Milhaud, Poulenc, Auric, Sauguet, Roland-
Manuel, Messiaen, and others, nothing contemporary
is coming out of France.

B426.   Lemarchand, Jacques.   "Charivari Courteline au Théâtre
des Ambassadeurs."   **Combat,** 27 April, 1946, 2.
Brief citation about the amusing music by Sauguet
in **La Voiture versée** (W376).

B427.   Lesure, François.   "Sauguet."   **Enciclopedia della
spettacolo.**   Rome: Maschere, 1954.
Brief biographical sketch with a list of stage
works for which Sauguet wrote incidental music.

B428.   Levinson, Adnré.   **Les Visages de la danse.**   Paris:
Bernard Grasset, 1933.
David (W15) contains a good overture, but after
that the composer hesitates between Bach and Offenbach.

B429.   Leygue, Louis.   **Discours de M. Louis Leygue.**   Paris:
Institut, 1976.
Leygue, Président de l'Académie, introduces

Sauguet to the assembled members of the Académie as
part of his initiation to the Académie des Beaux-Arts.

B430.   Lido, Serge. **Ballet II.** Paris: Art et Industrie,
        1952.
        Brief reference to **Cordélia** (W29).

B431.   -----. **Ballet VI.** Paris: Art et Industrie, 1956.
        Brief reference to **Le Caméléopard** (W33).

B432.   -----. **Ballet d'aujourd'hui.** Paris: Vilo, 1965.
        Brief references to **Pâris** (W39).

B433.   -----. **Ballet panorama.** New York: Macmillan, 1961.
        Brief references to **La Dame aux camélias** (W35)
        and the 1961 production of **La Nuit** (W17).

B434.   Lidova, Irène. "Alonso crée 'La Dame aux camélias.'"
        Les Saisons de la danse no. 35 (June, 1971): 4-5.
        Citation for the Ballet National de Cuba's per-
        formance at Bordeaux, 22 May, 1971, of **La Dame** (W35).

B435.   -----. **Dix-sept visages de la danse française.** Par-
        is: Art et Industrie, 1953.
        Brief references to **Les Forains** (W25) and **La Ren-
        contre** (W26).

B436.   -----. **Roland Petit.** Paris: Lafont, 1956.
        Brief references to **Les Forains** (W25).

B437.   -----. **Trente ans de ballets français.** Paris: Vilo,
        1969.
        Brief references to **Image à Paul et Virginie** (W23),
        Les Mirages (W24), **Les Forains** (W25), **Pâris** (W39), and
        Les Amants de Teruel (W355).

B438.   Lifar, Serge. **La Danse.** Paris: Denoel, 1938.
        Lifar considers **La Chatte** (W14) the most perfect
        or most "Balanchinian" ballet at this time of his life.

B439.   -----. "Fin de saison chorégraphique à l'Opéra." **Le
        Figaro,** 7 August, 1942, 4.
        A discussion of the film **Symphonie en blanc** (W331).

B440.   -----. "Les Trois grâces du XXe siècle: Légends et
        Verité.** Paris: Buchet-Chastel, 1959.
        Lifar describes details concerning the production
        of **La Chatte** (W14).

B441.   Lonchampt, Jacques. "Henri Sauguet, Orphée de 80 ans."
        Le Monde, 2 February, 1981, 17.
        Sauguet is not as much at ease in the large clas-
        sic forms, and he sometimes seems ill at ease here by
        the wish to write a true concerto in the normal clas-
        sic or romantic manner, notably in the cadenza. But
        one becomes more interested in the musical ideas
        which, at moments, emerge from the haze and then fade
        too quickly away for our taste. We prefer passages
        where Orphée sings and charms or foils the savage

beasts. There is also in the slow movement a moving page which curiously reminds us of the loneliness of the Berg concerto. See: W77.

B442.   Lonchampt, Jacques. "La Mort d'Henri Sauguet. Une fan-
        taisie mêlée d'ombres." **Le Monde**, 24 June, 1989, 20.
        Obituary. Lists of honors include Académie des
        Beaux-Arts, Société des Auteurs et Compositeurs Dra-
        matiques (president), Académie du Jazz, Académie du
        disque français, Officier de la Légion d'Honneur,
        Grand Officier de l'Ordre du Mérite et Commandeur des
        Arts et Lettres, Société du Droit de Reproduction du
        Musique (honorary president).

B443.   -----. "Les Musiciens et leurs projets." **Le Monde**,
        22 February, 1962, 12.
        Sauguet's projects at the time of the interview
        included **Vie des campagnes** (W259), **Monelle de la nuit**
        (W439), and the **3rd Piano concerto** (W79).

B444.   -----. "La Musique." **Le Monde**, 9 February, 1968, 12.
        La Chartreuse de Parme (W4) contains a very pas-
        sionate lyricism which is deployed throughout, es-
        pecially in the last two acts. It's easy to look at
        this work as old fashioned, out of date, or merely as
        a pastiche, but one must look closer to see its lyri-
        cism and unique use of established tradition.

B445.   -----. "La Musique--Les Adieux de Doda Conrad." **Le
        Monde**, 20 March, 1965, 16.
        Doda Conrad, who premiered Sauguet's **Le Cornette**
        (W208) and **L'Espace du dedans** (W195), retires from
        performance. In his farewell appearance he performs
        works by his friends Poulenc, Auric, Françaix and
        Sauguet.

B446.   -----. "Musiques du printemps." **Le Monde**, 19 May,
        1981, 1.
        Of the **Quartet no. 3** (W100) Lonchampt says: Per-
        haps not since Debussy has there been a quartet that
        struck you so much with its colors and perfumes, with
        treat arms full of polyphonies glistening like flowers.
        Moving pages in memory of his friend Jacques Dupont,
        inspite of certain slightly banal developments, con-
        stantly display new freshness of character, ranging
        from profound outbursts to vehement sadness wherever
        necessary.

B447.   -----. "La 'Quatrième symphonie' d'Henri Sauguet."
        Le Monde, 2 December, 1971, 18.
        The **Fourth Symphony** (W71), called "The Third age,"
        by Henri Sauguet is very moving. The spirit, the
        playfulness, the poetry, the youthfulness, carefully
        sifted through a melancholy haze, mixed in with a
        sort of march, not really unrelenting as lyric, in-
        deed, epic, empty time, but also transfigured. Per-
        haps the middle slow movement has a more ordinary
        development, but his score is more complex than others,
        written with a light hand without disowning the past,

gives a very harmonious image of its author. It
watches, with a bittersweet tonality, toward the
future.

B448.   London, Kurt. **Film music.** New York: Arno, 1970.
        "Of Sauguet we so far only know the music for
L'Herbier's **L'Epevier** (W326).   We can see that here
are great possibilities for the future; and it is
one of many mysteries surrounding the French film
industry that this talented composer has been given
so few chances to show his worth." From the author's
preface of 1936.

B449.   Lyon, Raymond.   "Quatuor à cordes #2." **Le Courrier
        du disque microsillon** 7, no. 47 (3 October, 1948):
        8-9.
        Review of Vega C35 A171 (D56).   "This is a moving
composition, compelling, but not sad.   The **Quartet**
(W91) is beautiful throughout.

B450.   -----.   "Quelques disques de Grand Prix 1948." **Les
        Lettres françaises** no. 212 (10 June, 1948): 6.
        Les Forains recording (D49) on the Polydor label
barely wins out over Saint-Saëns' <u>Namouna</u> for the
Grand Prix du Disques Charles-Cros.

B451.   M., B.   "La Musique." **L'Europe nouvelle** no. 565 (3
        December, 1928): 1665.
        Sauguet is restrained in **David** (W15) by the design
of a series of tableaux, but he still offers a series
of agreeable dance numbers.

B452.   MacDonald, Nesta. **Diaghilev observed by critics in
        England and the United States 1911-1929.** New York:
        Dance Horizons Books, 1975.
        References to performances of **La Chatte** (W14) re-
viewed in <u>The Sphere</u> (2 July, 1927), <u>The Queen</u> (22
June, 1927), <u>Observer</u> (19 June, 1927), and <u>Morning
Post</u> (16 June, 1927).

B453.   Machabey, Armande.   "Le Triptyque." **L'Information
        musicale**, 29 January, 1943, 189.
        Machabey singles out the Baudelaire cat songs
which Sauguet set in **Six mélodies sur des poèmes symbolistes** (W239) as music which agrees with the poetry.

B454.   Maggie, Dinah.   "Bordeaux, la ville qui chante et qui
        danse avec la 'Symphonie Allégorique.'" **Combat,**
        22 May, 1951, 2.
        Poetic description of the town and the festivities
of the 1951 Mai musical de Bordeaux which featured **Les
Saisons** (W28).

B455.   -----.   "La Chorégraphie de Massine dégage une atmos-
        phere de bucolique rêverie." **Combat,** 22 May, 1951,
        2.
        A review of **Les Saisons** (W28) which emphasizes the
work as a complete theater piece.   When the **Symphonie
allégorique** (W57) was originally premiered Sauguet

found it necessary to add something extra in the form of sound effects. Now, as a ballet, everything is there to satisfy the eye and the ear. Nothing distracts from any other thing.

B456.   Magnan, Henry. "Christian Bérard n'est plus." **Le Monde. Section hebdomadaire,** 11-17 February, 1949, 4.
   Brief citations of Sauguet's works with Bérard on **La Nuit** (W17), **Les Forains** (W25), **La Rencontre** (W26), **La Folle de Chaillot** (W375), and **Dom Juan** (W379).

B457.   -----. Les Spectacles--Avec Louis Jouvet." **Le Monde,** 4 August, 1945, 7.
   In an interview which previews **La Folle de Chaillot** (W375), Jouvet mentions that the music will be by Sauguet.

B458.   Malherbe, Henri. "Le Ballet de l'Opéra en voyage." **Les Lettres françaises** no. 232 (4 November, 1948,: 6.
   An account of the Paris Opéra ballet's trip to the United States. They will include **Les Mirages** (W24) in their repertoire.

B459.   -----. "Le Bruit et la fureur de la danse." **Les Lettres françaises** no. 238 (16 December, 1948): 6.
   Never has Henri Sauguet put together such powerful rhythms or such clear expressiveness as in **La Rencontre** (W26). All is completely under control of his fantasy, from confident parading to inexperienced anguish. One does not know of better orchestration, more ingenious work which mixes together all the sonorities to the best effect. Henri Sauguet has entered into full mastery.

B460.   Manchester, P. W. "New York City Ballet, at State Theater New York season begins Nov. 18, 1966." **Dance news** 50, no. 1 (January, 1967): 9.
   This garland (W41) should have been put aside to wither unobtrusively after its appearance at a private benefit performance last April.

B461.   Manildi, Donald. "Sauguet: Piano music." **American record guide** (November/December, 1988): 77.
   Of the Billy Eidi performance of selected Sauguet piano music (D26) Manildi suggests that they are nicely laid out for the player's hands and the instrument's sonority, but not especially memorable. They make pleasant, undemanding listening and will undoubtedly be of interest to pianistically-oriented Francophiles wanting to explore new territory.

B462.   Marchesseau, Daniel. **Marie Laurencin.** Paris: Fernand Hazan, 1981.
   Brief reference to **Les Roses** (W13).

B463.   Mari, Pierrette. "A Besançon: Illustration de la musique contemporaine." **Les Lettres françaises** no.

841 (15-21 September, 1960): 8.
L'Oiseau a vu tout cela (W209), in our opinion, is
carried away with the description of a subject deliberately cruel and barbarous. Henri Sauguet has, moreover, avoided this pitfall of placing accentuation on
realism by giving emphasis to the interior drama of
the man about to die. His work, therefore, has force
without brutality, pathos without horror. The style
is well sustained, glazed with pleasant touches of
poetry.

B464. Mari, Pierrette. "Dans l'édition--L'Oiseau a vu tout
cela." **Le Guide du concert** 44, no. 386 (28 March,
1963): 745.
This jumble of writing provides a fabric of harmonic base over which the song declares, with warmth,
the dramatic recitation of Jean Cayrol. There is
something very strange and full of penetrating com-
passion about it. Accents of pathos are not lacking.
See: W209.

B465. -----. "Dans l'édition musicale--L'Oiseau a vu tout
cela." **Le Guide du concert** 43, no. 330 (17 November, 1961): 406.
This bird, which witnessed the suffering of human
pain, inspired the most exquisite and sensitive melodies. The harmonies of the accompaniment are dis-
cretely original and contrast and support it in a
style that results in unity. The voice of the baritone is placed within the range of the strings, in
juxtaposition sometimes dissonant, but always full of
tasteful espressiveness. See: W209.

B466. -----. "Entretien avec Marguerite Long." **Les Lettres
françaises**, no. 1,002 (7 November, 1963): 8.
The tenth Thibaud-Long contest will be headed by
Darius Milhaud as President and Henri Sauguet as Vice-
President.

B467. -----. "Le VIIIe Festival de Besançon." **Le Guide du
concert** 41, no. 283 (7 October, 1960): 95.
Henri Sauguet has set this cantata (**L'Oiseau a vu
tout cela**-W209) in a style deliberately stark, but it
lacks nothing of the power and expressiveness of the
poetry.

B468. -----. "Marguerite Long et le piano." **Les Lettres
françaises** no. 902 (4 January, 1962): 6.
Vasso Devetzi plays Sauguet's **Concerto no. 1** (W75)
at an Orchestre Pasdeloup concert, and Sauguet holds
an "animated dialogue" with Long about the value of
competitions and winner's performances.

B469. Marion, Dénis. "Les Amoureux sont seuls au monde."
Combat, 18 September, 1948, 4.
There is nothing else to say about the film (W340)
except to extend condolences to Louis Jouvet, Renée
Devilliers and Dany Robin for their participation in
the heartbreaking story, and especially to Henri

Sauguet whose successful music has made the viewing of this film pleasant.

B470.   Markevitch, Dimitry. **The Solo cello: A bibliography of unaccompanied violoncello literature.** Berkeley, Calif.: Fallen Leaf Press, 1989.
Brief reference concerning the **Sonate** (W172) by the man who commissioned the work and premiered it.

B471.   Markevitch, Igor. **Etre et avoir été.** Paris: Gallimard, 1980.
Several references to the good frienship they shared in the Hôtel Nollet days. Markevitch orchestrated some pages of **La Contrebasse** (W3) to help Sauguet meet his deadline.

B472.   -----. **Point d'orgue; entretiens avec Claude Rostand.** Paris: Julliard, 1959.
Markevitch helped copy the score of **Le Contrebasse** (W3) and may have orchestrated part of the Overture, perhaps as part of a lesson from Vittorio Rietti.

B473.   Marnold, Jean. "Musique." **Mercure de France** no. 632 (15 October, 1924): 524-531.
Les Roses (W13) is without the slightest interest.

B474.   Martin, John. "Ballet: Markova as Giselle." **New York Times**, 21 April, 1955, 35.
Notice that the Ballet Theater will present **La Rencontre** (W26) at the Metropolitan Opera House.

B475.   -----. "Ballet: 'The Sphinx' bows." **New York Times**, 22 April, 1955, 21.
Brief review of the New York performance of **La Rencontre** (W26).

B476.   -----. "The Dance: Art of Jooss." **New York Times**, 5 November, 1933, sec. 9, 2.
Serge Lifar, in his American debut, performs **La Chatte** (W14).

B477.   -----. "The Dance: Diaghileff's group." **New York Times**, 8 June, 1930, sec. 9, 6.
Brief description of **La Nuit** (W17).

B478.   -----. "The Dance jubilee." **New York Times**, 29 August, 1948, sec. 2, 5.
Paris Opéra Ballet will perform **Les Mirages** (W24) during its appearance at the International Dance Festival, 21-30 October, 1948.

B479.   -----. "The Dance: Next fall's celebrity." **New York Times**, 7 May, 1933, sec. 9, 6.
A brief description of Serge Lifar's career which cites **la Nuit** (W17) in the Cochran 1930 revue.

B480.   -----. "Lifar makes debut; Diaghileff protege." **New York Times**, 6 November, 1933, 17.
The final number of the evening was **La Chatte** (W14).

B481.   Massine, Léonide. **My life in ballet.** London: Mac-
         millan, 1968.
         References to Soirées de Paris (which contained
         Les Roses--W13), **La Chatte** (W14), and **David** (W15) and
         a biographical sketch of Sauguet.

B482.   Mattfeld, Julius. **A Handbook of American operatic**
         premieres 1731-1962. (Detroit Studies in Music Bib-
         liography no. 5) Detroit: Information Coordina-
         tors, 1963.
         Reference to the 27 July, 1962, U. S. premier of
         Le Contrebasse (W3) at the Wheeler Opera House in
         Aspen, Colorado.

B483.   Maulnier, Thierry. "Ou Supervielle reinvente Robin-
         son." **Combat,** 13 November, 1952, 2.
         Henri Sauguet's music is very agreeable. See:
         W387.

B484.   Maur, Karin von. **Salvador Dalí, 1904-1989.** Stuttgart:
         Gerd Hatje, 1989.
         Reference to **Le Sacre de l'automne** (W32).

B485.   Meisner, N. "Obituary." **Dance and dancers** no. 473
         (1989): 40.

B486.   Menasce, Jacques de. "henri Sauguet." **Musical quar-**
         terly 36 (January, 1950): 114-124.
         One of the best and most accessible articles on
         Henri Sauguet. After a brief biography Menasce links
         Sauguet to neo-romanticism. The analytic portion of
         the article focuses on **La Rencontre** (W26), **Cinq poèmes**
         de Max Jacob (W246), and the **Second String Quartet**
         (W91).

B487.   -----. "Patrons." **New York Times,** 23 October, 1949,
         sec. 2, 7.
         During Menasce's six-month tour of Europe he en-
         countered a number of patrons of music. Among them
         were Comtesse Jean de Polignac who included (among
         others) Henri Sauguet as her friend.

B488.   Menger, Pierre-Michel. **La Condition du compositeur**
         et le marche de la musique contemporaine. Paris:
         La Documentation française, 1982.
         The study, financed by La Fondacion SACEM, suggests
         that older composers receive more performances than
         younger ones. The older generation, such as Sauguet,
         Auric and Milhaud, who are symphonic composers, have
         long been active in music for the stage and for films.
         A general survey of all members of SACEM includes a
         comment that Sauguet is considered reactionary.

B489.   Merlin, Olivier. "Le Ballet de l'Opéra s'est-il four-
         voyer à New York?" **Le Monde,** 9 October, 1943, 8.
         Despite the lack of general support since its re-
         turn from New York and Washington, the Ballet de
         l'Opéra has been adventuresome in presenting ballets
         like **Les Mirages** (W24) and Le Chevalier et la Damoiselle.

B490.   Merlin, Olivier. "Créations chorégraphiques." **Le
        Monde**, 9 May, 1952, 8.
        Cordélia (W29) by Henri Sauguet and John Taras
        weaves the poetry of a dream and the shadows of a
        nightmare a little in the style of **La Nuit** (W17), **Les
        Forains** (W25), and Rendevous (**La Rencontre?**)

B491.   -----. "La Dame aux camélias à l'Opéra. **Le Monde**,
        5 February, 1960, 12.
        Merlin finds the action as relentless as the
        guillotine, and Sauguet lacks the ability to decapi-
        tate it in **La Dame** (W35).

B492.   -----. **L'Opéra de Paris**. Fribourg: Hatier, 1975.
        Commentary concerning **Les Mirages** (W24) includes
        a photography of participants preparing the production
        of the ballet. They are: Auric, Jacques Dupont,
        Lifar, Gabriel Dussurget, Sauguet and Cassandre. Con-
        cerning **David** (W15) Merlin comments that Ida Rubin-
        stein sought to seduce the old companion in arms of
        Diaghilev: Stravinsky, Ravel, Sauguet, Alexandre
        Benois, Massini, Bronislava Nijinska, to her ballet
        company.

B493.   -----. "Un Mois faste pour le ballet." **Le Monde**.
        Section hebdomadaire, 9-15 December, 1949, 4.
        During the month of November **Les Forains** (W25) was
        performed by the Ballets des Champs-Elysées.

B494.   -----. "Nouvelle danseuse étoile de l'Opéra--Nina
        Vyroubova, sera-t-elle une Chauviré?" **Le Monde**.
        Section hebdomadaire, 24-30 March, 1950, 5.
        A sketch of Vyroubova's career. Will she be ready
        to take over the lead in **Les Mirages** (W24)?

B495.   -----. "La Rentrée du corps de ballet de l'Opéra."
        Le Monde, 25 September, 1952, 13.
        The Ballets de l'Opéra returns to Paris with a
        full season. **Les Mirages** (W24) with its skillful com-
        bination of choreography and music and sets, still
        seems a hit.

B496.   -----. "Reprise des 'Mirages.'" **Le Monde**, 28 Sep-
        tember, 1962, 15.
        Les Mirages (W24) is resurrected, and the critic
        says that he certainly would not have returned without
        the marvelous, nostalgic music of Henri Sauguet.

B497.   Michaut, Pierre. **Le Ballet contemporain, 1929-1950**.
        Paris: Plon, 1950.
        Brief references to **Les Roses** (W13), **David** (W15),
        La Chatte (W14), **Fastes** (W19), and **La Nuit** (W17) Con-
        cerning **Les Mirages** (W24) Sauguet's music was a com-
        pletely successful accompaniment, very clear, which
        had the easy transparency of a song upon which the
        choreographer could model his dances. About **Les
        Forains** (W25) it's success was really extraordinary.
        Concerning **La Rencontre** (W26) it was remarkably suc-
        cessful because of the power of its music and the

direction and eloquence and appropriateness of the
mythic scenery.

B498.   Michaut, Pierre. "Critique du cinéma--L'Honorable
Catherine." **L'Information musicale**, 12 February,
1943, 203.
Sauguet's score gives the Rose Pavillion scene an
excellent atmosphere. See: W332.

B499.   Milhaud, Darius. "The Brilliant impressario." **Modern
music** 7, no. 1 (December/January, 1929-1930): 12-15.
During the last season Diaghilev called upon a
still younger element, Henri Sauguet for **La Chatte**
(W14) and Nabokov for his Ode with choruses.

B500.   -----. "'La Chartreuse de Parme' à l'Opéra." **Ce
Soir**, 18 March, 1939, 12.
A favorable review by a friend who likens Sauguet
to Berlioz or Bizet. See: W4.

B501.   -----. "Les dernières œuvres d'Erik Satie et les
premières œuvres d'Henri Sauguet." **Les Feuilles
libres**, 5, no. 37 (September/October, 1924): 46-48.
After commenting about Satie's latest works Mercure and Relâche, Milhaud then compares Sauguet, one
of the youngest musicians of France, to the well-
established Satie. Sauguet takes his inspiration from
Chopin, but his taste for simplicity and proportions
derive directly from Fauré, Debussy, and especially
Satie. General references are made to the **Françaises**
(W141), songs on texts by Cocteau, Copperie, Gabory,
and Radiguet, the flute **Sonatine** (W102), a nocturne
and **Danse des matelots** (W44), and **Le Plumet du Colonel** (W1). He notes, in particular, Sauguet's melodic
facility and his surety of taste. "His music has
something of the quality of a siamese cat." See:
W225, W226, W227, W228 concerning the above-mentioned
songs.

B502.   -----. "The Day after tommorrow." **Modern music** 3,
no. 1 (November/December, 1925): 15-17.
Sauguet has never succumbed to the influence of
jazz. Chopin is his chief influence. The stamp of
his personality is especially marked in the military
opera-bouffe **Le Plumet du Colonel** (W1). It may be
said that this is badly orchestrated, but should one
expect to find a boy of twenty-two orchestrating pages
of perfect balance in his first attempt? All the music of this score is pleasing, and that is itself
rare enough.

B503   -----. **Entretiens avec Claude Rostand**. Paris: Julliard, 1952.
In speaking of music criticism he refers to Sauguet's as intelligent and caustic.

B504.   -----. **Etudes**. Paris: Claude Aveline, 1927.
Chapters of particular importance in this collection of writtings are: "La musique française dupuis

la guere," "Un Semaine à Paris au printemps de 1925,"
"Jean Wiener," and "Les tendances de quelques jeunes
musiciens français."

B505.   Milhaud, Darius. **Ma vie heureuse.** Paris: Pierre
Belfond, 1973.
Besides quotes from his earlier Notes sans mu-
que (B509), Milhaud writes about stage music including Sauguet's **Irma** (W361), of the 1937 Universal Exposition, which had as one of its by-products A L'exposition (See W153), and his experiences at the Aspen
Festival where Sauguet was also a guest (See W3, W62,
and W201). After Milhaud's war-time exile he returned
to France where Sauguet was helpful in bringing him
up to date about such things as the death of Max
Jacob.

B506.   -----. "La Musique--A l'O.S.P.: Le 'Concerto grosso'
de Igor Markevitch et 'La Nuit' de Henri Sauguet."
L'Europe nouvelle no. 670 (13 December, 1930): 1795-
1796.
La Nuit suite (W47) is a work where the heart
speaks with modesty mixed with tenderness. All the
poetic feelings are revealed in this symphonic poem
with an exquisite purity.

B507.   -----. **Notes sans musique.** Paris: Juillard, 1949.
Translated by Donald Evans under the title **Notes
without music.** New York: Da Capo, 1970.
Milhaud considered Sauguet the most gifted of
l'Ecole d'Arcueil. He refers to **Le Plumet du Colonel**
W1), **La Chatte** (W14), **La Chartreuse de Parme** (W4),
and a recording of **La Voyante** (D41).

B508.   -----. "'La Nuit' de Henri Sauguet." **L'Europe nouvelle** no. 635 (2 April, 1930): 570.
In **La Nuit suite** (W47) the orchestration is extremely restrained; each timbre keeps its expressive
value intact and is always presented to us in its
purest element.

B509.   -----. "Paris opera just before the occupation."
Modern music 18, no. 1 (November/December, 1940):
45.
The performance of Henri Sauguet's delightful **La
Chartreuse de Parme** (W4), with costumes and settings
stamped with the sure taste of Jacques Dupont, was
one of the most beautiful moments of this renaissance
in opera.

B510.   -----. "'Le Plumet du Colonel' par Henri Sauguet."
L'Europe nouvelle no. 583 (13 April, 1929): 477.
On each page, on each line, in each measure of
the score (W1) there is a spate of uninterrupted melody or ideas bouncing from place to place, connected
together with an imagination and a grace of the most
youthful freshness. All the requisite qualities of a
comic opera are found here in certain blossoming. The
most tender scene of Isabelle, the too-young wife of

the jealous colonel, the constant interruptions of the comic hero, the arrival of the creole who charms us like she charms the enchanted bird, all this with a sense of lively and flowing theater. Milhaud continues and speculates about the possibility of a performance in the future by the Frankfurt Opera.

B511. Miller, Phillip L. **The Guide to long playing records.** New York: Knopf, 1955.
Brief review of R.E.B. 2 (D51) and Doda Conrad's performance of **Visions infernales** and **Mouvements du cœur.**

B512. Montboron. "Grands concerts--Grande salle Pleyel--La Récital Janine Charrat et Roland Petit." **L'Œuvre,** 17-18 April, 1943, 4.
"I especially preferred the **Paul and Virgine** (W23) with music by Henri Sauguet on this recital."

B513. Montu, Suzanne. "La Suite à quatre mains et à deux pianos au XXe siècle." **Revue international de musique française** no. 15 (November, 1984): 101-111.
In **Les Jeux de l'amour et du hasard** (W127) there is simultaneously a compromise and a synthesis of the classic and romantic suite. From a very romantic point of view the composer expresses with infinite poetry and sincerity the happiness in his life at this period.

B514. Mootz, William. "'Les Trois Lys' is 30 years too late." **Louisville Courrier-Journal,** 26 September, 1954.
Concerning the symphonic movement (W61) "it recalls some of those creations of the 1920s which were still thought clever in the 30s, suddenly discovered to be woefully empty in the 40s, and are no longer played in the 50s."

B515. Mosk. "Ce Siècle a 50 Ans." **Variety,** 26 April, 1950, 22.
Brief plot summary and evaluation of the film (W344) with music by Auric and Sauguet.

B516. -----. "Julie De Carneilhan." **Variety,** 24 May, 1950, 20.
Brief plot summary and evaluation of the film (W345) with music by Sauguet.

B517. Mouron, Henri. **A. M. Cassandre.** New York: Rizzoli, 1985.
References to **Les Mirages** (W24) including a plate illustrating the stage set.

B518. Moussinac, Léon. **The New movement in the theatre.** 1931. Reprint. New York: B. Blom, 1967.
Brief references to **La Chatte** (W14).

B519. "Les Musiques qui viennent." **L'Information musicale,** 12 September, 1941, 11.

In response to a question about what he is doing in the world of music today, Sauguet replies that he is working on **Péché de jeunesse** (W328) and **La Gageure imprévue** (W5).

B520.   Mussy, Georges. "Concerts & récitals." **Le Figaro,** 1 April, 1930, 6.
At l'O.S.P. Pierre Monteux presented an unpublished work by Henri Sauguet, **La Nuit suite** (W47). "Indescriminately, we see people who are downcast and also several impressions of nocturnal life. A waltz intervenes like a blurred memory. M. Monteux conducted this score with a kindly and easy hand."

B521.   Myers, Rollo. **Modern French music; its evolution and cultural background from 1900 to the present day.** Oxford: Basil Blackwood, 1971.
Contains a biographical sketch of Sauguet.

B522.   "New publications." **Musical courrier** 143 (1 March, 1951): 28.
The **Quartet no. 2** (W91) is a lyrical work conceived along traditional lines. The first movement is an elegant Andantino capricioso; the second is marked Lento molto expressivo, and has a real lyric grace. A waltz, with several ponticello effects, forms the third movement; and an Andante moderato concludes the work.

B523.   "New publications in review." **Musical courrier** 143 (1 March, 1951): 27.
One look at the music for **Visions infernales** (W250) is enough to identify the contemporary Gallic technique --a pointed style of writing, clear melodic lines, rich but not cloying harmonizations, and the ghost of Debussy hovering over all.

B524.   "New works by living composers." **Music news** 41 (February, 1949): 4.
Notice of Doda Conrad's 28 December, 1948, Town Hall recital which included **Visions infernales** (W250).

B525.   "News from the world--Paris." **Ballet today** 9, no. 9 (October, 1956): 7.
The reviewer was disappointed in **Le Caméléopard** (W33) because the choreography didn't include any real dancing.

B526.   "Notes et informations--Les Ballets de Mme Ida Rubinstein." **Le Figaro,** 7 December, 1928, 6.
David (W15) is an extraordinary impression of biblical poetry.

B527.   "Nouvelles brève à l'étranger." **Le Guide du concert** 31, no. 14 (18 May, 1951): 265.
Henri Sauguet is noted as elected a member of the National Institute of Arts and Letters in New York.

B528.   "Obituary." **Boston Globe,** 23 June, 1989, 83.

B529.   "Obituary." **Musik und Gesellschaft** 41 (August, 1989):
        446.

B530.   "Obituary." **Das Orchester** 37 (September, 1989): 992.

B531.   "Obituary." **Times,** 26 June, 1989, 16.

B532.   "Obituary." **Variety** 335 (5 July, 1989): 110.

B533.   Oenslager, Donald. **Stage design.** New York: Viking
        Press, 1975.
        Brief references to **Ondine** (W364).

B534.   "Les Œuvres." **Nouvelle revue musicale** 33 (June/July,
        1924): 212.
        Brief reference to **Les Roses** (W13).

B535.   Ollivier, Eric. "Hommage à Lifar." **Réalités** 382
        (December, 1977): xxiv.
        Les Mirages (W24) performed at L'Opéra de Paris
        as part of a tribute to Serge Lifar.

B536.   "Ondine." **Theatre arts monthly** 23, no. 9 (September,
        1939): 623.
        Brief reference to the play (W364) and its pro-
        duction.

B537.   "Opera tonight; workshop tomorrow." **Aspen Times,** 26
        July, 1962.
        La Contrebasse (W3) performed by the Opera Workshop
        of the Aspen Music School. The opera was staged by
        Madeleine Milhaud. Jennie Tourel performed **La Voyante**
        (W201) and the **Symphony no. 3** (W62) was performed on
        Sunday.

B538.   Orwen, Gifford P. "Henri Sauguet: Visions Infernales,
        Les Pénitents en Maillots Roses." **Notes** 8, no. 3
        (March, 1951): 398.
        In **Visions infernales** (W250) "Regates mysterieuses"
        stands out with a breadth and sweep despite a macabre
        subject. Vocally and textually "Le Petit paysan" and
        "Exhortation" have a poignancy enhanced by hauntingly
        repetitious patterns in the accompaniment. In these
        two pieces Sauguet's predilection for a vocal line of
        nearly recitative simplicity counterpointed against a
        relatively intricate texture in the accompaniment is
        noticable. In **Cinq poèmes de Max Jacob** (W246) "A une
        Sainte le jour de sa fête" combines subtle rhythmic
        patterns with an insouciant refrain and an unexpected
        codetta into an altogether original song.

B539.   Osborne, Charles. **The Dictionary of opera.** New York:
        Simon and Schuster, 1983.
        Brief biographical sketch.

B540.   P., L. "Frantsayskie myszkanty v Moskve." **Sovetskaîa
        muzyka** 27 (January, 1963): 126-127.
        An account of the visit to the Soviet Union by
        Sauguet, Auric, D. Lesur, R. Boucher, and M. Hoffmann.

B541.   "Paris." **Musical courrier** 161 (April, 1960): 31.
        Over the pretty score of **La Dame aux camélias**
        (W35) hovers, from time to time, the shadows of such
        romanticists as Liszt, Chopin and Johann Strauss. The
        music is logical, varied, frequently audacious, and is
        wonderfully danceable, thanks to its fine rhythms and
        its dramatic melodies.

B542.   **Paris, 1937-1957.** Paris: Centre Georges Pompidou,
        1981.
        References to **Ondine** (W364) and **La Folle de Chail-
        lot** (W375).

B543.   Pâris, Alain. "La Symphonie française de 1918 à nos
        jours." **Courrier musical de France** no. 68 (1979):
        137-139.
        Sauguet's symphonies (W53, W57, W62, W71) are con-
        sidered humaine. His music is colorful and trans-
        parent. They reject the aggressive quality of sound
        prevalent in this era, but they do not appear out of
        place.

B544.   **Paris-Moscou, 1900-1930.** Paris: Centre Georges Pom-
        pidou, 1979.
        References to **La Chatte** (W14).

B545.   Parisot, Raoul. "Un 'Première' d'Henri Sauguet." **Le
        Guide du concert** 42, no. 317 (9 June, 1961): 1227.
        Plus loin que la nuit et le jour (W38) compared
        to a twilight tale, extremely sensitive and poetic.
        It has become, thanks to the voice and the dance, a
        ravishing spectacle which the public has warmly ap-
        plauded. "There is little left to describe about the
        daring and ability in the acting-out of the story and
        the dance. It is incontestably a 'Sauguet feeling,'
        a color which is personally expressive to this musi-
        cian."

B546.   Pascal, Claude, "A l'Opéra Comique—'Gageure imprévue.'"
        L'Œuvre, 9 July, 1944, 2.
        The opera (W5) is set in a classic form, somewhat
        like the <u>Devin du village</u>, with beautiful arias. The
        critic, however, found it difficult to hear the words
        because the orchestra was too heavy.

B547.   Passek, Jean Loup. **Dictionnaire du cinéma.** Paris:
        Librairie Larousse, 1986.
        Brief biographical sketches of many of the French
        film community with whom Sauguet worked. Claude Mi-
        chel Cluny contributes a brief biographical sketch and
        appreciation of Sauguet's work in film music.

B548.   Peckham, Anson W. "Sauguet--Poulenc--Auric--Préger--
        Milhaud: Mouvements du Cœur; Sauguet: Visions In-
        fernales." **American record guide** 15 (May, 1950):
        310.
        Review of R.E.B.2 (D51). Concerning the **Visions**
        (W250) "Sauguet's music is effectively mated to the
        words, a further example of the present-day French

leadership in the field of serious song writing."

B549.   Persichetti, Vincent.   "Music for band and orchestra."
Notes 12, no. 1 (September, 1955): 656.
The Concerto d'Orphée (W77) is a "refreshingly
lyric and sensitive work with transparency of thought.
In maintaining a certain 'classic' formal equilibrium
Sauguet relies too often on measured accompaniment
figures; the piece is in want of contrapuntal interest
and spontaniety of rhythmic ideas. The gloomy is too
plesant and the carefree too moody. Although there
are several finely molded passages, the over-all work
lacks the beauty it is describing."

B550.   "Petit dictionnaire des compositeurs contemporains."
Almanach de la musique 1950, 209-210.
Reference to Sauguet, and a works list.

B551.   Petit, Raymond.   "Latin gaiety today."   Modern music
9, no. 2 (January/February, 1932): 74-78.
"I am thinking of Sauguet, for instance, whose
Plumet du Colonel (W1), opera bouffe performed fairly
recently by Mme. Beriza, revealed much verve and true
comic invention, but who development, as Contrebasse
(W3), a sketch given this year by Balieff, clearly
showed, seems arrested because he has not acquired
sufficient formal perfection."

B552.   Petit, Roland.   "L'Accord du mouvement et de la mu-
sique."   Avant scène ballet danse 15 (1984): 34-36.
An illustrated article by Petit relating the
necessity to coordinate movement and music when crea-
ting a ballet. The article also contains contribu-
tions by Sauguet, Jean Robin, Boris Kochno, Gabriel
Dussurget, Jean-Michel Damasse, Marcel Landowski,
Marius Constant, Erté, Edmonde Charles-Roux, and Henri
Dutilleux, all of who collaborated with Petit. See:
W25 concerning Les Forains in which Petit danced.

B553.   Pfunke, Peter C.   "Sauguet: Les Forains; Concerto no.
1."   American record guide (November, 1983): 45.
A review of Le Chant du Monde LCX-78300 (D17).
The Concerto (W75) is a tepid affair, quite conservative and generally romantic in style. Skillfully
crafted, it is a pleasant but not very exciting work.
Les Forains (W25) is even frothier, with moments that
border on the banal; it is a fairly high-spirited
score in the manner of latter-day Offenbach.

B554.   Philidor.   "Les Disques--Musique contemporaine."   Le
Monde, 15 April, 1959, 12.
Commentary about the four discs which were awarded
the Grand Prix de l'Académie Charles Cros. "Let us
end with another French composer. His Quartet no. 2
(W91) has grace and delicacy. The Lento molto expressivo is a lament which is bathed in hope. A review
of Vega C35 A171 (D56).

B555. Pierhal, Armand. "La Musique enregistrée--Ballets de
       Poulenc et de Sauguet." **Preuves** 3, no. 25 (March,
       1953): 94.
           Review of Polydor LP 540003 (D49). **Les Forains**
       (W25) is a work of maturity. It has always been popu-
       lar and remains one of the best achievements of the
       composer.

B556. Pierre, José. "Au temps du 'Bœuf sur le toit.'" **Œil**
       no. 311 (June, 1981): 52-57.
           Brief reference to **Les Roses** (W13).

B557. Pierre-Petit. "Boule de suif." **Le Figaro**, 18 Decem-
       ber, 1978, 8.
           The production of the opera (W9) has undeniable
       charm where intelligence and imagination are united
       to give us great pleasure. In spite of a few little
       faults, easily erased, it is an entertainment of ex-
       cellent quality.

B558. -----. "Henri Sauguet est mort." **Le Figaro**, 23 June,
       1989, 41.
           An obituary which includes a tribute subtitled
       "Un musicien de cœur et d'esprit."

B559. Pinzauti, Leonardo. "A colloquio con Henri Sauguet."
       Nouva revista musical italiana 4, no. 2 (March-June,
       1970): 482-487.
           An interview with Sauguet on the occasion of the
       performance of **La Voyante** (W201) at the Maggio musicale
       di Firenze (1970). Pinzauti questions Sauguet about
       his early career and his aesthetic attitude toward
       Schoenberg and others like Boulez, Berio, Nono, and
       Stockhausen.

B560. Plaut, Fred, and Rose. Papers. Yale University, New
       Haven, Connecticut.
           Contains letters from Sauguet and photographs of
       Sauguet during a visit to New York City.

B561. Pistone, Daniele, ed. **Le Théâtre lyrique français,
       1945-1985.** Paris: Librairie Honoré Champion, 1987.
           References to operas by Sauguet A table cites
       thirteen recordings of five different operatic works
       by Sauguet. An article entitled "Opéra: 'pour' ou
       'avec' les enfants" by Sauguet in Cahiers de l'anima-
       tion musicale no. 9 (September, 1978) is also cited.

B562. Polignac, Princesse Edmond de. "Mes amis musiciens."
       La Revue de Paris 71 (August/September, 1964): 97-
       105.
           The Princesse discusses her interactions with mu-
       sicians and her role in encouraging new music. She
       considers Sauguet as the principle representative of
       l'Ecole d'Arcueil and lists **Les Jeux de l'amour et du
       hasard** (W127) as dedicated to her.

B563. Porcile, François. **Présence de la musique à l'écran.**
       Paris: Cerf, 1969.

References to **Farrebique** (W337) on the Vega 30
A98 recording (D55).

B564.   Porter, Andrew. "Music of today--Henri Sauguet's 'Les
            Caprices de Marianne.'" **Musical events** 9, no. 9
            (September, 1954): 24-28.
            "The most interesting piece of new music, however,
        and the highest of the Festival was Henri Sauguet's
        latest opera, **Les Caprices de Marianne** (W6). I ad-
        mired this enormously." Sauguet's light, lyrical,
        flexible music seems an ideal partnership with Mus-
        set's lines.

B565.   Poulenc, Francis. **Correspondance, 1915-1963.** Paris:
            Editions du Seuil, 1967.
            A selection of letters which includes correspon-
        dence exchanged by Poulenc and Sauguet between 1923
        and 1962.

B566.   -----. **Diary of my songs.** Translated by Winifred
            Radford. London: Golanz, 1985. Originally pub-
            lished as Journal de mes mélodies (Paris: La So-
            ciété des amis de Francis Poulenc, 1964).
            Preface to the original edition by Henri Sauguet.
        Also contains a brief biographical sketch of Sauguet
        and a selected discography.

B567.   -----. **Entretiens avec Claude Rostand.** Paris: Jul-
            liard, 1954.
            References to Sauguet, especially the night in
        Hyères when **La Voyante** (W201) was premiered. Present
        at the event, besides the hosts, the Noailles, were
        Bruñuel, Giacommetti, Igor Markevitch, Christian Bé-
        rard, the Aurics, Nicolas Nabokov, Poulenc and Sauguet.
        Poulenc liked Sauguet's music, which he considered
        between the generation of Les Six and that of Messiaen.
        "It has a very authentic personality without tricks
        or mannerisms. With only the aid of his poetic sen-
        sitivity Sauguet has summed up a certain climate of
        our era, very near to the work of Christian Bérard."

B568.   Pourchet, Maurice. "The 1951-52 Ballet season in
            Paris." **Ballet annual** 7: 102-107.
            The Ballets des Champs-Elysées revives **La Ren-
        contre** (W26).

B569.   Pourtales, Guy de. "Musique." **Marianne,** 22 February,
            1933, 15.
            With his **Jeux de l'amour et du hasard** (W127) Henri
        Sauguet puts us in mind of some five or six illustrious
        people some time before. It is Chaminade in 1933. It
        suddenly seems to us like a finely worked out Scarf
        Dance adjusted to today's taste, less of the melody
        than of the effect: all honey and guaranteed pure
        sugar. I'll wager that a part of the audience had a
        spell cast upon it.

B570.   "Premier Festival international de la R.T.F." **Combat,**
            6 August, 1954, 2.

La Voyante (W201) with Elda Ribetti as the soloist
is scheduled for the first program (30 August) of the
Festival international de la Radio et de la Télévision.

B571.   "Le Programme du festival d'Aix-en-Provence." Le Monde,
18 June, 1954, 12.
Forecast of the festival program which included
Les Caprices de Marianne (W6).

B572.   Prunieres, Henry. "Chroniques et notes--Les Théâtres
lyriques--Les Ballets russes." La Revue musicale 8,
no. 9 (1 July, 1927): 48-51.
The score of La Chatte (W14) is a model of the
genre. It is very agreeable music, very rhythmic, of
a melodic form which recalls from time to time Offenbach and Léo Délibes.

B573.   -----. "New Prokofieff ballet--'Pas d'Acier' produced in Paris by Diaghileff Company--Other novelties." New York Times, 26 June, 1927, sec. 8, 4.
Brief reference to La Chatte (W14) which was also
on the program.

B574.   -----. "Paris music in May." New York Times, 1 May,
1927, sec. 8, 6.
Brief reference to the Paris premier of La Chatte
(W14).

B575.   -----. "Paris music varied." New York Times, 19 June,
1927, sec. 7, 6.
Concerning La Chatte (W14), it is a very pleasing
score in the style of traditional French operetta.
It is very agreeable, very naïeve and not without melodic spontaniety.

B576.   "Quatuor à cordes en re majeur." L'Information musi-
cale, 30 May-6 June, 1942, 626.
Brief analytical description of the Quartet no. 1
(W81) which was about to be premiered.

B577.   Quéant, Gilles. Encyclopédie du théâtre contemporaine.
Paris: Olivier Perrin, 1959.
Quéant's work is essential to the study of theater
in France during the first half of this century. Of
particular interest are the essays by Jacques Damase
("Les Ballets russes et suédois") which discusses La
Chatte (W14); Marie-Françoise Christoul ("Lifar et le
ballet") which refers to Les Mirages (W24); Rose-Marie
Madoues ("Jouvet et Bérard") which cites La Folle de
Chaillot (W375), Dom Juan (W379), Tartuffe (W382), and
Les Fourberies de Scapin (W381); Jean Robin and André
Coffrant ("Les Ballets du Champs-Elysées") which refers
to Les Forains (W25) and La Rencontre (W26); and
Pierre-Aimé Touchard ("Giraudoux, Jouvet, Bérard")
which cites Ondine (W364).

B578.   -----. Théâtre de France. Paris: Olivier Perrin,
1950-1956 (6 vols.)
Vol. 2 contains information concerning Comme il

vous plaira (W386); vol. 3 for **Robinson Crusoë** (W387)
and vol. 6 cites **Les Caprices de Marianne** (W6), **Caméléopard** (W33) and **Suites d'une course** (W389).

B579. R., F. "What Paris thought of two ballet companies."
Ballet today 5, no. 6 (June, 1952): 20.
The score for **Cordélia** (W29) is considered rather
feeble.

B580. Rapin, Maurice. "'Comme il vous plaira' marquera un
changement d'orientation de la Salle Luxembourg."
Le Figaro, 6 December, 1951, 6.
Brief reference to Sauguet's music for the play
(W286).

B581. -----. "En Hommage à André Gide." **Le Figaro**, 15
June, 1949, 4.
In **Le Retour de l'enfant prodigue** (W362) it was
the admirable music of Henri Sauguet which was not
modified in the evening's tributes.

B582. -----. "Pour monter 'Le Tartuffe' Louis Jouvet n'a
maintenu qu'une tradition." **Le Figaro**, 23 January,
1950, 6.
For the play (W382) Henri Sauguet composed some
discrete background to lighten up the denouement, thus
making it seem like a divertissement.

B583. Rebatet, Lucien. "La Musique--Les Concerts." **L'Action
française**, 24 March, 1939, 4.
Rebatet finds **Le Chartreuse de Parme** (W4) long,
monotonous and old-fashioned.

B584. "Reception chez Heugel." **Le Guide du concert**, 38, no.
184 (14 February, 1958): 765.
Sauguet and Milhaud sign contracts with the publishing house of Heugel which hosts a reception for
them.

B585. Rèche, Albert. "Un Cantate chorégraphique de Sauguet."
Le Figaro, 18 May, 1961, 23.
The audience which awaited this choreographic cantata written by Henri Sauguet on a poem by his coun-
tryman Louis Emié, **Plus loin que la nuit** (W38), was
not disappointed. The moving, gentle, mysterious and
sensitive form of the poetry was in total accord with
the radiant music of Sauguet and the choreography of
Jean-Jacques Etcheverry. The authors of the success
cannot be dissociated from each other. The a cappella
mixed chorus went far to underline the pantomime of
the three stars of the ballet of the Grand Théâtre de
Bordeaux.

B586. -----. "Marcel Dupré et Henri Sauguet au Festival de
Bordeaux." **Le Figaro**, 22 May, 1951, 6.
The apotheosis of this Mai musical was the premier
of the **Symphonie allégorique** (W28) by Henri Sauguet.
Enchantingly symbolic, this symphony, so full of grace,
and charm, united music, dance and song.

B587. "Les Revues." **Le Guide du concert** 16, no. 27 (4
April, 1930): 762.
Excerpts from the reviews of the premier of the
orchestral suite from **La Nuit** (W47) on 30 March, 1930.
P. Dambly says that "The natural sparseness of M.
Sauguet seems to offer here a slight suspicion of slen-
derness." Paul Le Flem thinks that the work assures
the "success of the score and its author." L. Aubert
considers it "a peaky little work."

B588. Rey, Etienne. "La Chronique dramatique--M. et Mme.
Roméo." **L'Œuvre** 22-23 July, 1944, 3.
The critic singles out the incidental music for
the play (W374) for special notice.

B589. Reyna, Ferdinando. **Histoire du ballet.** Paris: Aimery
Somogy, 1964.
A good, compact survey of ballet through history.
Reyna cites **La Chatte** (W14), **David** (W15), **Les Mirages**
(W24), **Les Forains** (W25), **La Rencontre** (W26), **La Dame
aux camélias** (W35), and **Caméléopard** (W33) along with
a biographical sketch of Sauguet.

B590. Richard, Roger. "Sur les ondes 'L'Oiseleur et la
Fleuriste' d'Armand Lanoux." **Combat**, 14 December,
1950, 2.
"Henri Sauguet's music (W416) pleasantly aids
Lanoux's text in transporting the listener to the
world where flowers sing and birds smell pretty."

B591. Richardson, Philip J. S. "Les Ballets des Champs-
Elysées." **Dancing times** no. 428 (May, 1946): 390.
Les Forains (W25) gives us the "first glimpse of
realism and deeper character than the company has so
far given us." The company danced for five weeks at
the Adelphi Theatre.

B592. -----. "La Rencontre." **Dancing times** no. 470 (November, 1949): 69.
Brief citation to **La Rencontre** (W26) and its performance in London.

B593. -----. "Yvette Chauviré." **Dancing times** no. 566 (No-
vember, 1957): 63.
Cover photo and story about **La Dame aux camélias**
(W35) and Chauviré's appearance in the ballet.

B594. Rivoyre, Christine de. "A la Comédie-Française-Lux-
embourg." **Le Monde**, 9-10 December, 1951.
Henri Sauguet's music for **Comme il vous plaira**
(W386) is as clear and light as a spring.

B595. -----. "L'Actualité chorégraphique." **Le Monde**, 24
March, 1951, 7.
Announcement of the program for the Mai musical
de Bordeaux which featured **Les Saisons** (W28).

B596. -----. "L'Actualité chorégraphique dans le monde."
Le Monde. Section hebdomadaire, 23-29 March, 1951, 5.

Nothing was undertaken by the Grand Ballets du
Marquis de Cuevas during the New York season last au-
tumn; they are beginning to rehearse a ballet by Henri
Sauguet, Les Quatre Saisons (W28).

B597. Rogeri. "Suite Royale." **Music journal** 23 (February,
1965): 106-107.
Henri Sauguet created a remarkably original composition (W159) for solo harpsichord while drawing
heavily on the legacy of the highly developed seven-
teenth century French keyboard style. The frequent
"echo" effects and other small contrasts, together
with ornate passage work, arabesque figurations, and
ritornello-form elements assure the composer's sure-
ness of his stylistic roots.

B598. Roland-Manuel. "Les Ballets des Champs-Elysées.
Combat, 18-19 March, 1945, 2.
The occasion of the unforgetable, nostalgic and
delicious **Forains** (W25) of Henri Sauguet serves today to gather together the trained stars.

B599. -----. "Les Ballets des Champs-Elysées." **Combat**, 12
November, 1948, 4.
A single unpublished ballet **La Rencontre** (W26),
based on a scenario by Boris Kochno, accounts for a
score which can be numbered among the best. The best
conceived, the best written, the most clearly arranged, and the most poetically allusive work which
this musician of great taste and ballet sense has
given us. Sauguet excells, moreover, in translating
the image and choreographic idea into the musical
symbol.

B600. -----. "Ballets russes." **Revue Pleyel** no. 45 (June,
1927): 289-290.
The music for **La Chatte** (W14) has much freshness,
charming frankness and grace. This young man possesses
among other things, the gift of melody which Euturpe
reserves only for her favorites. There are not many
young men who appear better suited than M. Henri Sauguet to write so easily the free and singing music
and to present to dancers a resonant carpet.

B601. -----. "'Les Forains' ballet d'Henri Sauguet." **Combat**, 16 October, 1945, 2.
Concerning the orchestral suite from **Les Forains**
(W52), it is the balance and perfection of the ensemble
which makes for the charm and value. The nostalgic
music has liveliness, and the richness of invention
is sustained.

B602. -----. "Les Mirages." **Combat**, 28 January, 1945, 2.
Concerning the orchestral suite from **Les Mirages**
(W49), the music possesses the virtue of melody.

B603. -----. "Mozart compositeur mediterranéen au Festival
d'Aix-en-Provence." **Combat**, 1 August, 1949, 2.
Season included **String quartet no. 2** (W91) premier.

B604.   Roland-Manuel. "Musiques de ballet 'Les Mirages'
        d'Henri Sauguet à l'Orchestre national." **Combat**,
        22 December, 1945, 2.
            Concerning the orchestral suite from **Les Mirages**
        (W49) "The composer gives us here a symphonic ballet.
        Sauguet, moreover, has much in common with the master
        of the 'Belle au bois dormant,' and I believe that
        the comparison would please him as much to hear it as
        I was pleased to say it.

B605.   Rosenthal, Harold, and John Warrack. **The Concise Ox-
        ford dictionary of opera.** 2nd ed. London: Oxford
        University Press, 1979.
            Brief biographical sketch of Sauguet with a selec-
        tive works list.

B606.   Rostand, Claude. "Au Festival de Berlin--Romantisme
        et art abstrait." **Le Monde**, 6 October, 1957, 14.
            Concerning **La Dame aux camélias** (W35) Sauguet
        gives us one of the most remarkable, moving and poetic
        scores. It is cast in an expressive climate which
        suits the subject exactly and places us in an ambiance
        of rejuvenated romanticism with complete delicacy.
        It touches everything directly. But the musical lan-
        guage employed by the composer is not archaic, quite
        to the contrary. It rejuvenates , for the most part,
        the usual style of M. Sauguet. Melodically, harmoni-
        cally especially there is invention, brainwaves,
        changes of direction and a great novelty which con-
        stantly radiates novelty and dazzling freedom of
        writing.

B607.   -----. "Les Caprices de Marianne." **La Table ronde**
        no. 81 (1954): 149-152.
            A lengthy review of the action in the opera (W6)
        which concludes: "In brief, a complete and enticing
        success on the poetic scale. One which marks a most
        interesting originality."

B608.   -----. "Le Cornette." **La Table ronde** no. 50 (Feb-
        ruary, 1952): 175-178.
            Throughout the grand recitative of the score
        (W208) M. Sauguet has treated it in a mixture of
        styles of the epic and the ballade while always pre-
        serving a direct, lyric tone. It is doubtless because
        of the length of the work that it was conceived as a
        recitative rather than as a symphonic poem. In this
        sense it is probable that the composer tried to ease
        the strain on the singer by placing the burden on the
        orchestra that permits the singer to be more an ob-
        server.

B609.   -----. **Dictionnaire de la musique contemporaine.**
        Paris: Larousse, 1970.
            Brief biographical sketch of Sauguet.

B610.   -----. "Dumas' Camille theme of new ballet." **Musi-
        cal America** 80 (March, 1960): 15.
            Sauguet's music (W35) eludes the conventions which

we find in most ballets. It is a score of extraordinary poetic delicacy, without big, superficial effects, without brilliant climaxes, all in subtle
nuances and profoundly romantic in character. The
musical language, lightly touched with atonality, is
very personal and extremely free. After Verdi's fa-
mous arias, which are in everyone's ears, it was difficult and risky to illustrate musically the pathetic
adventures of Marguerite. Yet Sauguet has succeeded
with much taste and originality in this score which
is one of his best works.

B611.   Rostand, Claude. "Musique contemporaine à Aix-en-
         Provence." **La Table ronde** no. 69 (September, 1953):
         153-158.
              Rostand describes the programatic aspects of the
         Concerto d'Orphée (W77) and comments about the jux-
         taposition of diatonic and atonal writing. He is
         quick to point out that the atonal writing is not
         twelve-tone composition. He further questions why
         Sauguet did this. Was it because the composer wanted
         the concerto to be more like its neighbors on the pro-
         gram? "All in all, it is a strong, handsome score,
         but perhaps it deserves to be better developed."

B612.   -----. **La Musique française contemporaine.** Paris:
         Presses Universitaires de France, 1952. Translated
         by Henri Marx as **French music today.** New York:
         Merlin Press, n.d.
              Contains a biographical reference to Sauguet and
         the Arceuil School which stresses the composer's
         highly personal language, his growth and maturity,
         and the originality of his melodic ingenuity. Es-
         pecially noted are **La Voyante** (W201), **La Chartreuse
         de Parme** (W4), **La Rencontre** (W26), adn **Les Saisons**
         (W28).

B613.   -----. **Petit guide de l'auditeur de musique. Les
         chefs-d'œuvres du piano.** Paris: Plon, 1950.
              Brief biographical sketch and references to the
         Sonate (W145), **Pièces poétiques** (W151), and the **Con-
         certo in a** (W75).

B614.   "Soirée d'opéras bouffes à l'Opéra de Marseille."
         Le Monde, 30 November, 1956, 12.
              Refering to **La Contrebasse** (W3), it is buffonery,
         full of genuine poetry. It is astonishing that it has
         not figured in the repertory more often of the lyric
         theater.

B615.   -----. "Symphonie allégorique." **La Table ronde** no.
         43 (July, 1951): 172-174.
              Speaking of **Les Saisons** (W28), we have here, in
         effect, a ballet score composed not with rhythmic in-
         spiration, but one which has as a subjective base,
         conceived with expressive sentiment. Departing from
         the appearance of the seasons he writes of the soul
         of the seasons, and in this the orchestra is treated
         with much transparancy, lightness and color.

B616.   Roy, Jean. "Hommage. Henri Sauguet, souvenirs d'en
        France." **Le Monde de la musique** no. 125 (September,
        1989): 38-39.
            A tribute to Sauguet followed by excerpts from
        the composer's memoirs and an announcement of the pub-
        lication of them as La Musique, ma vie.

B617.   -----. **Musique française. Presences contemporaines.**
        Paris: Debress, 1969.
            Lengthy biographical portrait with a works list
        and a discography.

B618.   -----. "Sauguet." **Encyclopédie de la musique.** Paris:
        Fasquelle, 1961.
            Biographical sketch with works list.

B619.   Sabin, Robert. "Ballet Theatre." **Dance observer** 22,
        no. 6 (June/July, 1955): 84.
            Description and cast for the 21 April performance
        of **La Rencontre** (W26). "The music was mediocre but
        servicable."

B620.   -----. "Ballet Theatre marks 15th anniversary." **Mu-
        sical America** 75 (May, 1955): 5.
            See B621 above for identical comment.

B621.   -----. "Henri Sauguet concert, Museum of Modern Art,
        April 23." **Musical America** 73 (May, 1953): 22.
            "Like Poulenc, he writes with a nonchalance, a
        melodic charm, and a transparency of style that many
        more 'serious' composers might envy. Sauguet is a
        romanticist at heart; he does not hesitate to compose
        long, rhythmically inert movements in which the moods
        drift by like summer clouds. But there is always me-
        lodic shape and sumptuous harmony in his work. Like
        Fauré, he can graze cliches without ever falling into
        them."
            Perhaps the most characteristic and fascinating
        piece on the program was **La Voyante** (W201).
            The **Second Quartet** (W91) is "exquisitely scored
        and harmonically interesting throughout. Its weak-
        ness consists in its looseness of form, its lack of
        rhythmic propulsion and variety, and its neglect of
        contrapuntal development. But, static as it is in
        part, it is lovely music."
            Bocages (W92) is "expertly scored and full of de-
        lightful passages, even if it is rather aimless."
            La Chèvrefeuille (W245) contained neither poems
        nor music which were very original or compelling, but
        "both were elegant."
            "It was a mistake to attempt **La Nuit** (W17) upon
        the tiny stage; it was rather like watching a company
        attempt a performance of Les Sylphides in a clothes
        closet. The music seemed pulseless, though not with-
        out atmospheric charm."

B622.   Sabrie, Jean-Charles. **Cinéma français, les anées 50.**
        Les longs métrages réalisés de 1950 à 1959. Paris:
        Centre Pompidou/Economica, 1987.

Brief references to **Don Juan** (W348), **Lorsque l'enfant paraît** (W349), **Œufs de l'autruche** (W350), and
Tu es Pierre (W352).

B623.   Sachs, Maurice. **The Decade of illusion. Paris, 1918-
1928.** New York: Knopf, 1933.
A brief character sketch reveals Sauguet to be
"thin, sharp, biting, as he had an astonishing gift
for entertaining. Only in him or Paul Smara have I
known repartee so lively or so cruel. But one must
judge by more than appearances; the deep sensitivity
enclosed in his music revealed a wealth of sentiment
which doubtless he had some reason for dissimulating."

B624.   Sadoul, Georges. **Dictionaire des films.** Paris:
Seuil/Microcosme, 1978.
References to **Farrebique** (W337) and Sauguet's con-
tribution to the film .

B625.   Salter, Lionel. "Diaghilev at Monte Carlo." **Gramophone** no. 688 (September, 1980): 552.
La Chatte (W14) contains "ballet music of a more
conventional sub-Délibes kind." <u>See</u>: D33.

B626.   -----. "Exposition Paris, 1937." **Gramophone** no. 788
(January, 1989): 1190-1191.
In **La Nuit coloniale** (W153) "Sauguet rambles past
the Expo's colonial pavilions, picking up whiffs of
their exoticism." <u>See</u>: D30.

B627.   Samazeuilh, Gustave. "Les Concerts." **La Revue heb-
domadaire** 41, no. 32 (6 August, 1932): 108-115.
Listing of the composers who have written msuic
for the benefit concert of Nikitina and her partner,
Witback. They include Stravinsky, Prokofiev, Satie,
Nabokov and "even Sauguet." <u>See</u>: W18.

B628.   -----. "Les Concours du Conservatoire et du Prix de
Rome--Derniers concerts--Festivals et saison.--Deux
livres." **La Revue hebdomadaire** 43, no. 33 (18 August, 1934): 372-377.
Marie-Thérèse Holley performs a program which includes music by Monteverdi and unnamed song(s) by Sauguet.

B629.   -----. "La 'Grande saison' de Paris." **La Revue hebdomadaire** 44, no. 30 (27 June, 1935): 492-499.
The orchestral suite from **Fastes** (W48) was conducted by Inghelbrecht at one of the Concerts de La
Sérénade.

B630.   -----. "Le 'juin' Parisien." **La Revue hebdomadaire**
42, no. 27 (8 July, 1933): 237-242.
"On the other hand, one can only say about his
other ballet, **Fastes** (W19), that M. Sauguet's mani-
festly limited technical resources and his musical
invention hardly permit the degree of sumptuousness
to which he aspires.

B631.   Samazeuilh, Gustave.   "Opéra--Quelques récitals et
séances de musique de chambre." **La Revue hebdomadaire** 41, no. 11 (12 March, 1932): 229-241.
   "M. Sauguet and the indefatigable Jane Bathori
presented a series of songs entitled **Polymètres** (W234)
among which "La Double rougeur" and "La Vide" seem to
me to be adequate reflections of their titles." He
also performed in the role of Baron Méduse in Satie's
Piège de Méduse on this concert. His "Debut on the
stage seems to assure him of a brilliant future as an
actor. Accept this as an omen . . . ."

B632.   Sarnaker, Benedict.   "Sauguet: Les Forains. Concerto
no. 1 for piano and orchestra." **Hi-Fi News and record review** 26, no. 5 (May, 1981): 83.
   Review of Chant du Monde LDX 78300 (D 17). The
music for **Les Forains** (W25) is easy to listen to and
very attractively and skillfully shaped and orchestrated. It is also richly varied although this very
variety makes it less than ideal for listening right
through without the intended visual stimulus. About
the **Concerto** (W75): "This is a shapely, pseudo-Roman-
tic work distinguished by its elegance, clarity and a
delicate (and deep) lyricism."

B633.   Sarraute, Claude.   "Les Ballets de Jean Babilée sur
la scène du Théâtre des Champs-Elysées." **Le Monde,**
19 July, 1956, 10.
   A review of the company and an announcement of its
program which will include **Le Caméléopard** (W33).

B634.   -----. "La Danse--Janine Charrat et son Ballet de
France." **Le Monde,** 27 November, 1964, 14.
   There was beautiful unanimity in **Pâris** (W39).

B635.   "Sauguet." **Dictionnaire des hommes du théâtre français
contemporains.** Paris: Olivier Perrin, 1967.
   Biographical sketch.

B636.   "Sauguet." **Enciclopedia della musica.** Milan: Riz-
zoli/Ricordi, 1972.
   Biographical sketch.

B637.   Schloezer, Boris de.   "A propos de La Chartreuse de
Parme." **La Nouvelle revue française** no. 308 (May,
1939): 894-896.
   Schloezer believes that **La Chartreuse** (W4) is not
great opera, but at least it is enjoyable.

B638.   -----. "Chronique musicale." **La Nouvelle revue française** no. 130 (1 July, 1924): 112.
   The spring season was full of promises that French
music was alive and in full flower. "Among these promises, one of the most significant was **Le Plumet du
Colonel** (W1) by Sauguet, a little comic opera in one
act. If this young musician has the courage to work
and to resist the attentions of his friends, he will
do very great things."

B639. Schloezer, Boris de. "Chronique musicale." **La Nou-velle revue française** no. 167 (1 August, 1927): 244-248.
Schloezer looks at **La Chatte** (W14) with many references to **Le Plumet du Colonel** (W1). "Sauguet owes much to Satie and to his colleagues, but he can do better than they because the charm of his music lies in his melodic abundance.

B640. -----. "Les Spectacles du Théâtre Beriza." **La Revue musical** 5, no. 8 (June, 1924): 243-244.
Le Plumet du Colonel (W1) was a welcome contrast to Berner's work (La Carosse du Sacrament). "I believe that the young composer deserves most of the credit (for the evening), upon the condition that he works and perfects his technique, still very elementary. Sauguet has an undeniable melodic gift, truly novel and interesting rhythmic ideas and a great sense of the theater."

B641. Schlumberger, Jean. "Avec 'La Tentation de Tati' j'ai laché les renes à la fantaisie." **Le Figaro**, 16 February, 1949, 4.
The play (W380) contained very witty and refined incidental music by Sauguet.

B642. Schneider, Louis. "La Musique." **La Revue de France** 7, no. 13 (1 July, 1927): 175-177.
"The mystery remains as to why the score (for **La Chatte--W14**) was entrusted to a youth: M. Henri Sauguet, whose score was an academic retrograde which paid homage to Théodore Dubois or Charles Lefebvre, if they are still around, provided only a background in front of which the dancers could describe geometric figures in space."

B643. Schneider, Marcel. "A Aix-en-Provence, première audition mondiale des 'Caprices de Marianne,' opéra de Sauguet." **Combat**, 23 July, 1954, 2.
Schneider's review of **Les Caprices de Marianne** (W6) is extensive. "Two possibilities were open to Sauguet, either the magnification or the simplificaiton of the scenario. That is, to typecast the characters, accentuate the buffonery or the carnaval atmosphere, strengthen the secondary roles, or, on the contrary, give amplitude to the pathos of Celio and to the dramatic liveliness of Octave. He preferred the poetic option, thoughtful and sensitive musician that he is." A synopsis of the plot follows along with the arrangement of musical materials and the treatment of the recitatives, arias, duos, etc., so that everything seems more like a lyrical conversation than like a number opera. Schneider compares some of the qualities he found in **Les Caprices** to some he heard in the **Concerto d'Orphée** (W77) with its extremely free tonality and how this works with a lighter orchestration. There is much that is very subtle and very refined in this personal adaptation of atonality. "The **Caprices** is the best work by Sauguet."

B644.   Schneider, Marcel. "Aix et Orange en 1974." **La Nou-
        velle revue française** 44, no. 263 (1974): 126.
        Summer festivals are gradually adding new works
        to their programs. Sauguet is beginning to appear on
        them. Composers such as Sauguet, whom he has met at
        the Aix Festival, find it important to attend them.

B645.   -----. "Au Festival de Bordeaux." **Combat**, 19 May,
        1961, 8.
        Concerning **La Plus loin que la nuit et le jour**
        (W38), Sauguet has "told us in confidence that it is
        a portrait of the soul and the countryside around the
        Gironde. It is made up of fondness, sweetness, and
        calm contemplation. No one could have said it better.
        The music suggests a lyric, elegaic soul embued with
        the vision of nature and borders upon a religious
        feeling.

B646.   -----. "Au Festival de Bordeaux qui s'ouvira le 20
        mai, l'art lyrique cedera le pas aux ballets."
        Combat, 7 May, 1951, 2.
        A schedule for the Mai musical de Bordeaux includes
        the premier of Sauguet's **Saisons** (W28).

B647.   -----. "Le 'Ballet de France' aux Champs-Elysées--La
        Musique." **Combat**, 27 November, 1964, 11.
        Sauguet's ballet, **Pâris** (W39), is separated beau-
        tifully into melodic elements which one can easily
        distinguish between, even though they are pasted to-
        gether. The five variations are ingeniously worked
        out and portray the characteristics of each partici-
        pant, especially that of Vénus which is best worked
        out and developed. The final Pas de deux between
        Pâris and the unknown maiden is preferred, and it al-
        lows Sauguet a free hand in his lyricism. It is his
        twenty-fifth ballet score and still remains easily
        recognizable from the others. For its charm, fluidity
        of writing and evocative poetry **Pâris** joins **Fastes**
        (W19), **Cordélia** (W29), and **La Rencontre** (W26).

B648.   -----. "'Cordélia' et "Coup de feu' de Sauguet et
        d'Auric." **Combat**, 10-11 May, 1952, 2.
        Cordélia (W29) is an enchantment which is divided
        into tenderness, compassion, idyl, dreaminess; the
        score can also be valued by itself for the poetic and
        emotional lyricism that it sustains. It is conceived
        of as a symphonic legend and a dream, and as such, it
        unfolds without interruption. It was created as much
        for the ear and the heart as for the eye. Sauguet
        has composed a truely danceable ballet.

B649.   -----. "La Danse." **La Nouvelle revue française** 51,
        no. 300 (1978): 166-170.
        The excellent music for **Les Mirages** (W24) by Sau-
        guet stands between fantasy and dream and holds ev-
        erything together in a fascinating spectacle.

B650.   -----. "Festival d'Aix-en-Provence, 1953." **Combat**,
        29 June, 1953, 8.

Preview of the Festival program which includes the premier of the **Concerto d'Orphée** (W77).

B651.   Schneider, Marcel. "Festival Sauguet." **Combat,** 10
            June, 1963, 11.
            Concerning **Le Cornette** (W208): "There are certain
         affinities between Sauguet and Rilke which are main-
         tained from beginning to end."
            The **Third Piano Concerto** (W79) resembles a fantasy
         for piano and orchestra. The unity is realized, ac-
         cording ot the composers avowal "outside the thematic,
         melodic and rhythmic elements." It is here that we
         recognize the characteristic of Sauguet: "transform
         with sounds, an emotion and a poetic vision."
            The **Golden Suite** (W93) is a succession of elegaic
         and tender canticle, a very ingeniously varied song,
         and an ironic and unselfconscious march.

B652.   -----. "La Guirlande de Campra ou la Nouvelle Guir-
            lande de Julie." **Combat,** 6 August, 1952, 2.
            In the **Variations** (W60) "the Minuet by Sauguet is
         a long development, then a delicious arabesque, giving
         rise more and more to reveries, visions of the dance
         and the poetry of yesterday."

B653.   -----. **Henri Sauguet.** Paris: Ventadour, 1959.
            An early biography (in French) of Sauguet with a
         works list and a discography.

B654.   -----. "Henri Sauguet." **Combat,** 8 March, 1961, 9.
            L'Oiseau a vu tout cela (W209) ends on a solemn
         tone, nearly mystical in its gravity and spirituality.
         The way in which it passes, from the peaceful begin-
         ning to the animated ending, through nobleness of faith
         or courage, connected by subtle linkages, is ample
         testimony to the unanimous admiration which Sauguet
         deserves.
            In **La Nuit des rois** (W397) Sauguet has written
         pages which seem as if they had been written by Eliz-
         abethan composers and recall the melodies he composed
         for the poems by Max Jacob (W246).
            Listeners will be surprised to hear a song by Sau-
         guet, written in a style similar to that on the theme
         of his **Forains** for Edith Piaf (i.e., **Le Chemin des
         forains**--W297). **Un Seul poème** (W308) was composed on
         a poem by Denise Bourdet for a television program,
         "Les Muses s'amusent," hosted by Claude Roy.

B655.   -----. "La Musique de Sauguet restaure le lyrisme
            romantique." **Combat,** 22 May, 1951, 2.
            Les Saisons (W28) is a fresco in sound which is
         somewhere between pure music and opera. Musically it
         leaves **Forains** (W25) and **Mirages** (W24) long behind it
         and is nearer to the **String quartet** (W91) and some
         scenes in **Le Chartreuse de Parme** (W4). The "Nocturne
         du Rossignol" forms the lyrical acme of the symphonie.
         Thanks to a knowledgeable and unfettered writing, a
         chromatism full of langor, the dissonances, which nev-
         er fall into discord, romantic lyricism remains.

B656.   Schneider, Marcel. "Musique moderne à Aix-en-Pro-
         vence." **combat**, 30 July, 1953, 2.
             The **Concerto d'Orphée** (W77) was "written at the
         request of M. Strobel, but Sauguet had long been temp-
         ted by the lyrical, charming and elegant quality of
         the violin, and to write such a composition for it."
         The three movements are connected in a sort of lyri-
         cal meditation where fantasy and freedom are given
         free rein. The rhythmic and atonal tendencies of the
         introduction return incessantly during the course of
         the concerto and form a continual ambiguity. Sauguet
         tried in this work to give expression to a new style,
         reshelving that of **La Rencontre** (W26), which discon-
         certed those who admired **Saisons** (W28), **Forains** (W25),
         and **Mirages** (W24) and the **Concerto for piano** (W75).
         "This is a most refined and subtle style which tries
         less to please than to envelope the spirit in an air
         or seduction."

B657.   ------. "Quatrième Symphonie." **Combat**, 2 December,
         1971, 11.
             The three traditional movements which make up
         this new symphony (W71) each possess their own beauty
         and individual character. They are equally balanced
         because all movements were conceived as a whole.

B658.   ------. "Rostropovitch joue Britten et Sauguet." **Com-
         bat**, 16 December, 1964, 9.
             The **Mélodie concertante** (W80) is composed in a
         single gesture with subtle and natural interweavings
         at the same time. It is a sad and joyous meditation.
         His ambiguous harmony and vague tonality create a
         powerful presence which evokes and creates an atmos-
         phere of lyricism, tenderness, and the dream at which
         Sauguet excels.

B659.   ------. "60ème anniversaire de Henri Sauguet." **Com-
         bat**, 24 November, 1961, 9.
             The three movements of the **Concerto d'Orphée** (W77)
         are interconnected in a true poetic meditation. It is
         a very free rhapsody which evokes ancient lyricism and
         the sovereignty of inspiration.
             The **Third Symphony** (W62) is a "noble, persuasive,
         moving, subtle, and delicate work." The great success
         of the symphony is its variety.
             The last scene of the orchestral suite from **La
         Dame aux camélias** (W65) has something spectral and
         fairy-like, which makes it an "anti-Traviata," and
         assures the lyrical unity of the ballet.

B660.   ------. "Vasso Devetzi et Sauguet." **Combat**, 16 Octo-
         ber, 1962, 11.
             Vasso Devetzi returns to Paris and plays Sauguet's
         First Concerto (W75). The critic regrets that young
         pianists only play Prokofiev or Bartók when a home-
         grown composer of so much talent does not receive his
         fair share of performances.

B661.   Schneider, Marcel. "La Vita musicale all'estero--
         Francia." **Musica d'oggi** 3 (April, 1960): 178-179.
           Henri Sauguet has conceived **La Dame aux camélias**
         (W35) as an "anti-Traviata." The music has something
         spectral and magic in its quality. He has achieved
         this by incorporating bitonality, polytonality, and
         all the resources available to musicians today.

B662.   Schonberg, Harold. "Music: Henri Sauguet visits As-
         pen." **New York Times**, 23 July, 1962, 18.
           "**La Contrebasse** (W3) is a delightfully frothy mix-
         ture in the tradition of Offenbach and Poulenc. Light,
         giddy, very sophisticated melodically pert, it is a
         real charmer."
           The **Third Symphony** (W62) is entirely different.
         Here "he is serious and has attempted a broad style
         that completely avoids the music-hall atmosphere and
         motion-picture associations of many of his other
         works."
           "If there is an influence it is Honegger rather
         than Poulenc. There is something muscular about the
         writing, though it must be said that the symphony con-
         tains none of the 'angry man' outbursts found in
         Honegger. Climaxes there are in plenty, but never
         hysteria or rhetoric. Complicated rhythmic devices
         are handled with tact, and the symphony as a whole is
         the work of a serious, skilled composer."

B663.   -----. "Musical softball. Students play the faculty
         at Aspen with Brahms in the background." **New York
         Times**, 29 July, 1962, 7.
           Notice for the American premier of Sauguet's
         Third Symphony (W62).

B664.   -----. "A new vein. Once a mining town, Aspen now
         finds riches as music and sports center." **New York
         Times**, 22 July, sec. 2, 7.
           Notice that Sauguet is at Aspen for a visit, and
         that his **Third Symphony** (W62) and **La Contrebasse** (W3)
         will be performed.

B665.   "The School of Arcueil and Young France." **Larousse
         Encyclopedia of music.** New York: World Publishing,
         1971.
           Brief account of younger composers in France, in-
         cluding Sauguet.

B666.   Schwerke, Irving. "Paris finds some glowing pages in
         world premiere of Sauguet's opera." **Musical cour-
         rier** 119 (15 April, 1949): 5.
           In **La Chartreuse de Parme** (W4) "one had the im-
         pression of being in the presence of a score that was
         neither young nor old, neither reactionary nor revo-
         lutionary, neither radical nor conservative.
           The composition has some ravishing pages, some
         that are ingratiatingly fresh, some that are almost
         hot with passion's glow, others, such as the cradle
         song and Fabrice's aria in the tavern scene, that are
         burdened with real beauty."

B667.   Searle, Humphrey. **Ballet music.** New York: Dover,
         1973.
              La Chatte (W14) contains some "not very distin-
         guished music by Henri Sauguet."
              Les Forains (W25) is "adequate for its purpose
         but hardly more than that; Sauguet has never been a
         particularly inspired composer."

B668.   "Une Semaine chorégraphique riche en creations."   **Le**
         Monde, 6 May, 1952, 9.
              Notice of the premier of **Cordélia** (W29).

B669.   Shearer, Moira. **Balletmaster. A dancer's view of**
         George Balanchine. London: Sidgwick and Jackson,
         1986.
              Numerous citations to **La Chatte** (W14), **Fastes**
         (W19) and Sauguet.

B670.   Siclier, Jacques.   "La Télévision--Le Prince et le
         mendiant." **Le Monde,** 7 September, 1965, 9.
              What we have here is a tentative expression of
         pure television, but the fusion of the two elements,
         choreography and dramaturgy, has, most of the time,
         an artificial character.   If the work is charming, it
         is more because of its visual effects than for the
         direction, which is a compromise between theater and
         cinema.   See: W40.

B671.   Siohan, Robert.   "Experiences musicales." **Le Monde,**
         4 June, 1959, 12.
              "For my part, I accord special mention to **Aspect**
         sentimental (W324) of Henri Sauguet, most nearly like
         recognizable music, and infinitely poetic."

B672.   Smith, Cecil.   "Sauguet, Henri: Visions Infernales."
         Musical America 70 (1 November, 1950): 32.
              "These are not important songs (W250), but they
         are skillfully and cleanly written with excellent
         French prosody and with the sensitive taste that marks
         Sauguet as an inheritor of the viewpoint and composi-
         tional practices of Fauré and Satie."

B673.   Snook, Paul A.   "Sauguet: 'L'Oiseau a vu tout cela--
         Cantata. Garden Concerto. Sonate d'église.'" **Fan-**
         fare 13, no. 3 (January/February, 1990): 290.
              In **L'Oiseau** (W209) "Sauguet's vocal line is inti-
         mate and expressive, and his writing for string or-
         chestra is both sweet and sinewy, as the flow of the
         music requires."
              The **Garden Concerto** (W81) "embodies the full gamut
         of Sauguet's esthetic, as he so acutely and epigram-
         matically describes it: 'lightness is not frivolity,
         depth is not solemnity, simplicity is not poverty,
         transparency is not emptiness, liberty is not chance.'"
              Typical of so many of Sauguet's compositions, in
         the **Sonate** (W82) a group of small sequences slowly and
         repeatedly build up into larger musical paragraphs or
         stanzas.   See: D8.

B674.   Snook, Paul,   "Sauguet: String quartet no. 2, no. 3."
        Fanfare 9, no. 4 (March/April, 1986): 22-23.
        The **Quartet no.** 2 (W91) "projects that special
        aura of pensive contemplation, shot through with sud-
        den volatile changes of emotional gear that charac-
        terizes Sauguet's idiom."
        The **Quartet no.** 3 (W100) utilizes quasi-conver-
        sational tone, but with more pungent and soulful in-
        flections: the polytonal textures are denser, the
        thematic ideas more cursive, and the overall atmo-
        sphere more highly charged. It is fraught with the
        radiant trills, hypnotically repeated modulations and
        gently sighing cadenced lyricism, which convey Sau-
        guet's unerring sense of serene and mournful mystery
        with near-immediacy of a speaking voice." See: D24.

B675.   Solar, Jean. **Maurice Thiriet.** Paris: Ventadour,
        1957.
        Thiriet classes Sauguet with the giants of film
        music when it was at its peak. They were the spiri-
        tual inheritors of the French trandition which derives
        from Costeley, Couperin, and Rameau.

B676.   Sordet, Dominique. "Chronique musicale." **L'Action
        française,** 31 March, 1939, 4.
        A defence of the music, the opera, and the com-
        poser in response to Lucien rebatet's attack on **La
        Chartreuse de Parme** (W4) in the previous week's is-
        sue of the paper. See: W585.

B677.   Spencer, Charles. **Cecil Beaton. Stage and film de-
        signs.** London: Academy Editions, 1975.
        References to **Landscape with figures** (W394).

B678.   Spychet, Jerome. **Clara Haskil.** Lausanne: Payot,
        1975.
        After meeting Haskil at one of the Princesse de
        Polignac's soirées Sauguet asks her to play his **First
        Piano Concerto** (W75). He prepares a two-piano version
        for her which is quite different from any other. Af-
        ter Paul Collaer's, Jean Doyen's and Jeanne-Marie
        Darre's performances of the concerto Haskil plays it
        in Paris, Lausanne and Geneva in 1937.

B679.   Stein, E. "France--Paris--La Contrebasse." **Opera**
        (London) 9 (January, 1958): 39.
        Sauguets score (W3) is unpretentious and sweetly
        ingratiating. The spirit of Messager never hovers at
        too great a distance."

B680.   Stepánek, Vladimir. "Nová díla na parížských scénách
        a pódiích." **Hudebne rozhledy** 13, no. 3 (1960):
        240-241.
        A lengthy review (in Czech) concerning music in
        Paris and the production of **La Dame aux camélias** (W35).

B681.   ------. "Premiéra Sauguetovy kantáty." **Hudebni rozh-
        ledy** 14, no. 4 (1961): 601.
        A Czech review of **L'Oiseau a vu tout cela** (W209).

B682.   Strasbourg (City). **Les Ballets russes de Serge de Diaghilev 1909-1929.** Strasbourg: Ancienne Douane, 1969.
Illustrations of all the participants in the creation of **La Chatte** (W14) including comment that Sauguet "wrote music perfectly adapted to the purpose of the ballet."

B683.   Straus, Noel. "Tribute by Conrad to Goethe, Chopin." **New York Times,** 7 November, 1949, 33.
Sauguet's prelude formed an effective introduction to **Mouvements du cœur** (W251), and his postlude brought the set to an impressive close.

B684.   Stravinsky, Igor. **Selected correspondence.** New York: Knopf, 1985.
The orchestration of **La Chartreuse de Parme** (W4) is "remarkable and consistent from beginning to end, with no weak moments, no lack of imagination."

B685.   Stravinsky, Vera, and Robert Craft. **Stravinsky in pictures and documents.** New York: Simon and Schuster, 1978.
Stravinsky first heard Sauguet's music in 1924. After that he frequently mentioned him as the outstanding contemporary French composer. In Prague in 1930 Stravinsky made a point of recommending Sauguet.

B686.   Strazzula, Gaetano. "Sauguet." **Filmlexicon degli autori e delle opere.** Rome: Bianco e Nero, 1964.
Brief biographical sketch and a list of the composer's music for films.

B687.   Strobel, Heinrich. "Neue Opern aus drei Landern." **Neue Rundschau** 50, pt. 1 (June, 1939): 605.
Concerning **La Chartreuse de Parme** (W4) "the composer has taste, rhythmic sense, discretion, melodic feeling (similar to Gounod and to the older Italian school), a sense of form and a purely French feeling for declamation.

B688.   Strongin, Theodore. "Julia Marlowe on Harpsichord scans music of the 20th century." **New York Times,** 16 December, 1964, 51.
Sauguet's **Suite** (W159) has deliberate references to the great French keyboard tradition of the 1700's. "There are decorations, sweeping passages for emphasis, episodes that contrast in sonority, and other recognizable devices. But the concomitant flavor is the composer's own, and it is remarkably reflective and serious for him."

B689.   -----. "Modern music by Marlowe." **New York Times,** 23 May, 1965, sec. 10, 15.
"Mr. Sauguet bathes his **Suite** (W159) in the sounds of the 18th century. But he uses his awareness of the harpsichord's royal past to form entirely new thoughts. The movements are in turn, majestic, fanciful--and forceful, too--and over each one hangs a wry, bitter-

sweet air, a sad nobility." Review of Decca 10 108
(D28)

B690. Stuckenschmidt, Hans Heinz. "American artists launch
new Berlin Hall." **Musical America** 77 (1 November,
1957): 8-9.
"For 'The Lady of the Camellias' (W35) Henri Sauguet has summed up for his music all the magic of his
melody, schooled by Massenet. He lets the dance sing,
so to speak, and he mirrors the spirit of the waltz,
which dominates the score, in many facets. The delicate orchestration also softens the dissonances. The
whole thing is an echo of the 19th century, in which
Sauguet is more at home than in the present."

B691. "Succès d'Yvette Chauviré à Berlin." **Le Monde**, 3 October, 1957, 13.
Brief notice concerning the success of **La Dame aux
camélias** (W35).

B692. "Symphonie en blanc." **L'Œuvre**, 28-29 November, 1942,
4.
Brief article about the film (W331) including the
particulars and the fact that it was one of the best-
attended French films of the season.

B693. Taper, Bernard. **Balanchine, a biography.** New York:
Times Books, 1984.
Citations for **La Chatte** (W14) and **Fastes** (W19).

B694. "Théâtre Sarah-Bernhardt." **Annuaire des artistes** 37
(1928): 178.
La Chatte (W14) contained "attractively poetic and
graceful music, carefully orchestrated. It was free
and supple like his young fancy.

B695. Thomas, René. "Christian Bérard." **Larousse mensuel**
no. 416 (April, 1949): 241-243.
Citations for **La Chatte** (W14), **La Nuit** (W17), **La
Folle de Chaillot** (W375), **Dom Juan** (W379), **Les Four-
beries de Scapin** (W381), **Les Forains** (W25), and **La
Rencontre** (W26).

B696. Thomson surprise guest on 'Meaning' panel." **Aspen
Times**, 27 July, 1962, 3.
Virgil Thomson, who arrived unexpectedly at the
Festival, helped Darius Milhaud to translate Sauguet's
remarks concerning Debussy's La Mer. Others consti-
tuting the panel were Walter Piston, Charles Jones,
and Walter Susskind.

B697. Thomson, Virgil. "French landscapes and figures."
Modern music 16, no. 1 (November/December, 1938):
17-22.
The theater aesthetic of **La Chartreuse de Parme**
(W4) is taken directly from Verdi and Gounod. "Its
vocal line is fluid and lyrical. Instrumentally it
is Neo-Romantic, which also means fluid and lyrical.
It has good numbers, effective theatrical situations

and the finest French workmanship. It should be a
success like <u>Faust</u> or <u>Carmen</u>. Maybe not the first
time. Neither <u>Faust</u> nor <u>Carmen</u> was. But certainly
eventually. Because France is longing for a really
French opera once again and **Chartreuse** is exactly
that."

B698.   Thomson, Virgil. "Igor Markevitch, Little Rollo in
Big time." **Modern music** 10, no. 1 (November/Decem-
ber, 1932): 19-23.
Thomson compares Igor Markevitch's <u>Concerto grosso</u>
to a Haydn symphony, Sauguet's **La Nuit** (W17) and Stravinsky's <u>Renard</u>.

B699.   -----. "More and More from Paris." **Modern music** 16,
no. 4 (May/June, 1938): 229-232.
"What is important about **La Chartreuse de Parme** (W4)
is that, with all the trouble Henri Sauguet and Armand
Lunel gave themselves to get the book on to the stage
at all, the result is not any form of dramatic effec-
tiveness that we are used to. The dialog lacks pep,
in spite of the use wherever possible of Stendhal's
text, and there is no action. The whole thing is rather like a recital in costume.
It is intimate like a recital. I mean the music
is intimate and interior, like lieder music. The continuity is all in the vocal line, which is almost hys-
terically sensitive and emotional."

B700.   -----. **Music reviewed, 1940-1954.** New York: Vintage
Books, 1967.
In a review for the New York <u>Tribune</u>, dated 9 May,
1953, Thomson states that he considers Sauguet one of
the founders of neo-Romanticism. He cites in particular Sauguet's ability to write vocal music and the
moving sincerity of his music. Thomson recommends
Sauguet to American audiences.

B701.   -----. **Music with words. A composer's view.** New
Haven: Yale University Press, 1989.
"The French composers of our time have, in fact,
like their predecessors, virtually all composed for
both the singing and dancing stage. Hence, the abun-
dant theatrical production of Sauguet."

B702.   -----. "Now in Paris." **Modern music** 10, no. 2 (March/
April, 1933): 141-148.
Thomson writes of neo-Romanticism in Paris and cites
La Chatte (W14), **Le Plumet du Colonel** (W1), and **La
Chartreuse de Parme** (W4). Sauguet "is not of the Con-
servatoire tradition and has brains and taste."

B703.   -----. Papers. Yale University, New Haven, Connecticut.
The papers include a large body of correspondence
exchanged between Sauguet and Thomson between 1927 and
1982.

B704.   Thomson, Virgil. "Paris news." **Modern music** 11, no.
         1 (November/December, 1933): 42-45.
             Concerning **Fastes** (W19): it "contains delicious
         music, rich, gay, but unfortunately it is orchestrated
         for the chamber rather than the theatre. The matter,
         however, is fine, the fabrication ingenious."

B705.   -----. **A Portrait album.** Joseph Silverstein, violin.
         Nonesuch, D 79024.
             No. 7 on the album is entitled "Sauguet from life."

B706.   -----. "Sauguet from life." **Eight portraits for vio-
         lin alone.** London: Boosey & Hawkes, 1981.
             Dated 5 November, 1928. Premiered by Lucien
         Schwartz at Salle Majestic, Paris, 14 November, 1928.

B707.   -----. **Virgil Thomson.** New York: Knopf, 1966.
             Thomson's general physical description of Sauguet
         is not very flattering, but he "composes with lyrical
         spontaneity."

B708.   Thoresby, Christina. "Prokofieff's 'The Flaming Angel'
         scores at Venice contemporary festival." **Musical
         America** 75, no. 5 (1 November, 1955): 5.
             The Sauguet **Symphony** (W62), "an ambitious and ca-
         pable work in the Tchaikovsky tradition, evoked either
         serious approval or emphatic rejection from musicians
         and public."

B709.   "Trio Jacques Canet." **L'Information musicale,** 17 Oc-
         tober, 1941, 179.
             Unidentified "Mélodies" by Sauguet (probably **Six
         mélodies sur des poèmes symbolistes--W239**) to be per-
         formed by Sauguet and Olga Luchaire on 17 October,
         1941.

B710.   "Le Triptyque." **L'Information musicale,** 13 March,
         1942, 849.
             At a Le Triptyque Concert in the Salle Chopin,
         Comtesse Jean de Polignac, Paul Derenne and Sauguet
         performed the **Trois duos** (W240) on 19 March, 1942.

B711.   "Le Triptyque." **L'Information musicale,** 18 December,
         1942, 146.
             The history of the Triptyque concerts, founded in
         1934, is related. To celebrate an anniversary, repre-
         sentatives from various groups appear at the concert
         and make short speeches. Sauguet represents l'Ecole
         d'Arcueil.

B712.   "Trois comédies gaies." **Le Progrès** (Lyon), 29 October,
         1945, 2.
             Agnès Capri's group performs three comic pieces in
         Lyon: Sancta Simplicitas, and two scenes by Courte-
         line, **Les Bonnes occasions** (W241) and **Sigismond** (W367).
         Sauguet's music for the latter two is considered a
         delicious parody.

B713.   Vaillat, Léandre. **Ballets de l'Opéra de Paris.** Paris:
Compagnie française des arts graphique, 1947.
In Sauguet's **La Chartreuse de Parme** (W4) the Duch-
ess of Sanserverino hosts a salon in her residence.
Part of the evening contains a ballet in which Solange
Schwarz danced. This extract from Act I, scene 3, was
performed at La Scala (Milan) in 1939. Vaillat refers
to it as a "musical moment which one will want to re-
member."

B714.   Vallas, Léon. "Au théâtre." **Nouvelle revue musicale**
22, no. 6 (April, 1924): 166-167.
Le Plumet du Colonel (W1) is a "little comic work
without pretension by the young Henri Sauguet."

B715.   -----. "Au théâtre." **Nouvelle revue musicale** 21, no.
8 (June/July, 1924): 212.
Vallas considers **Les Roses** (W13) as "one of the
insignificant scores which were presented during the
bizarre performances of the Soirées de Paris."

B716.   -----. "Au théâtre." **Nouvelle revue musicale** 26,
no. 2 (Decmeber, 1928): 52.
Commenting about **David** (W15), "The reputation that
this young composer enjoys in certain circles remains
a surprise to us. **La Chatte** (W14) seems to us to have
a certain dullness. It does not appear that **David** is
able to cause us to modify this impression since it
was created in a manner that is truly too elementary
and infantile."

B717.   -----. "L'Ecole d'Arcueil." **Nouvelle revue musicale**
22, no. 6 (April, 1924): 168.
The troup leaves a "lamentable impression of musical amateurs who are forced to imitate the lesser works
of the younger members of Les Six."

B718.   -----. "Jeunes musiciens." **Nouvelle revue musicale**
21, no. 9 (August/September, 1923): 167-168.
The songs of Sauguet are full of invention and
charming detail, but they "seem to me rather badly
balanced and a bit long. But two of his **Françaises**
(W141) for piano are entirely successful, with vivacity, written in perfect taste. For my part, I look
upon them as two true successes of a very interesting
evening which did not lack for revelations."

B719.   Var, Lucien. "Musique contemporaine." **Les Lettres
françaises** no. 952 (22 November, 1962): 10.
Review of a new recording of Satie's <u>Socrate</u> on
Le Chant du monde (LDX-A-8292). Sauguet conducts the
recorded performance and writes the program notes.
He "Keeps the orchestra in strict limits in the spirit
of the work" and is perfect for the job. "This recording must not be allowed to escape the vigilant
attention of the Grand Prix du Disque's jury."

B720.   Vickers, Hugo. **Cecil Beaton. The authorized biography.** London: Weidenfeld and Nicolson. 1985.

Brief references to **Landscape with figures** (W394) and the music by Sauguet.

B721.   Vignal, Marc, ed. **Dictionnaire des grands musiciens.** Paris: Larousse, 1985.
Biographical sketch and brief works list.

B722.   "Vladimir Vlasov: Concerto no. 1. Henri Sauguet: Mélodie concertante." **Audio** 56, no. 1 (January, 1972): 71.
Sauguet's music is "hardly a model of briefness. His **Mélodie** (W80) meanders for an unconscionably long time and, considering that the composer is conducting (he's 70), it sounds very old fashioned. At first. But Sauguet has what Vlasov hasn't: Sincerity and honesty. His basic melodic idea, too, is strong, sinewy and good for sober development. The longer you listen, the more modern this music sounds. The man is not great, but he is real and so is his music--if you have the patience to stick out its length." <u>See</u>: D39.

B723.   Volta, Ornella. **Satie seen through his letters.** (translated by Michael Bullock) London: Marion Boyars, 1989.
The epistolary biography gives evidence of Satie's introduction of the L'Ecole d'Arcueil to Rolf de Maré, and the impressario's part in sponsoring the group's first concert at the Théâtre des Champs-Elysées.

B724.   Vuillermoz, Emile. **Histoire de la musique.** Paris: Arthème Fayard, 1973.
Brief references to Sauguet's salon activity and his interest in Pierre Schaeffer's discovery of electronic music.

B725.   Wahl, Marie. "Portrait d'un couturier. Christian Dior." **Les Lettres françaises** no. 277 (15 September, 1949): 7.
Recounts Dior's interest in music and his musical friends like Milhaud, Poulenc and Sauguet, which he made during the late 1920s.

B726.   Waldemar, George. "Paris Ballet." **Art news**, 45 (September, 1946): 20.
Waldemar describes **Les Forains** (W25) as a pantomime in choreographic style; a work vibrant with life, wherein the classic dance is directed toward new and original ends.

B727.   Warnod, André. "Avant de parcourir la France Louis Jouvet torne 'L'Ecole des femmes.'" **Le Figaro**, 17 January, 1941, 4.
Louis Jouvet and Madeleine Ozeray tour the unoccupied zones of France with sections of **L'Ecole des femmes** and selections of songs and dances, particularly from **Ondine** (W364), from other works.

B728.   Warnod, André. "Charivari Courteline." **Le Figaro**, 4
        April, 1946, 2.
        Brief reference to **La Voiture versée** (W376) as
        part of the "Charivari" program.

B729.   -----. "La Nuit." **Le Figaro**, 21 April, 1949, 4.
        The music participated on equal footing in the
        work. "It is exactly what is called for to evoke the
        populous street and the world apart peopled by strange
        personages, passing by each other with echoes of com-
        plaints at the crossroads." See: W17.

B730.   -----. "L'Œuvre de Christian Bérard." **Le Figaro**,
        14 February, 1949, 4.
        Obituary for Bérard which cites **La Folle de Chail-
        lot** (W375), **Les Fourberies de Scapin** (W381), **Les Fo-
        rains** (W25), and **La Rencontre** (W26).

B731.   -----. "Serge Lifar nous dit comment il a conçu la
        realisation de son film documentaire sur la danse."
        Le Figaro, 13 March, 1942, 4.
        Sauguet has written music expressly for it. At
        the outset Lifar warns that **Symphonie en blanc** (W331)
        is a documentary, and it demonstrates dance technique
        and how a ballet is produced. Don't look for a plot
        or a romance.

B732.   -----. "Spectacle dansé et chanté." **Le Figaro**, 9
        May, 1952, 6.
        Brief reference to the premier of **Cordélia** (W29).

B733.   Weissmann, John S. "Music survey--The visit of Sau-
        guet." **Musical events** 16, no. 6 (June, 1961): 30.
        At the French Institute's 95th concert at Morley
        College the Twentiety Century Ensemble performs music
        by Sauguet. Adele Leigh is the soloist in **La Voyante**
        (W201), which is conducted by Sauguet. "This is music
        which convinces by its taste and refinement. Sauguet
        shows himself a master of instrumental and harmonic
        colours. Even more perfect example of his discrimi-
        nating Gallic art was his more recent work." The com-
        position is unnamed, but is probably **L'Oiseau a vu
        tout cela** (W209).

B734.   Williams, Peter. "French dressing." **Dance and danc-
        ers** 16 (February, 1965): 20-25.
        Sauguet's score for **Pâris** (W39) "never seemed to
        quite make up its mind whether to be satirical and
        witty or pretentious."

B735.   Williamson, Audrey. **Contemporary ballet.** London:
        Rockleff, 1946.
        Les ballets des Champs-Elysées visits London's
        Adelphi Theatre in April, 1946, and performs **Les Fo-
        rains** (W25).

B736.   Willis, John. **Dance world.** New York: Crown, 1966-
        The annual cites as follows:
        v. 1: **Guirlande de Campra** (W41) in the repertoire

of the New York City Ballet.
    v. 2: "Love begins on childhood wings" credits
music by Sauguet, but the author has found no other
citation to this.
    v. 5: Minnesota Dance Theatre incorporates **La
Rencontre** (W26) into its repertoire.
    v. 6: Leonard Fowler Ballet performs "Pictures
for six" in New York. Here again, the author can
find no other citation to the work.
    v. 7: **La Rencontre** (W26) still in the repertoire
of the Minnesota Dance Theatre which it performs at
the Jacob's Pillow Dance Festival in July, 1971.
    v. 9: **La Rencontre** (W26) was still in the Min-
nesota Dance Theatre's repertoire as of 1974.

B737.   Wilson, G.B.L. **A Dictionary of ballet.** New York:
        Barnes and Noble, 1961.
            Biographical sketch of Sauguet and references to
        La Chatte (W14), **Les Mirages** (W24), and **Les Forains**
        (W25).

W738.   Wiser, John D. "Exposition Paris 1937." **Fanfare** 12,
        no. 4 (March/April, 1989): 365.
            Brief reference to **La Nuit coloniale sur les bords
        de la Seine** (W153) on the Bennet Lerner recording.
        See: D30.

B739.   -----. "Milhaud: Suite provençale; Poulenc: Aubade,
        Concerto chorégraphique; Sauguet: Les Forains."
        Fanfare 9, no. 1 (September/October, 1985): 185.
            Review of Le Chant du monde LCD 278.300. See:
        D15.

B740.   Wolff, Stéphane. **Un Demi-siècle d'Opéra-Comique, 1900-
        1950.** Paris: André Bonne, 1953.
            Full particulars for **La Gageure imprévue** (W5) and
        its twelve performances at the Opéra-Comique.

B741.   -----. "France--Last season in retrospect." **Opera**
        (London) 21 (January, 1970): 61-62.
            "The new season opened with the revival of a del-
        icate and subtle work, **La Gageure imprévue** (W5), a
        kind of musical conversation which Henri Sauguet based
        very cleverly on a text by Sedaine.

B742.   -----. "Grenoble." **Opera** (London) 19 (May, 1968):
        379.
            La Chartreuse de Parme (W4) is performed during
        the winter olympics of 1968. It is a "Delicately ro-
        mantic work and contains some pleasant tunes which
        are elegantly developed through its ten scenes. The
        'Berceuse' is one of the most successful numbers in
        the score."

B743.   -----. **L'Opéra au Palais Garnier (1875-1962); les
        œuvres, les interpretes.** Paris: L'Entr'acte, 1962.
            Numerous citations for operas and ballets by Sau-
        guet which were performed at the Opéra de Paris. In-
        cluded are: **La Chartreuse de Parme** (W4), **La Chatte**

(W14), **David** (W15), **Les Mirages** (W24), **Trésor et magie**
(W30), and **La dame aux camélias** (W35).

B744.   Wolff, Stéphane. "Théâtre Charles-de-Rochefort: Eu-
gene Oneguine--Le Plumet du Colonel." **Le Guide du
concert** 40, no. 274 (27 May, 1960): 718.
      Le Plumet (W1) "is a charming, happy little act,
full of fantasy, by Henri Sauguet who composed it with
extreme grace and taste."

B745.   "Yvette Chauviré applaudie à Berlin." **Le Figaro**, 2
October, 1957, 12.
      La Dame aux camélias (W35) returns to Paris after
its great success in Berlin. Chauviré will continue
in the lead role in both Paris and at La Scala in
Milan.

B746.   Yvon, Francine. "Hommage à Henri Sauguet." **Le Monde**,
15 September, 1971, 25.
      Udo Reinemann performs **L'Oiseau a vu tout cela**
(W209) at the Festival de Saint-Emilion, and Sauguet
introduces André Boutard and Gérard Faisandier who
perform songs by Sauguet's friends Poulenc, Satie and
Milhaud.

B747.   ------. "La Musique--Le Troisième Festival de Saint-
Emilion." **Le Monde**, 30 September, 1969, 17.
      In its third year the Festival, "which has known
considerable success, affirms a quality to which,
from the beginning, its founders Henri Sauguet and
Gérard Faisandier, have striven. For this year Henri
Barraud dedicated a concert to Berlioz which was
composed of rarely heard songs and diverse literary
texts by the composer. Henri Sauguet evoked the spirit of Jean Cocteau, the Choryphæus of Les Six for a
program which featured the Quintette à vent de Paris,
and the young singer Danièle Fontanille." (Sauguet's
Six fanfares--W94--was probably part of this program.)

B748.   Zamora, Juan Guerreo. **Historia del teatro contempo-
raneo.** Barcelona: Juan Flors, 1961.
      Brief reference to the collaboration of Sauguet
and Max Jacob on **Un Amour de Titien** (W2) in 1928.

Appendix I:
Alphabetical
List of Compositions

Appendix I is an alphabetical list of Henri Sauguet's compositions. Working titles, final titles, and alternate titles are included. The "W" numbers which follow each entry refer to corresponding numbers in the "Works and Performances" section of this volume.

A Jean Voilier, W163.
A quoi rêvent les jeunes filles, W373
A saint Lazare, W431
Adonis, W410
Agathe de Nieul l'espoir, W417
Alentours saxophoniques, W97
Altitudes, W280
Les Amants de Teruel, W355
Un Amour du Titien, W2
Amour et sommeil, W282
L'Amour peintre, W363
Un Amour qui ne finit pas, W400
Les Amoureux sont seuls au monde (film), W340
Les Amoureux sont seuls au monde (song), W295
Andantino, W104
Les Anémones, W306
L'Ange Dudule, W422
Les Animaux et leurs hommes, W224
L'Arbre, W43
Aria d'Eduardo poeta, W287
Arthur Rimbaud, W320
L'As de cœur, W37
Aspect sentimental, W324
Au cyprès que j'ai fait planter la-bas, W212
Au pied de l'arbre, W357
Au revoir monsieur Grock, W343
L'Auberge de la belle étoile, W429
Les Aventures d'Ulysse, W421

Ballade, W110
Le Ballade de Covendale, W447
Barcarolle, W106
Beauté, retirez-vous, W205
Berceuse créole, W1

Clochemerle, W339
Comme à la lumière de la lune, W311
Comme il vous plaira, W386
La Compagnons de Baal, W443
Complaint, W200
Concert à trois pour Fronsac, W99
Concert des mondes souterrains, W79
Concerto d'Orphée, W77
Concerto no. 1, W75
Concerto no. 2, W76
Concerto no. 3, W79
La Concierge, W392
Les Contemporains, W156
La Contrebasse, W3
Cordelia, W29
Cordelia suite, W59
Le Cornette, W208

Dagueréotype, W312
La Dame aux camélias, W35
La Dame aux camélias suite (orchestra), W65
La Dame aux camélias suite (piano, four hands), W129
Dans la maison de paix. W321
Danse d'Arles, W95
Danse des matelots, W44, W143
La Danse éternelle, W331
David, W15
David suite, W46
De mal en pis, W368
Les Délices des enfants, W140
Le Désert de l'amour, W445
Destin, W438
Deux airs à manger, W253
Deux chansons, W260
Deux chansons sur des poèmes d'Alain Saury, W262
Deux chansons sur des poèmes de Pierre Olivier, W252
Deux mélodies romantiques, W233
Deux mélodies sur des poèmes de Paul Valéry, W247
Deux mélodies sur des poèmes de Robert Gaillard, W256
Deux mouvements pour archets, W68
Deux pièces pour orgue, W131
Deux poèmes d'Antoinette d'Arcourt, W238
Deux poèmes de Jules Romains, W219
Deux poèmes de l'Intermezzo de Heine, W235
Deux poèmes de Rabindranath Tagore, W237
Deux poèmes de René Laporte, W254
Deux poèmes de Shakespeare, W232
Deux sonnets de Louise Labé (orchestra), W89
Deux sonnets de Shakespeare, W261
Dialogues dans le Loir-et-Cher, W404
Divertissement de chambre, W85
Dix images pour une vie de Jeanne d'Arc, W409
Documents lumière Angleterre-Amérique, W360
Dom Juan, W379
Le Dompteur dompte, W20
Don Juan, W348
Du troisième âge, W71
Un Duo, W121

Image d'Epinal, W347
Imploration, W319
L'Imposteur, W439
Ingeborg, W370
Inscription pour un portrait, W278
Irma, W361
Isis poignardée, W302

Je sais qu'il existe, W266
Je suis heureuse, W298
Je vous salue Marie, W187
Les Jeux de l'amour et du hasard, W127
J'habite le silence, W216
Les Jours se suivent, W265
Julie de Carneilhan, W345

La Laboureur, W277
Lancelot du Lac, W424
Landscape with figures, W394
Lente valse d'amour inquiet, W35
Léonce et Lena, W406
Le Lit, W391
Lorsque l'enfant paraît, W349
Love poem, W316
Luisa de San-Felice, W441

Ma belle forêt, W190
Machinchouette, W401
Madrigal, W204
La Marchande d'anémones, W306
Marche (au Lieutenant Pourchasse), W452
Marie-Antoinette, W378
Le Marin et la sirène, W11
Marine, W274
Max Jacob de Quimper, W440
Méditation à la mémoire de J. Cocteau, W101
Melmoth réconcilié, W437
Mélodie concertante, W80
La Mémoire en marche, W451
Menuet galante, W96
La Mer est loin de Vienne, W313
Messe jubilatoire, W184
Les Mille et une nuits, W426
Les Mirages, W24
Les Mirages suite, W49
Mon bien, W257
Monelle de la nuit, W435
Monsieur Cendrillon, W423
Monsieur de Pourceaugnac, W428
Monsieur et Madame Roméo, W374
La Mort de Danton, W407
La Mort de la dame aux camélias, W35
Mosaïques, W351
Mouton blanc, W192
Mouvement de valse modéré, W128
Mouvements du cœur, W251
Les Mules du Vice-Roi, W430
Musique de scène pour le spectacle de Jean Tardieu, W322
Musique de scène pour Les Temps du verbe de Jean Tardieu, W323

Pie Jésus, W189
Pièce (untitled), W157
Pièces poétiques pour les enfants, W151
Les Pierres vivent, W210
Plainte, W108
Plein ciel malgache, W346
Plumes, W226
Le Plumet du Colonel, W1
Plus loin que la nuit et le jour, W38, W193
La Plus longue nuit de l'année, W420
Le Poème sans heros, Prélude de, W315
Polymètres, W234
Porte-bonheur, W213
Portrait-souvenir de Virgil Thomson, W167
Pour Lucrèce, W405
Pour Nicolas, W318
Pour un cyprès, W212
Prélude, W135
Prélude de le poème sans héros, W315
Préludes, W139
Premier aspect sentimental, W324
Premier de cordée, W336
Premier scherzo, W144
Première danse nègre, W123
Près du bal (ballet), W16
Près du bal (chamber ensemble), W84
Près du bal (piano), W149
Présence, W283
Prière dans le soir, W310
Prière nuptiale, W130
Le Prince et le Mendiant, W40
Promenades espagnoles, W69
Pronostics de Nostradamus, W220

Quatre chœurs, W196
Quatre poèmes de Schiller, W231
Quatre sonnets de Francis Jammes, W269
Quatre-vingt-dix notes, W181
Quatre-vingt notes, W457
Les Quatres saisons, W191
Quatrième française, W142
Quatuor à cordes (unfinished), W83
Quatuor à cordes no. 1, W87
Quatuor à cordes no. 2, W91
Quatuor à cordes no. 3, W100
Quelques trilles pour les treilles, W179

Reflets sur feuilles, W73
La Reine aux cheveaux d'or, W124
La Rencontre, W26
La Rencontre suite, W56
Requiem æternam (a cappella chorus), W182
Requiem æternam (chorus and organ), W188
Le Retour de l'enfant prodigue, W362
Rêve d'Isa, W325
Réverance à Jean-Sebastian Bach, W122
Rêverie concertante, W96
Rêverie symphonique, W36, W66
Rivière, W281

Symphonie de ballet, W33
Symphonie de la montagne, W50
Symphonie de marches, W70
Symphonie en blanc, W331
Symphonie expiatoire, W53
Symphonie I.N.R., W62
Symphonie no. 1, W53
Symphonie no. 2, W57, W191
Symphonie no. 3, W62
Symphonie no. 4, W71

Le Tabac à priser, W270
Tableaux de Paris, W58
Tartuffe, W382
La Tempête, W388
Les Temps du verbe, W323
Tendres canailles, W418
La Tentation de Tati, W380
Terre sauvage, W338
Théâtre 1950, W383
Les Thibault, W448
Tistou-les-pouces-verts, W10
Toast à Henri Barraud, W197
Tombeau d'un berger, W255
Le Tonnelier, W330
Les Trente-sept sous de Monsieur Montaudoin, W412
Trésor et magie, W30
Trio, W90
Trois chants de contemplation, W211
Trois chants d'ombre, W263
Le Trois cygnes, W222
Trois duos, W240
Trois églogues, W136
Trois élegies, W258
Trois françaises, W141
Trois innocentines, W264
Trois lieder, W268
Les Trois lys, W61
Trois mélodies sur des poèmes de Schiller, W229
Trois mélodies sur des poèmes d'Abeille Guichard, W243
Trois mélodies lyriques sur des textes frivoles, W249
Trois nouvelles françaises, W143
Trois pièces pour alto, W177
Trois pièces pour piano, W134
Trois poèmes arméniens, W218
Trois poèmes de Jean Cocteau, W225
Trois poèmes de Pierre-Albert Birot, W199
Trois poésies, de Jean Cocteau, W223
Trois poésies de Raymond Radiguet, W227
Trois préludes, W175
Tu es Petrus, W183, W352
Tu es Pierre, W183, W352

Uriel, W434

Valse, W109
Valse anachronique, W169
Valse brève, W128
Valse des si, W305

Appendix II:
Chronological
List of Compositions

The "W" numbers following each title refer to corresponding numbers in the "Works and Performances" section of this volume.

1917   Deux pièces pour orgue, W131

1918   Esquisses, W132
        Le Passeur, W133

1919   Trois poèmes arméniens, W218
        Première danse nègre, W123

1920   Le Tabac à priser, W270
        Deux poèmes de Jules Romains, W219
        Pronostics de Nostradamus, W220
        Carmen, W271
        Trois pièces pour piano, W134
        Oceano roof, W221

1921   Les Trois cygnes, W222
        Trois poésies de Jean Cocteau, W223
        Prélude, W135
        Trois églogues, W136
        Les Animaux et leurs hommes, W224
        Complaint, W200

1922   Paul et Virginie, W137
        Cinq inventions, W138
        Plumes, W226
        Trois poésies de Raymond Radiguet, W227
        Bergerie (text by Radiguet), W272
        Fausse alerte, W273
        Marine, W274
        Préludes, W139
        Hommage à Charlot, W124
        Les Délices des enfants, W140

1923   Le Marin et la sirène, W11
        La Vieille image, W275
        Halte, W276

        Bonsoir retraite, W125
        Sonatine pour flûte et piano, W102
        Trois françaises, W141
        Quatrième française, W142
        La Laboureur, W277

1924   Le Plumet du Colonel, W1
        La Fortune de Venise, W12
        Inscription pour un portrait, W278
        Equipe de France, W279
        Altitudes, W280
        Rivière, W281
        Les Roses, W13

1925   Deux poèmes de Jean Cocteau, W225
        Sonate pour violon et piano, W103
        Viñes aux mains de fée, W126
        Danse des matelots, W44
        Cirque, W228
        Trois nouvelles françaises, W143
        Premier scherzo, W144

1926   Irma, W361
        Sonate en ré majeur, W145
        Nouvel album pour la jeunesse, W146
        Trois mélodies sur des poèmes de Schiller, W229

1927   La Chatte, W14
        Six sonnets de Louise Labé, W230
        Quatuor à cordes (unfinished), W83

1928   Un Amour du Titien, W2
        La Chatte suite, W45
        David, W15
        David Suite, W46
        Quatre poèmes de Schiller, W231

1929   Romance en ut, W147
        Feuillets d'album, W148
        Près du bal, W16
        Près du bal (piano version), W149
        Près du bal (chamber version), W84
        Deux poèmes de Shakespeare, W232
        Amour et sommeil, W282
        Présence, W283
        La Nuit, W17
        La Contrebasse, W3

1930   Deux mélodies romantiques, W233
        La Nuit suite, W47

1931   Divertissement de chambre, W85
        Chant nuptial, W150
        Polymètres, W234

1932   La Voyante, W201
        Deux poèmes de l'_Intermezzo_ de Heine, W235
        Caprice, W18
        Herbst, W284

Les Ondines, W285
Enigme, W202
Les Jeux de l'amour et du hasard, W127

1933   Le Retour de l'enfant prodigue, W362
Fastes, W19
Fastes suite, W48
L'Epervier, W326
Chanson de marin, W286
Cinq poèmes de Hölderlin, W236

1934   Pièces poétiques, W151
Petite messe pastorale, W185
Concerto no. 1, W75
Andantino, W104
Aria d'Eduardo poeta, W287
Le Sicilien ou l'amour peintre, W363

1935   La Fortune enchantée, W327
Suite pour clarinette et piano, W105
Nocturne, W152

1936   La Chartreuse de Parme, W4
Barcarolle, W106
Les Enfants du ruisseau, W288

1937   Deux poèmes de Rabindranath Tagore, W237
Nuit coloniale sur les bords de la Seine, W153

1938   Deux poèmes d'Antoinette d'Arcourt, W238
Six mélodies sur des poèmes symbolistes, W239
Les Ombres du jardin, W203

1939   Ondine, W364
Le Dompteur dompte, W20
Trois duos, W240

1940   L'Ecole de la médisance, W365
Les Perses, W366
Cantique en trio, W86
Marche (au Lieutenant Pourchasse), W452
Cantique à saint Vincent, W186
Pastorale de septembre, W154
Sigismond, W367
Les Bonnes occasions, W241

1941   Léonce et Lena, W406
La Mort de Danton, W407
Un Bouquet à la main, W289
Quatuor à cordes no. 1, W87
Cartes postales, W21
Péché de jeunesse, W328
Cinq images pour un Saint Louis à Damiette, W408
La Cigale et la fourmi, W22
Sur les chemins de Lamartine, W329
La Gageure imprévue, W5

1942   Neiges, W244
De mal en pis, W368

Le Tonnelier, W330
Petite chanson, W107
Six interludes, W88
Symphonie en blanc, W331
Madrigal, W204
Image à Paul et Virginie, W23
L'Honorable Catherine, W332

1943   L'Honorable Monsieur Pepys, W369
Beauté, retirez-vous, W205
Les Mirages, W24
Les Mirages suite, W49
Ma belle forêt, W190
Deux sonnets de Louise Labé, W89
Le Cirque enchanté, W333
Ingeborg, W370
Dix images pour une vie de Jeanne d'Arc, W409
Trois mélodies sur des poèmes d'Abeille Guichard, W243
Je vous salue Marie, W187
Fumée légère, W290
Le Charron, W334
Adonis, W410
Force et faiblesse, W244
La Part de l'enfant, W335

1944   Le Pendu, W371
Passe-temps, W372
Premier de cordée, W336
Symphonie de la montagne, W50
A quoi rêvent les jeunes filles, W373
Sérénade, W206
Le Sport et l'esprit, W411
Offrande à Hermès, W291
Monsieur et Madame Roméo, W374
La Chèvrefeuille, W245
Bêtes et méchants, W292
Chant funèbre pour de nouveaux héros, W207
Cinq poèmes de Max Jacob, W246
Image à Paul et Virginie (orchestra), W51

1945   Les Forains, W25
Les Forains suite, W52
Les Trente-sept sous de Monsieur Montaudoin, W412
Symphonie expiatoire, W53
Deux mélodies sur des poèmes de Paul Valéry, W247
Eaux douces, W293
La Folle de Chaillot, W375

1946   La Voiture versée, W376
Farrebique, W337
Bergerie (text by Chabrillac), W294
Six poèmes d'André de Richaud, W248
Trio, W90
Les Saisons et les jours, W54
Victor, W377

1947   Marie-Antoinette, W378
Trois mélodies lyriques sur des textes frivoles, W249
Les Enfants terribles, W413

Terre sauvage, W338
Petite marche, W155
Pepe et Carmelita, W414
Les Amoureux sont seuls au monde (song), W295
Dom Juan, W379

1948   Clochemerle, W339
Les Amoureux sont seuls au monde (film), W304
Quatuor à cordes no. 2, W91
Concerto no. 2, W76
Visions infernales, W250
La Rencontre, W26
La Rencontre suite, W56
Le Chalet tyrolien, W296
Stèle symphonique, W55

1949   Entre onze heures et minuit, W341
La Tentation de Tati, W380
Les Quatres saisons, W191
Les Fourberies de Scapin, W381
Ouvrages du fer, W342
Bocages, W92
Symphonie allégorique, W57
Mouvements du cœur, W251
Valse brève, W128
La Pharmacienne, W415
Le Chemin des forains, W297
Au revoir monsieur Grock, W343
Plainte, W108

1950   Ce siècle a cinquante ans, W344
Julie de Carneilhan, W345
Tartuffe, W382
Espièglerie, W156
Théâtre 1950, W383
Valse, W109
Je suis heureuse, W298
Tableaux de Pars, W58
L'Oiseleur et la fleuriste, W416
Agathe de Nieul l'espoir, W417
On pleur aussi dans le Midi, W299

1951   Pas de deux classique, W27
Le Rois lépreux, W384
L'Ecole des hommes, W385
L'Eternelle chanson, W300
Les Saisons, W28
Tendres canailles, W418
Deux chansons sur des poèmes de Pierre Olivier, W252
Comme il vous plaira, W386
Deux airs à manger, W253

1952   Cordélia, W30
Cordélia suite, W59
Robinson Crusoë, W387
Le Cornette, W208
Trésor et magie, W30
Variations sur un thème de Campra, W60
Le Cardinal aux chats, W31

Robinson Crusoë, W419
Chanson de la fille de bar, W301
Isis poignardée, W302
Cinq mars, W303
Concerto d'Orphée, W77
Mouton blanc, W192
Octave valse, W78

1953   Plein ciel malgache, W346
La Plus longue nuit de l'année, W420
Le Sacre de l'automne, W32

1954   Les Trois lys, W61
Sur un page d'album, W304
Requiem æternam, W188
Les Aventures d'Ulysse, W421
Les Caprices de Marianne, W6
L'Ange Dudule, W422
Monsieur Cendrillon, W423
Lancelot du Lac, W424
Deux poèmes de René Laporte, W254

1955   La Tempête, W388
Musique de scène pour le spectacle de Jean Tardieu,
   W322
Symphonie no. 3, W62
Les Suites d'une course, W389

1956   Musique de scène pour Les temps de verbe de Jean Tar-
   dieu, W323
Un Voix sans personne, W390
Images d'Epinal, W347
Le Grand écart, W425
Valse des si, W305
Don Juan, W348
Le Caméléopard, W33
Lorsque l'enfant paraît, W349
Sonate pour violoncelle, W172
Les Mille et une nuits, W426
Variation en forme de berceuse, W63
Tombeau d'un berger, W255
La Marchande d'anémones, W306
Image pour Maria Freund, W307
Le Lit, W391
Petit air tendre, W453
La Concierge, W392

1957   Les Cinq étages, W34
Les Cinq étages suite, W64
Premier Aspect sentimental, W324
La Nuit des rois, W393
La Dame aux camélias, W35
La Dame aux camélias suite, W65
Les Folies amoureuses, W427
Les Œufs de l'autruche, W350
Chant de l'Oiseau qui n'existe pas, W173
Pie Jésus, W189

1958   Monsieur de Pourceaugnac, W428

Pièce (untitled), W157
C'est ça l'amour, W454
La Solitude, W36
Rêverie symphonique, W66
Deux mélodies sur des poèmes de Roger Gaillard, W256
Petit vœu musical, W425
Mon bien, W257
Soliloque, W174
L'Auberge de la belle étoile, W429
Mosaïques, W351

1959   Les Mules du Vice-Roi, W430
Tu es Pierre, W352
A saint Lazare, W431
Landscape with figures, W394
La Dame aux camélias (piano, four hands), W129
Le Zébu du zoo, W423
Trois élégies, W258
Requiem æternam, W182
Un Seul poème, W308

1960   Carlota, W395
Ballade, W110
L'Oiseau a vu tout cela, W209
Paul Valéry, W353
Robinson, W396
L'As de cœur, W37
L'As de cœur suite, W67
Plus loin que la nuit et le jour (ballet), W38
Plus loin que la nuit et le jour (chorus), W193

1961   La Nuit des rois (new version), W397
Le Chevalier de Brûle-Flame, W433
Othello, W398
Vie des campagnes, W259
Uriel, W434
Deux chansons, W260
Harmonie du soir, W158

1962   France, W354
Les Amants de Teruel, W355
Rêve d'Isa, W325
Monelle de la nuit, W435
L'Ecole de la médisance, W399
Prière nuptial, W130
Suite royale, W159

1963   Un Amour qui ne finit pas, W400
France (new version), W356
Concerto no. 3, W79
Golden suite, W93
Christine, W436
Celui qui dort, W309
Soledad, W7
Mélodie concertante, W80
Mélmoth réconcilié, W437

1964   Deux mouvements pour archets, W68
Au pied de l'arbre, W357

Promenades espagnoles, W69
Deux sonnets de Shakespeare, W261
Oraisons nuptiale, W160
L'Esprit de l'escalier, W161
La Chanson du soir, W162
Sonatine bucolique, W111
Machin-chouette, W401
Pâris, W39

1965   Destin, W438
Cinq chansons sur des poèmes de Louis Emié, W195
Ecce homo (film), W358
Ecce homo (chorus), W183
L'Espace du dedans, W195
L'Heure de verité, W359
Le Prince et le mendiant, W40
L'Imposteur, W439
Quatre chansons sur des poèmes de Louis Emié, W196
Toast à Henri Barraud, W197
A Jean Voilier, W163
Le Bestiaire du petit Noé, W164

1966   Symphonie de marches, W70
Max Jacob de Quimper, W440
Le Souvenir, déjà, W198
La Guirlande de Campra, W41
Prière dans le soir, W310
Luisa de San Felice, W441
Trois poèmes de Pierre-Albert Birot, W199

1967   Chant pour un ville meurtrie, W210
La Bonifas, W442
Le Roi Cymbeline, W402
Comme à la lumière de la lune, W311

1968   Les Compagnons de Baal, W443
Documents lumière Angleterre-Amérique, W360
Dagueréotype, W312
Scènes d'amour, W403
La Mer est loin de Vienne, W313
Le Songe de Dona Clara, W444

1969   Le Désert de l'amour, W445
La Fille qui dit "non," W446
Deux chansons sur des poèmes d'Alain Saury, W262
Trois chants d'ombre, W263
Six fanfares, W94
Danse d'Arles, W95
Menuet galante, W96
La Ballade de Covendale, W447
Trois innocentines, W164

1970   Trois préludes, W174
Les Jours se suivent, W265
The Garden's concerto, W81
Fado, W314

1971   Trois chants de contemplation, W211
Sonatine aux bois, W112

Symphonie no. 4, W71
Romance pour un soir à Saint-Emilion, W113
Petite valse du Grand échiquier (orchestra), W72

1972   Les Thibault, W448
Sonatine pour clarinette et piano, W114
L'Oiselet vert, W449
Pour un cyprès, W212
Choral varié, W176
Trois pièces pour alto, W177

1973   Petite valse du Grand échiquier (piano), W165
Je sais qu'il existe, W266
Dialogue dans le Loir-et-Cher, W404
Musiques pour Claudel, W178
Le Pain des autres, W8

1974   Salavin, W450
Porte bonheur, W213

1975   Six pièces faciles, W115
Pour regarder Watteau, W166
Sonatine en deux chants et un intermède, W116
Prélude de la poème sans héros, W315

1976   Elisabeth de Belgique, la reine aux cheveau d'or, W214
Alentours saxophoniques, W97
Oraisons, W98
Love poem, W316
Chant du feu, W317

1978   Les Sept chansons de l'alchimiste, W267
Boule de suif, W9
Cantilène pastorale, W117

1979   Reflets sur feuilles, W73
La Solitude (new version), W42
Concert à trois pour Fronsac, W99
Non morietur in æternam, W118
Quatuor à cordes no. 3, W100
Pour Nicolas, W318

1980   Tistou-les-pouces-verts, W10

1981   L'Arbre, W43
Imploration, W319
Sonate crépusculaire, W119

1982   Trois lieder de Jean Tardieu, W268
Par-delà les étoiles, W215
Portrait souvenir de Virgil Thomson, W167
Pour Lucrèce, W405
Pâques fête de la joie, W455
Quelques trilles pour les treilles, W179

1983   Messe jubiliatoire, W184
Méditation à la mémoire de J. Cocteau, W101
Le Souvenir de Déodat, W168
Quatre-vingts notes, W548

        La Mémoire en marche, W451

1984   Un Fleur, W120
        Un Duo, W121

1985   Sonate d'église, W82
        Réverence à Jean-Sebastien Bach, W112
        J'habite le silence, W216
        Valse anachronique, W169
        Cadence, W180
        Arthur Rimbaud, W320

1986   Ombre de Venise, W176
        Quatre-vingt-dix notes, W181
        Musique pour Cendrars, W217
        Septembre (piano), W171

1987   Septembre (orchestra), W74
        Quatre sonnets de Francis Jammes, W269
        Dans la maison de paix, W321

Index

Lower case Roman numerals refer to the "Preface," Arabic numerals refer to the "Biography," numbers preceded by "W" refer to "Works and Performances" citations, "S" numbers refer
to "Writings by Henri Sauguet," numbers preceded by "D" refer
to citations in the "Discography," and numbers preceded by
"B" refer to citations in the section "Writings about Henri
Sauguet and his Works."

Abott, Alain, W176, D1
Abravanel, Maurice, W19
Absil, Jean, D59
Académie des Beaux-Arts, 9,
  B429, B442
Académie du disque français,
  B442
Académie du Jazz, 9, B442
Académie Français, B429
Achard, Marcel, W401, S86
Adrouin, François, W331
Æschylus, W366
Agostini, Philippe, W347,
  W352
Agrupacíon Choral de Camera
  de Pamplona, W38
Aguet, William, W301, W413,
  W419, W422, W423, W432
Akhmatova, Anna, W315
Alard, Jean-Delphin, D40
Albanese, Francesco, W6
Algaroff, Youly, W17, B366
Allard, Maurice, D19
Allard, Roger, W410
Allegret, Marc, W360
Alley, Jean, W10
Alonso, Alicia, W35
Altman, Karen, B237
Amade, Louis, W320
American Ballet Theatre, W26
Amiel, Josette, W24

Les Amis de la Musique de
  Chambre, W246
Amitiés artistiques de Brux-
  elles, W212
Ancelin, Pierre, W118, W121,
  B16
Andia, Rafael, W178, B233
André, Farnz, W53, W62, W66,
  W75, W208, B121
Annenkov, Georges, W3
Anouilh, Jean, W397
Ansermet, Ernest, W1, S2, S3,
  S4, S5, S19, S174, S177
Apollinaire, Guillaume, W270
April, Roland, W34
Aristophanes, S39
Armer, Paul, S167
Arnal, Camille, W440
Arnaud, Michel, W370, W406,
  W407
Arnoux, Alexander, W336, W103,
  W182
Arnoux, Robert, W341
Artigues, Georges, W275
Aspen Festival, 9, W3, W62,
  W201, B482, B537
Association symphonique de
  Chambre de Paris, W81
Astruc, Yvonne, S162
Atterberg, Kurt, S151
Auber, Brigitte, W349
Aubert, L., B587

About the Author

DAVID L. AUSTIN is Architecture and Art Librarian at the University of Illinois at Chicago. He has contributed articles to *Symphony Orchestras of the United States* (Greenwood Press, 1986) and *The New Grove Dictionary of American Music.*

Recent Titles in
Bio-Bibliographies in Music

Ned Rorem: A Bio-Bibliography
Arlys L. McDonald

Richard Rodney Bennett: A Bio-Bibliography
Stewart R. Craggs, compiler

Radie Britain: A Bio-Bibliography
Walter B. Bailey and Nancy Gisbrecht Bailey

Frank Martin: A Bio-Bibliography
Charles W. King, compiler

Peggy Glanville-Hicks: A Bio-Bibliography
Deborah Hayes

Francis Poulenc: A Bio-Bibliography
George R. Keck, compiler

Robert Russell Bennett: A Bio-Bibliography
George J. Ferencz

György Ligeti: A Bio-Bibliography
Robert W. Richart

Karel Husa: A Bio-Bibliography
Susan Hayes Hitchens

Ferruccio Busoni: A Bio-Bibliography
Marc-André Roberge

Frank Bridge: A Bio-Bibliography
Karen R. Little

Otto Luening: A Bio-Bibliography
Ralph Hartsock

John McCabe: A Bio-Bibliography
Stewart R. Craggs

Lukas Foss: A Bio-Bibliography
Karen L. Perone